Within Me, Without Me

About the Author

Sue Wells is a birth mother and lives in Bristol. She was born in Dunedin, New Zealand in 1947 and studied anthropology at the University of Otago. At 21 she travelled overland to the UK, where she now works as a social worker, counsellor and writer. She is a trustee and member of the Natural Parents Support Group. Sue is married to a psychotherapist and has three daughters.

Her purpose in writing this book is to highlight the benefits of openness in adoption by showing the damage that secrecy can cause. However, her birth daughter has requested anonymity and Sue Wells has therefore chosen not to identify her own story.

Within Me, Without Me
Adoption: an open and shut case?

Sue Wells

Scarlet Press

*For all those mothers who gave up
their children for adoption*

Published by Scarlet Press
5 Montague Road, London E8 2HN

Copyright © Sue Wells 1994

The author asserts her moral right to be identified
as the author of this work

British Library Cataloguing in Publication Data
A catalogue record for this book is available from the British Library

ISBN 1 85727 0428 pb
      1 85727 0479 hb

Designed and produced for Scarlet Press by
Chase Production Services, Chipping Norton
Typeset from author's disks by
Stanford DTP Services, Milton Keynes
Printed in Finland by WSOY

Contents

Acknowledgements

I want to thank all the birth mothers, adopted children, adopted adults and adoptive parents who contributed their experiences to this book with generosity, trust and enthusiasm.

I also thank those adoption groups, adoption agencies and workers in New Zealand, particularly in Auckland (Ron Benjamin), Hamilton and Dunedin Social Welfare, and in the UK the Natural Parents Support Group, Post-adoption Centre (London), After Adoption (Manchester) and Parent to Parent Information on Adoption Services, who have given me their help, time and encouragement. Also Eileen Preston in New Zealand for helping me so promptly to trace my daughter; Murray Ryburn for kindly interviewing me for my story.

I also thank New Zealanders Jonathan Hunt MP and Fran Wilde MP, whose perserverance and dedication culminated in the passing of the Adult Adoption Information Act 1985 that enabled me and thousands of other New Zealanders to be reunited with our lost children.

In particular I thank all the birth mothers who had the courage and trust to share their experiences. It has not been possible to include everyone's story and I would therefore like to thank individually those birth mothers whose stories do not appear:

- *in Auckland and Hamilton, New Zealand*: Di Marshall, Alison, Elisabeth, Natalie, Gail, Lilly, Jenny, Kim, Chris, Lara, Julie, Karen, Leonie, Heather, Jenny, Colleen, Geraldine;
- *in Wellington*: Jane, Jacki, Julie;
- *in Christchurch and Dunedin*: Cushla, Sandra, Lindy, Dena, Linda, Sara, Lyn.

I also thank:

- *adopted adults and children*: John, Barbara, Richard, Marion, Shona, Oenonie, Susie aged 15, Dufty jnr. aged 10;

- *adoptive parents*: Jan and John Ryan, the Garricks, Dufty and Mary Martin, Noeline, Alison Cleland;
- *natural grandparents*: David and Edith;
- *in the UK, birth mothers*: Veronica, Penny, Jenny, and Clare from the Post Adoption Centre, London; Ann, natural grandmother of Nathan; Alex, adoptive mother of Nathan; Jenny Harrison;
- the 262 birth mothers who participated in the questionnaire that has contributed towards a greater understanding of the impact on mothers of adoption.

Thanks to Scarlet Press and in particular Christine Considine for her respect and enthusiasm for the book.

Thanks to all my friends who have encouraged and inspired me, especially Angie, Doreen, Ken and Elizabeth; and special thanks to my husband Martin who enabled me to write this book not only by buying me a word processor but by supporting my taking time out to write it; to my younger daughters Anna and Sophie for their understanding of my lengthy absences and for their encouragement; and to my first daughter for helping me to resolve the past.

Foreword

Phillida Sawbridge, Director, Post-adoption Centre, London

Adoption became a legal process in England and Wales in 1926 and in Scotland in 1930. Nearly 900,000 adoption orders have been granted since that time. Responding to social and political trends, countless small voluntary agencies arranged hundreds of adoptions annually, joined in the 1950s by local authorities, newly empowered to do so too.

What do we know about the outcome of all these adoptions? How have we assessed whether such a provision, which transplants a child totally from one family into another, is viable or desirable? What do we know about the impact of such a basic piece of social engineering on the participants?

There continued to be an assumption, as Sue Wells says, that 'adopters did not need to know the mothers of the children, but instead needed protection from them, as did the children'. So all the arrangements were made in total secrecy, which was also considered the best protection for the mothers themselves, in terms of the shame and stigma of illegitimate births and 'giving away' of children.

Birth mothers, and still more birth fathers, only two of whom feature in this book, became faceless, anonymous beings. It is not insignificant that national self-help organisations for adoptive parents and adopted people came into being 15 or 20 years before one was finally set up by and for birth parents. Nobody dared to confess publicly that she had parted with a child for adoption – and academics and professional workers colluded with this secrecy and denial, and made no attempt to find out what had happened to all those women.

This book helps to fill that yawning gap. In circulating and analysing a questionnaire, and then interviewing a range of people, Sue Wells has gathered a wide variety of personal accounts, from both northern and southern hemispheres, and covering a span of 40 years. The people whose stories we read are representative of hundreds more, even though each is personal and unique. They illustrate, as no secondhand description could, the profundity of the experience for a mother who parts with her child, and the lifelong effects on her. They also highlight the desperation of women who know nothing of the subsequent lives of their children, even whether they are alive or dead. And many of the stories, in describing later reunions, show how tremendously difficult such encounters are, and how rocky the road to developing a new relationship. The case is strongly made for giving birth parents more rights, if only to information, and Sue Wells asks very pertinent questions about adoption as a tool of social control.

The debate about 'openness' in adoption has barely begun. This book adds substantially to that debate, in illustrating so powerfully what adoption has meant to many of the heretofore silent participants.

Introduction

'What has happened to my child? Is he or she dead or alive? Well and happy?' These are the questions that haunt those mothers like me, who felt they had no choice when they gave up their children for adoption to strangers – 'natural' mothers, 'unmarried' mothers or 'birth mothers' as we have come to be known. While I am not fond of the term 'birth mother', it does at least suggest to our children that they were born – each did *have* a mother who gave birth to them. Many adopted children (or 'adoptees' as they are sometimes called) know very little if anything about their roots. Their mothers have no names, no faces, no histories. They were 'chosen' by their adoptive parents, who in turn knew very little about them either. The mother, the birth mother, often knew nothing about the family her child was placed with, or what happened to him or her.

Some mothers will never know. Some dare not dwell on the subject. Some have sought professional help to cope with the anxiety of not knowing, or have succumbed to psychological or physical stresses. Some sit and wait. Some are still searching and hoping for a reunion. I am lucky. I have found my daughter. We have found each other. We are reunited.

Searching for a child you gave up for adoption is not made easy in Britain. Birth mothers do not have the same specific right as their relinquished (adult) children to access identifying information about them. Unless the agency who handled the adoption chooses to help obtain information or make contact, and this often means having the cooperation of the adoptive parents, birth mothers must sit and wait or resort to trying to crack the system themselves.

By contrast, the Adoption Act 1976 gave adopted adults in England and Wales the right to apply for their original birth certificates once they reach the age of 18. First they have to undergo compulsory counselling if they were adopted before November

1975, to ensure that basic information about their adoption is given in a helpful manner and that they understand the possible effects on themselves and others should they wish to make further enquiries about their birth families. Although it has always been possible to obtain copies of birth records without help, this can only be done if you know your original name. Most adoptees do not. In Scotland adopted people have always been able to get a copy of their original birth certificate once they reach 17.

Almost 20 years on, birth mothers still do not have the same right to know about their children as those children have to know about them. They were not consulted about the change in the law, yet their position was radically altered by it. The children they expected to know nothing about or ever have contact with were suddenly entitled to make contact with them once they turned 18.

Help offered is a lottery depending on where the birth mother lives and which agency handled the adoption. This is in spite of agencies having a responsibility – since 1976 and reinforced in the underlying principles of the Children Act 1989 – to provide a comprehensive service to all those involved in adoption. Secrecy has been implicit in adoption practice, including secrecy surrounding the identity of the adopters, but nowhere is it stated in legislation that an agency is unable to contact adoptive parents on behalf of a birth parent or relative. Any disclosure or response has always been at the discretion of the agency involved.

Until very recently the response of such agencies to birth mothers has been largely passive – noting enquiries from birth mothers and filing letters which their (adult) children would only receive once they had made contact themselves. While some agencies, especially voluntary ones, may offer birth mothers support, counselling and non-identifying information, others refuse to disclose any information or else make no response at all.

Recently a growing number of agencies are beginning to recognise the trauma attached to losing a child through adoption[1] – for many a lifelong grief that is not healed by time, successful careers, happy marriages or subsequent children – and are responding more actively to the increasing number of enquiries from birth mothers. They have revised their policies and look at each case individually; they will now consider making an approach to adopted adults, usually via the adoptive parents, and even to a child in special circumstances. In doing so these agencies provide safeguards such as counselling and intermediaries to see if both parties wish to meet, and obviate the need for birth mothers to search through records or hire private detectives.

Nevertheless, many birth mothers receive no help. Those desperate to trace their lost children search by themselves as a last resort because the agencies who handled the adoptions choose not to help. It is not illegal to search for someone, but it is time-consuming, surreptitious, laborious, complicated and expensive, often involving false leads and dead ends – hopes raised and shattered. The process can help to end years of wondering, worrying and pining, but such a system is inhumane and without any safeguards.

Another avenue open to birth mothers is to register a wish for contact with their relinquished children on the National Contact Register which came into effect in May 1991, but again, this is a passive position in that they must sit and wait for the adopted adults to make contact with them. Should the adoptee also register a wish for contact, he or she is given the name and address of birth relatives where a match occurs, but the relatives are not given his or her identity, only informed that contact has been made. The anticipation of contact can cause tremendous anxiety, hope or excitement in birth mothers. But the adoptee may choose not to pursue it immediately or possibly not to pursue it at all. The fee to register is also inequable – at the time of writing, £9.50 for adoptees, £27.50 for birth relatives.

Although adoption has existed in England and Wales since 1926, there has been virtually nothing known until recently about those in the adoption triangle considered to have lost the most. It is estimated that there are at least half a million birth mothers in Britain, yet we have maintained a position of silence, sorrow, secrecy and shame. In spite of pressure groups, submissions and 'consultations', we have made little impact on present proposals (not yet law) for legislation governing adoption law and practice contained in the White Paper *Adoption: The Future*, of November 1993.

Many birth mothers who have already experienced the closed, secret adoptions of the last 70-odd years were hoping for clear and positive changes in this White Paper, in line with the greater openness that is being offered to birth parents today, and for equality with adopted people's right to birth records, thereby redressing the imbalance that was created by the Adoption Act 1976.[2]

Adoption is a formal legal process, made through a permanent irreversible court order, in which all rights and duties relating to the child are transferred to the adoptive parents from the child's natural parents (or the local authority if it has assumed these responsibilities). A lawyer involved with projects concerning children's rights in the UK and NZ has written:

> Adoption has been linked to a legal conjuring trick. At the stroke of a pen the birth parents vanish and at the same moment the adoptive parents take their place. This judicial tinkering with family relationships is unique. Nowhere else in our law are the courts authorised to declare something to be what it demonstrably is not.[3]

Secrecy is a by-product of adoption, which was originally intended to legitimise children by finding homes for them. It developed to protect the privacy of all three parties involved: unmarried mothers and their children from the stigma of illegitimacy; adoptive parents from the taint of infertility and the possible interference of birth parents. Adopters were instructed to regard the children as if they were their own. Everyone was 'safe'. It was assumed that this was what everyone wanted. Birth mothers could make a fresh start and go away and forget that they had ever had their babies; adopted children should not know about their birth parents or the circumstances of their adoption; adopters did not need to know the mothers of the children, but instead needed protection from them, as did the children. Secrecy came to be regarded as simpler.

Views on the impact of secrecy on all those involved in adoption have changed, but Britain lags behind other countries such as New Zealand and some states in the USA and Australia when it comes to opening up records which were previously closed to birth relatives.

In 1964 in New Zealand I gave birth to a beautiful daughter. She was immediately taken away from me and put up for adoption. I was 17. Twenty-one years later it was decreed by an Act of Parliament (the Adult Adoption Information Act 1965) that birth relatives could be reunited. Birth records were opened up. With the prompt help and support of Social Welfare in New Zealand, my daughter and I have been reunited.

But what if I'd been a British birth mother – hoping, waiting, silent and anxious for my child to turn 18, maybe contacting me, maybe not, year in and year out, the thought always hovering near the surface, haunting me, saddening me probably for the rest of my life? Should birth mothers in Britain have the same right to open records?[4] And what about those hidden thousands in other parts of the western world who don't 'legally' exist either?

It was only when I began writing about my experience of loss and reunion in 1989 that I became aware of other birth mothers' experiences. Some wrote saying how much they wished they had the same right and help to search in Britain as I had had in New Zealand.

I therefore devised a questionnaire to see if their response was typical of birth mothers' feelings in the UK. Adoption was under review – a government body was set up in 1989 to look at adoption law and practice (its conclusions are in the White Paper referred to above). I wanted to help give birth mothers a voice, to express their views and feelings about relinquishing their children and how it has affected them. MPs in New Zealand knew the trauma attached to relinquishment because birth mothers told them. They became organised, formed pressure groups, wrote, informed the public. It took seven years to get the Information Act through the New Zealand Parliament. Why shouldn't it happen here as well?

A total of 262 birth mothers replied to advertisements in the press and adoption group newsletters, including some from Australia and Canada who had relinquished children in Britain. Some are associated with these adoption groups, most are not. Dates of the adoptions ranged from the 1930s to the present day. Many respondents added their own comments to the 43 questions asked. It was the first time, they said, they had communicated their thoughts and feelings about their children. Their replies are a real testimony to their experiences and cannot be ignored.

I decided to write this book after being overwhelmed by the poignant comments in the questionnaire. Some of the stories below are of these birth mothers but most come from people I made contact with through adoption support groups, adoption agencies and my own friends and acquaintances both in the UK and in New Zealand. Almost everyone in this book has been willing to use their own names, saying that they want to become visible after so many years of anonymity.

The book evolved further after I talked to adoption workers and counsellors in New Zealand about different types of adoption practice that exist there. I decided to compare the psychological and social effects on birth mothers, their children and their adoptive parents with the closed secret system I had known. Do those in the open system have a different experience, and if so in what ways?

This volume has therefore become the story of many birth mothers – and where possible their children and adoptive parents too. It is a story in which the details may differ, but for many the feelings experienced are the same: sadness, loss, guilt, shame and anger. For others, there is the sense that they chose the best alternative at the time – and for some there is eventual wholeness, resolution and joy.

The book is intended to help all those involved in, affected, touched by or curious about adoption to understand the effects of secrecy on themselves and their families and, by contrast, to understand the healthy relationships that can develop in open adoption. For birth mothers, it is aimed at enabling them to identify with the experiences shared by others. For our children, it is to let them know they have not been forgotten, erased from our memories. For pregnant women contemplating adoption and for adoptive parents, it is intended to show how the benefits of openness obviate the need for secrecy or pretence inherent in the closed system and can add an extra dimension to parenting. For professionals, it is to lead to an appreciation that adoption is about grief and loss and that good adoption practice, where adoption is considered the *only* option, should be better able to balance the interests of all three parties, as the stories of openness demonstrate.

The book is also intended for those involved with the increasing number of older children who are adopted today, often including those with special needs and those where the adoption is contested, usually when a child has been removed from his or her birth parents' home by the courts because of neglect or ill-treatment. Some openness by way of information would be humane, allowing those parents some reassurance about their child's progress, and, moreover, may benefit the adoptive family.

Likewise, in the case of children of reconstituted families whose contact with their non-custodial parent and extended family is severed as a result of divorce, or who are sometimes the subject of bitter disputes between parents – for these birth families and their children the need to maintain contact is the same as for those separated by adoption: to minimise feelings of rejection and loss and to maintain their own identity.

Secrecy in adoption in the recent past has been supplanted by secrecy inherent in some of the new birth technologies, like surrogacy, artificial donor insemination and, more recently, transplanting eggs from one female to another. Children are being created to meet the needs of parents in much the same way as they used to be 'found' for infertile couples to adopt. Some regard these children as commodities or possessions of their parents and feel they will have the same difficulties as adopted children, where information about the circumstances of their birth is concealed or withheld. This secrecy might be regarded as different from adoption as it takes place in a medical setting. As in traditional, closed adoptions, the plight of infertile couples today may overshadow and minimise the needs of the child and (where relevant) the birth mother. This book will help contribute to an understanding of the same need for openness, honesty and integrity.

References

1. Wells, S., 'Post-traumatic Stress Disorder in Birth Mothers' (1993), *Adoption and Fostering*, vol. 17, no. 2.
2. Natural Parents' Support Group (December 1992), *Response to 'Review of Adoption Law' – A Consultation Document*.
3. Ludbrook, R., *Adoption: Guide to Law and Practice* (1990), GP Books, Christchurch, New Zealand, p. 35.
4. Wells, S., 'What Do Birth Parents Want?' (1993), *Adoption and Fostering*, vol. 17, no. 4.

Part One
A Clean Break

But on the whole, morality as regards woman has nothing to do with ethics; it means sexual morality and nothing but sexual morality. To be a wayward girl usually has something to do with pre-marital sex; to be a wicked woman has something to do with adultery. This means it is far easier for a woman to lead a blameless life than it is for a man; all she has to do is avoid sexual intercourse like the plague.

Angela Carter, Wayward Girls and Wicked Women

The stories in the first and second parts of this book are about the experiences of those mothers – mainly in the 1960s and 1970s – like me, who gave up their children for adoption to strangers in New Zealand and in the UK. Many of us felt we had no choice. A total of 86 per cent of the 262 British birth mothers who responded to my questionnaire said they were pressurised by parents and social workers to go ahead with the adoption. And 200 (76 per cent) had second thoughts either before or after giving consent; of the remainder, many were unaware they could change their minds. Adoption was almost always presented as the only option.

Until recently birth mothers were told to go away and forget we had ever had our babies. We were too young, too immature, unsupported and, above all, we were not married; adoption was best for baby and best for us. We were placed in a double bind – 'If you love your child, you'll give him or her up.' In so doing we forfeited all rights to any contact or knowledge of our children. The stigma attached to having illegitimate children automatically made us unfit mothers; the families we had to offer were not 'proper' families and therefore we were undeserving of our children.

Having sex and being unmarried at that time was regarded as shameful. But my generation in the mid-1960s took the opportunity to enjoy dramatic social change, and peer group pressure included 'free love'. However, this was not acknowledged in New Zealand or in Britain at the time by a corresponding change in social policies; sex education, birth control and abortion were simply not available. Out of the 262 birth mothers who completed the questionnaire, 223 were not using contraception; the 39 who were, mainly used condoms; only twelve were using the contraceptive pill. Most (187) said they did not consider abortion, which was legalised in Britain in 1967, in New Zealand in 1977 and in the USA in 1973. Their average age at relinquishment was 20 – their present ages range from 22 to 81 and the average now is 45[1].

Unmarried mothers threatened both the idea and the ideal of marriage.[2] The nuclear family was the norm; single-parent benefits were not available in New Zealand or in the UK until the mid-1970s. The idea of children being brought up outside marriage was unthinkable. The shame and stigma attached to us was a powerful means of social control; we had to conform, caught up in the double standards of morality that to some extent still exist today.

Pregnancy was a confirmation of deviant and sinful behaviour. Those of us who were afraid, not smart, courageous or foolish enough to turn to the backstreet abortionists, were forced to continue the pregnancy, usually banished by our families, often to an unknown place and without any discussion or support. Banishment was a ritual, and symbolised the moral order of things. The idea of sin, says Joseph Campbell, puts you in a servile condition throughout your life.[3] We atoned by giving up our babies. In exchange we were expected to return to our 'former' place in society as if nothing had happened, unencumbered and no longer a family embarrassment, the past behind us, once again marriageable – after all, no man wanted 'soiled goods'. For many, this experience was never mentioned again.

The 'sin' we committed was grave and the price we paid was high – our virtue for our babies. But the gravest sin of all, which we realised too late, was the sin of giving up our children.

How does a birth mother begin to describe the loss of her child – a loss that does not fade with time, a loss that is exacerbated by a lack of information about him or her, a loss that is as irrevocable as death except there is no body, no funeral, no farewell, no comfort from family friends – while the child continues to live and grow elsewhere, with birthdays and Christmases as relentless reminders?

Some information – no matter how little – is the one factor that would have helped ease things for every birth mother in the years following relinquishment: the need to know what has happened to the child, some reassurance that the adoption had been 'best for baby'. Out of the 262 birth mothers surveyed, over half felt a clean break was not for the best because of the longterm emotional effects; 135 said they think about their lost children daily or frequently. Never knowing can generate terrible distress and anxiety, especially whenever tragic news of an adopted child is reported, like young men killed in the Falklands war. The burden of secrecy perpetuates the guilt, shame, bitterness and sorrow that many birth mothers still feel for the children for whom they were never allowed to grieve.

Almost all the 262 birth mothers said that information would have given them some peace of mind. Instead, many reported their physical and/or emotional health had been adversely affected: 207 (79 per cent) cited depression, anxiety, difficulties with relationships and establishing trust. This in turn has, for many, affected their interpersonal relationships with family and partners and their parenting of subsequent children. Some said relinquishing their children was the biggest mistake of their lives. One research study from Australia shows that for nearly half of the 213 birth mothers involved (48 per cent) relinquishment was the most stressful life event they had experienced and it was still affecting many of them years later; it also found that birth mothers are more prone to illness and nervous disorders than the rest of the population.[4]

Losing a child is probably one of the most traumatic losses anyone can experience. Bonds of love and attachment are formed in the womb. Unlike the case of a normal loss or bereavement, however, the grief reaction of a relinquishing birth mother is complex; she has participated at some level in the loss by signing consent to the adoption. This compounds the guilt, regardless of the lack of options or alternatives at the time.

Far from enabling us to make a 'fresh start', the loss of our babies and the subsequent denial of that loss by professionals (as well as birth mothers) has meant unresolved grief. We were expected to make the biggest decision of our lives at a vulnerable age and without any support or counselling. Most (205) of the 262 birth mothers surveyed said they had no counselling or support during or after their pregnancies. Of those who had some (57), only about half said this was provided by a social worker.

Unresolved grief for the many additional losses experienced at the time include being ostracised by family and friends, home and town, work; over half of those returning the questionnaire (149) said that after relinquishment they had never picked up where they had left off, and they felt different and distanced from their friends and family. Poor self-image and self-esteem were selected most often as areas of their lives that were most affected.

The 262 birth mothers were asked which words best described their feelings about the adoption in the first year or so afterwards; the most frequent words used were sadness, loss, grief, numb, depressed, guilty, angry, bitter. Many said they still experience the same feelings now.

At the time, most of us knew nothing or very little about childbirth; many endured the terror of it alone; some were expected to care for their babies for up to six weeks and did; some were expected not to see their babies or were 'allowed' just a glimpse, and acquiesced; it was assumed we would relinquish our babies and most of us did. It was also assumed that we wanted a clean break and total secrecy. What they did not tell us was that we would never forget the babies we gave birth to, in spite of the various ways we may have tried, and that it would affect us, often for the rest of our lives.

References

1. Wells, S., 'What Do Birth Mothers Want?', (1993), *Adoption and Fostering*, vol. 17, no. 4.
2. Howe, D., Sawbridge, P. and Hinings, D. (1992), *Half a Million Women: Mothers Who Lose Their Children by Adoption*. Harmondsworth: Penguin.
3. Campbell, J. *The Power of Myth* (1988), New York: Doubleday.
4. Winkler, R. and van Keppel, M. (1984), *Relinquishing Mothers in Adoption: Their Longterm Adjustment*, Melbourne: Institute of Family Studies, monograph no. 3.

1 Margaret

Margaret made contact with me after an article of mine was published in a national newspaper. We talked adoption. It was a new experience for me. I had skilfully managed to avoid the subject for over 20 years – until I was reunited with my daughter. Discussing our experiences highlighted the similarities in how we felt about losing our children, and also the differences in our adoption laws (New Zealand and British).

Margaret does not have the same right as I did to help her search for her daughter. Like other British birth mothers she is dependent on the placing agency to offer help and make contact, by acting on her behalf as an intermediary. She can search if she knows how to go about it, but does not have a specific right to do so. For her it has been a daunting task but one that she has accomplished. She now knows her daughter's whereabouts but hasn't attempted as yet to go any further. Like a lot of birth mothers she doesn't want to interfere in her daughter's life, particularly since she still lives with her adoptive parents.

Margaret has told her story many times, especially to workshops set up by Social Services for prospective adopters. She has also been very involved in the Post Adoption Centre in London where she has received counselling and support on an individual basis and in groups and is actively involved in campaigning for changes in the adoption law. She was one of the people who helped inspire me to write this book.

I think I knew I was pregnant as soon as I'd been to the party. I did actually know the bloke, we weren't complete strangers but we weren't exactly in a relationship. I had this horrible feeling I was pregnant and yet at the same time couldn't believe that something so pathetic and trivial had actually made me pregnant. So I kept thinking about it as just a bad dream. I was 18 at the time. It was 1965.

I had this fantasy that the baby was my ex-boyfriend's. We had been going out together for about a year. He was married. But he disappeared once he got me to bed. So part of me was also thinking it was his baby.

I can remember going to my friend's birthday party and my mum had bought me this white dress. I remember thinking this was very significant and that it meant I would actually come on and that I wouldn't be pregnant. But it didn't work.

I'd probably missed two periods before I told anyone. I was working as a nurse and I was on night duty. I was in a terrible state, not sleeping during the day. I was in a bad way and really worried. I got sent to sickbay and the doctor came and saw me. I told him and he was in fact very nice and suggested I go home and see my own doctor. So I did. I remember that train journey from Newcastle to Hexham. It was one of the most nightmarish train journeys in my life. There's some very pretty countryside through the Yorkshire Dales and I had this fantasy that I'd get off the train and I'd walk up the dales and some farmer would take me in. And then I wouldn't have to go home. I think that kept me from jumping off the train and killing myself. Telling my parents meant it'd be the end of an era when they thought I was all right. I was the youngest daughter who was their 'success'.

My mum met me at the station. She always did when I returned for my days off. We went for coffee as usual and I couldn't stop myself telling her. She was in a really bad way. She must've told my dad 'cos I didn't and he looked as if the world had fallen apart, ill and grey and cried a lot and hardly spoke to me. It was like a great disaster had occurred and befallen the family. After that weekend I knew I couldn't stay at home, not that they said I couldn't, but the atmosphere was so strained I knew I had to get away. It was just too stressful.

There was no way I was going to be able to have a baby and return with it to the house. It was inevitable it would be adopted. It was like a script that had been written. It didn't even get talked about. Not really. My mother was illegitimate and her mum had been as well, so there'd been a history of secrets and lies and children thinking that somebody was their parent who wasn't. It affected her a lot. She married my dad and had legitimate babies and felt that she had stopped the rot and I was potentially starting it again. So I couldn't have done anything that hurt her more. We had to protect her as children as we knew she'd been so hurt. The overriding feeling in the house was that she'd already suffered and it was our responsibility not to make her suffer anymore. So the only way to restore the status quo and pretend we were a moral family was to have the baby adopted. It was more about protecting my parents' fragility than what the neighbours thought.

I know I was very unhappy when I went to that party. It was a very grey time for me. I think that had a lot to do with it as well, in that parting with the baby for adoption was also parting with that grey time.

I went to see an almoner at the hospital and my mum came with me. Looking back I wish she hadn't, because I think the social worker might have asked me questions about how I felt about things and she'd have treated me differently. But instead it was all about practicalities. I ceased to be a grownup when I became pregnant and became their child again. It almost felt like a relief in some ways – someone telling you what to do.

I told the almoner I wanted to go away and she made an appointment for me to see the Moral Welfare Worker. I knew I'd be going to a mother and baby home. Most of them took you six weeks before and six weeks after, but she'd found me one that took you straight away, which was exactly what I needed – to get out as soon as possible. But I still had to wait a few weeks. I stayed on night duty for a while and slept a lot.

My own GP was a shit. He wouldn't verify during all this time that I was pregnant, even though I was booked into this home. Finally he gave me an examination and he did it very coldly and callously and hurt me. It was horrible. Then he said, 'Well that's well and truly fixed in place. Now you can't get rid of it, can you!' I'm sure he didn't verify it earlier as he thought I'd try and abort. I was mortified. Also he didn't get a chaperone into the room. He did it on his own and it made me feel like he was assaulting me. It was the first time I'd ever been examined and it was so painful and humiliating and in such a horrible context – to do with being bad and naughty. So it just felt like another humiliation on top of all the others.

I went to the home near Manchester from the February until September. It was a church-run home. You could give birth on the premises as well, unlike most of the other ones. When you arrived you were sent to an agency to find a job so you went out to work every day until six weeks before. I worked in a shop. You had to be out by 8.30 in the morning and you weren't allowed in till 5.30. But once you were in, you weren't allowed out again. You'd have been sent away if you broke the rules. And where would you have gone?

There was no support or anything like that among the women. We talked superficialities. We didn't talk about why we were there. We'd talk about the jobs and so on, but we learnt hardly anything about who we were before we came and we never talked about who we'd be after we left. You shared a room with three others and had to be in bed by 10. Lights were turned out at 10.15. And you weren't allowed to put the light on again. It was just like prison. At weekends you could go out between 2 and 4. You weren't allowed any visitors. You had to see them outside the home.

On Sunday morning you had to go to church. So here we were, hidden from the world in all this secrecy six days a week and on Sunday it could be anything up to 20 pregnant girls would all walk out, crocodile-fashion, to church! It was horrendous. One woman on the staff was OK in a Christian, do-goody way and the other was a pig. An absolute pig. She was in charge of all the administration as well as cooking the meals. We used to have a rota for housework and washing up in the evening. One of her little tricks was to turn the hot water off in the afternoon so that when you came to wash up there'd be no hot water. It'd be all cold and greasy and foul. Nothing was to be made easy! It was to be as difficult as possible. It was her way of operating. And she used to do these massive meals. Good, plain food. She was quite a good cook but you weren't allowed to leave the table until it was all eaten. So you'd have to sit there feeling sick and pregnant and eating roast potatoes that were bad for us. And no one ever challenged anything, apart from a few little things in a schoolgirl kind of way and that'd be the highspot of the moment.

We believed we were bad. No one challenged it because we thought that was the appropriate way to treat girls like us. And we were grateful that they took us in and fed us and housed us when we were so bad. And we were terrified of being chucked out. So your self-perception, your self-worth was absolutely non-existent. And there was no getting away from the fact that it was a religious establishment with prayers before meals and church.

We used to go to work each day pretending we were married. It was a whole other world in the daytime. You'd tell stories about where you were living. Hardly anyone told the truth. And then you'd return in the evening. We used to buy our wedding rings in Woolworth's and you had to keep polishing them 'cos they tarnished. They called us 'Mrs' at the agency when they paid us on a Friday so they all colluded with our being married.

The home was two big semis. When you gave up work you moved next door where the midwives were. And everyone was dying to move next door 'cos it meant it was getting near the end. It was almost like graduation. The day you gave up work you moved next door which meant you'd have six weeks to go. That's when the waiting really began. You weren't allowed out apart from the afternoon, so you were there all morning doing housework. We just made it up as nothing needed doing.

There was no preparation for birth. No books or anything. It was as if you were having a baby but you weren't. So you were there having a baby but it was the thing talked about least of all. The babies were the end result of what we were there for and they were to go to adoptive parents - and that was what it was about. It was nothing to do with *us* having babies.

Four weeks before the baby was due we had a checkup from the local doctor who oversaw the midwifery. I remember that very strongly. He didn't speak to us at all. He didn't acknowledge us by name or anything. He'd say to the midwife, 'Tell her to bend her knees,' or whatever and she'd then tell us. It was as if we were so bad, that he wasn't even allowed to speak to us. But it just felt like part of the system and what you expected. And he was very rough as well. It was very painful. Those of us waiting to see him would sit outside the clinic room on the stairs and those who were coming out would try and make a joke. He was just foul. I felt that my experience with a doctor during that time was almost like being raped. It was like 'I deserve to be hurt' and I wasn't a real person and the only part of me that existed was my genitals. I was just a body. And the midwife was colluding.

Then you waited to go into labour. By that time you had some idea of what was going to happen to you 'cos you'd heard it talked about. It was terrifying hearing the others give birth. The corridor was literally outside the labour ward. You also knew you'd try and make as little noise as possible so as not to frighten the ones to come. Some were only 14 or 15. It was obvious that from the way they talked that some of them didn't even know how they got pregnant.

When you went into labour you told the midwife, who confirmed it and shaved you. Then they went away. In some ways people might think it was an idyllic way to have a baby – with no intervention. You weren't made to lie on a bed or anything. So you could go to bed if you wanted to, but it wasn't 'cos they cared. It was because they didn't care. It could've been quite dangerous. The intervention was so minimal, I'm amazed no one died.

After that initial examination they didn't bother with you again until you wanted to push. No one had a forceps delivery or anything. But we all had an episiotomy. Everyone was cut.

I eventually retired to bed about 2 in the afternoon on the second day of my labour. It was called the 'lying-in room'. They left the door open and said to call. No one stayed with you and none of the girls was allowed to come and see you, so you were on your own with the door open. I really thought I was going to die. I just thought I wasn't going to live through it. There were no painkillers. At about 5 o'clock I got this pushing sensation and I called but no one came. So I ended up screaming, and eventually one of the girls who'd come up to use the toilet heard me and I asked her to get the midwife. I actually started pushing before there was a midwife there. Then they took me into the labour ward. I pushed for two hours. I remember saying, 'I think I'm going to die.' And I thought the baby was going to die as well. Eventually the midwife managed to drag her out with her hands. I was so torn! I needed about 15 internal stitches. I don't think they're allowed to use forceps without a doctor there. And they hadn't sent for him. It was just a nightmare!

She was born at 6.55 and was 8 lb 13 oz. Then they put her in a cot and asked what I was going to call her and put on a nametag. Then I went back to the 'lying-in room' and that's when the other girls were allowed to visit. You were also allowed hot chocolate. The only time you were ever allowed it. It was a treat. Then the midwife said a prayer by the bed. A healing-type prayer, a 'God forgive' type prayer for me and the baby. They were religious too. Then she was put in the nursery and I lay there and thought, 'Well, that's it now. I've got six weeks to go and then I won't be here any more.' And that's how I thought of it, that I wouldn't have to live there any more and I could go back home and pretend it never happened.

You weren't allowed to phone anyone. The only way they knew you'd had a baby was when they got your letter. So that could be a week later before you heard back. There were no cards or anything.

We had to feed the babies ourselves. I remember I didn't get to hold her until the next day when they taught me how to feed her. There was no night feeding. Nobody fed them. They were just left. You put them down at 11 o'clock at night and you weren't allowed back in until 6 in the morning. So they went eight hours without a feed. We used to have a wry joke and say it was for the adoptive parents so they could have an easy time of it. You could take them out between 2 and 5 o'clock. The only way you could be with your baby on your own was to take them out.

But the overriding feeling was actually getting out of that place. It really was. She did feel like my baby and yet she didn't. It felt like I was looking after someone else's baby. She always felt like someone else's because she was always going to be adopted and so I didn't let myself really recognise her as being mine although I can remember the physical feelings of her very strongly... her smell and feeling her breastfeeding and so on. All babies have their own smell regardless of whether you put powder on them ... and the warmth of their little heads and how it feels to have someone physically dependent on you. It's a very physical relationship I think at that stage. It's quite sensual.

I was programmed not to love her so I didn't let myself. It was built in, so I didn't have to think, 'I mustn't allow myself.' This was just a period in my life that was going to be over – and I was to go back and have another life. I used to look at other women who changed their minds and I felt they were on a different planet to me. I didn't feel like we were the same breed because I didn't know how you could be a woman who could decide to keep her baby. I wouldn't have known how to be one of those.

About half of them kept their babies, while I was there anyway. There were little peaks and troughs, a kind of knock-on effect. If one said, 'I'm going to,' how many others thought, 'If they can, I can.' The social worker from the adoption agency came and saw all those whose babies were a month old to ask if we were still going to have the babies adopted. Our little group of four said yes, but the following group all said no. After a few minimal questions she went away to match your child with adoptive parents. Then you'd hear from her within the next week whether she'd found a couple for your child and a little bit about them. Minimum details.

I said my baby was still for adoption and then she asked me if I had any special requests. Looking back I think she meant religion but I said off the top of my head that I'd like her to go to the same secondary school as me. The home wasn't all that far away from it. I'd said that because it represented a happy time of my life; I'd had some good friends there. But I didn't think it'd happen. She told me he was an accountant – her job wasn't mentioned – and they'd already adopted a little girl two years before. And then she indicated I might get my wish about the school. At the time it felt like very little information.

I can remember thinking from the time this couple was described to me that they were her parents, not me. Once there was a couple with an identity, then there was no way she was my child.

We had a few rituals that were imposed upon us, like once you'd given up work you had to go to church twice on Sundays and attend chapel every morning in the home. The day your baby was born you could actually choose the hymn that was sung in the morning service and they'd leave the doors open so you could hear and they'd sing it extra loud. That was the only acknowledgement that was given.

We had one or two self-imposed rituals and one of them was the day you left everybody would buy themselves a new outfit of clothes. And all the babies were always dressed in white – from top to toe. And looking back I suppose it was the nearest we got to a ceremony, like a christening or something. We actually symbolised this special day by our clothes. And perhaps the babies in white represented the innocence in this. They were moving from bad parents to good – and they were moving on in white. I think there was a lot of symbolism that was passed and we colluded with it.

The last week was quite occupied with the business of what one would wear and that took up a lot of time. Then we'd go into Sheffield and buy the sort of suit you'd wear at your child's christening. Something very smart, and you'd look very dressed up the day you left. I remember someone doing my hair for me and putting a lot of meaning into how I looked. The baby looked absolutely beautiful. Everything was brand new. I bought some little booties that had fur round them which was all soft and they were far too big so I put tissues in the toes. She looked gorgeous. And a lot of us took photos of each other before we left. I've got about half a dozen photos. They'd send them on to you. It's amazing, all that support and solidarity on the day you left.

The smartness was about bravado – we were going out to a new beginning. Our life was starting and we were showing the world we weren't bad any more. We were good again. And all of this wasn't explicit. You just saw it being done and you did it next. I remember we looked ever so respectable. I wore a bottle green suit with a straight skirt which was very fashionable, high heels and a grey short-sleeved sweater. I looked very smart. I gave it away

eventually but I wore it a lot. We all bought our clothes at this
'factory' shop. It was the only ritual that we devised for ourselves.
It was our choice, not theirs.

The day the babies were adopted was the day you left. The
adoptions took place in central Sheffield, which are also meeting
rooms and lots of people work there. To us it was the day of the
adoption but in fact it was where the baby was handed over. It
was a few miles away from the home. They organised a taxi for
you and the baby if you didn't have anyone to pick you up. You
paid for it though. I can remember young women leaving, carrying
beautifully dressed babies, climbing in taxis, looking a million
dollars and your suitcases were put in the taxi with you as you
weren't coming back. I suppose you could have gone off in the
taxi somewhere else, but no one ever did. If you've ever seen
pictures on the telly of women coming out of maternity hospitals,
like Lady Di, climbing into a car, the nurse holding the baby, the
baby's handed over and everyone waves – it was just like that.
You'd have thought they going off to the happiest celebration in
the world and we stood on the steps or leant out of windows and
waved goodbye. We'd never see them again.

The day I left, there were four of us and my mum and dad were
coming for me in the car. We were told to take one of the other
women, so the last few miles were spent in close proximity to
somebody else with their baby. It must've been worse for her 'cos
my parents were strangers to her. She was quite a character, tough
and quite rebellious. And she was potty about her baby. In the
end she was so hysterical in the car I had to give mum my baby
to hold while I held hers because she was so upset. The thing that
bothered me most was that dad would be angry 'cos he wouldn't
be able to concentrate on driving.

When we got there we were shown into a room with our babies.
I remember it was dark as there were no windows in it because it
has been partitioned. The adoptions took place every half hour
and mine was the last one. This woman came through for the first
baby and then half an hour later for the second and so on. So
although I had to wait so long I had my daughter for that much
longer. But I found it very difficult watching them, going through
theirs.

The adoptive couple were brought into the other half of this
room and then the church worker would come through the
dividing door and take the baby through and give it to the
adoptive couple who were on the other side of the partition.

That would have been the first time they had seen the baby. And off they went home with it.

The adoptive parents came for my baby at about half-past 3. They brought their little girl with them, as I could hear her voice. It just felt totally unreal. I felt numb. And my parents were out in the car, waiting. The adoptive parents were shown out first so we didn't bump into each other. And just as I was being shown out, my dad came down the corridor to look for me. In my memory, the corridor was very, very long, although I saw it quite recently and it's quite short. I remember walking along with him behind me and I looked back. I knew I wouldn't see the adoptors and the baby but I had to look back. And all I could see was my dad. And he said, 'What's the matter?'

It was a system that for them went absolutely smoothly. No one upset the applecart. If you decided to keep your baby then the social worker would discuss the practical things. I'm sure that the midwives approved more of those who kept than us, because they were being like proper mothers. I remember feeling jealous and I'm sure they were treated more warmly than us because once they'd made their decision they became 'normal' and we were abnormal even though everything had been geared to making us behave like that. So although I felt like they were from a different planet I also knew that they were better than me. They were being the right sort of mothers. But I couldn't imagine myself in their position. Looking back, the ones who kept their babies were those who had the most security to go back to and family support. Perhaps they were more emotionally mature than me as well.

That feeling of 'badness' never leaves you. The next few years were a frantic attempt to prove I wasn't bad. When I returned to my parents I mentally thought of myself as a virgin again. I was going to begin all over again. I needed to feel good. And for my parents' sake as well. Particularly them. They never mentioned it again. And my friends didn't want to know, were embarrassed if I tried to mention it. And no one wanted to see the photos. I felt so proud of her and to have produced such a beautiful baby. But it wasn't an ache.

I returned to nursing in a different place and started a whole new life. So that helped to cut off the past remarkably effectively. It was a great mechanism for pretending things hadn't happened.

Since then I've had depression and psychological disturbances, stresses and so on. But I've also had some happy times too. I think her conception and adoption were a symbol of lots of things that had been bad in our family which was very distressing to me. So its hard to separate it all out. But I know I felt such a heavy sense of shame about what I'd done that it was hard to even acknowledge it. That'd mean I'd have to start looking at it.

I think the worst effect on me was when I having my third child, Robert. I refused to recognise any link, but I can see it now. What I did was to pretend that Helen, the baby I gave for adoption, never existed. He was to be my second child. I couldn't do that with my second one as it was obvious that I'd had a child. So I didn't and no one asked any awkward questions. So my first child was 'present' then. But with Robert I denied she ever existed. At the time I saw it was a successful thing to do and thought, 'How wonderful! I can pretend I never had it.' She wasn't 'she' then – only 'it', that I'd given away. I thought that having him would make everything fit into place properly, respectably. So there was a complete denial of ever having had her.

I was profoundly depressed all the time I was pregnant with Robert and kept thinking there was going to be something wrong with him. Also my mum was very ill in hospital. When I had him there were lots of echoes of having Helen, like being on my own when I started pushing. I was haemorrhaging afterwards and was frightened I was going to die and I created absolute mayhem. Apparently I had psychosis and was quite mad for a while. The Sister came with an injection of paraldehyde which I knew would knock me out for days and I said, 'He isn't my second. He's my third!' She said, 'It doesn't matter' and I said, 'It does.' And then she knocked me out. When I came round a day or so later I never said any more about it. For years.

But I had told my two children about her when they were quite young so I haven't denied her to that extent. I was lucky that I managed to get a psychotherapist who got me to the stage where I was able to talk about her. I saw him for two and half years. It was almost as if he became her father because he cared about her. He thought she was highly important.

What lingers is the feeling of being bad, bad for being pregnant and bad for giving a child away. That has lasted for years. Adoption is painful, whatever the circumstances, but to have had some choice and support, to have felt more valued and to have been more open about it would have helped me. It wasn't till I joined a birthmothers' support group a couple of years ago that I seriously began to address the fact that I'd had her. And to hear about birth mothers' experiences, including reunions. That seemed like a fairytale, a fantasy.

My child in my head was still six weeks old, so in some ways I was quite angry that the assumption was we all wanted reunion. We didn't. We hadn't even come to terms with our children growing up. I think reunion is a long way down the line and you need to do a lot of thinking first. They saw that reunion would make them whole again or 'well' and I feel that for me it's part of a process. Reunion isn't always the answer and it can be an unrealistic investment. 'I've been waiting for it all these years' – I think I've been really lucky to have learnt from other people's experiences and paced myself accordingly.

I've also become involved in adoption on a wider scale and met adoptive parents and adoptees who think like I do and realise that we're not actually divided, it's often the professionals who divide us and we have a lot more trust in each other than people give us credit for. And that's been very healing. But the best thing that's happened to me is managing my own sense of reality – my openness is that I now know what her name is and where she lives. She is now real, she does exist – so if you've always been able to stay connected with that reality you must inevitably feel better about yourself.

After our interview in the summer of 1990, and after considerable thought, Margaret wrote to her daughter via an intermediary. On the day she posted the letter she arranged to have a party with her closest female friends. Her daughter replied almost at once and informed the intermediary that she was not wanting any contact at the moment.

2 Susan

I met Susan in New Zealand through a friend. She had never spoken to anyone before about her experience as a birth mother, apart from her husband and one friend who was with her at this interview. Susan is a birth mother. She had twin daughters, one of whom she kept. She is also adopted. Listening to her story it becomes clear that the two are inextricably linked, a connection she herself makes.

Susan's own Experience of Adoption

I always wanted to know from the time I was a little girl who I was … who I am. Mum and Dad were great – they were always open with me – explaining that I was the chosen one. They used to read me stories about the rabbit that adopted the opossum. They were fabulous parents and I had a very good upbringing. I had a brother five years older than me and we were quite competitive. I was more academic. But he worked hard and is now a successful businessman. But I always wanted to know who I was. I looked in the mirror and saw my nose going up. I looked in the mirror and I was tall. I couldn't identify myself with my mother and father. My personality was different. I threw tantrums, they didn't. I always knew I was different from them. For years I always thought my birth mother was better than these two, she had to be better. She was a film star, a model, an academic. Everything I wanted to be – I felt she was.

I remember when I was about 13 having a tantrum and my father saying, 'For God's sake, find her mother and send her to her.' Is it normal to feel like this? To still be feeling like this? I'm 40 years old!

When I was 19 I found out I was pregnant. I'd been working for a man who was very kind and caring and we had this wonderful affair. He taught me everything I know! Prior to this I'd had a bad accident and spent many months in hospital in Australia. I

17

returned home to New Zealand in the February. It was 1970. My
dad died in May. He didn't pick that I was pregnant and I couldn't
tell him. He was very caring about me and knew what I'd been
through. My parents were separated by this time and I went to
stay with my father's friend, June. She's a fabulous lady, we're still
in touch. She's like my mum.

Then I met this wonderful man and told everyone he was the
father. We didn't know at this stage I was having twins. I just got
larger and larger. But he was killed in a car accident three weeks
before we were to be married.

A short time later I went into hospital and had these twins. After
I'd put one of them up for adoption I knew then that I'd have to
find out who I was to try and cope with meeting my daughter at
some time in the future.

The years went on and I got married. We had no children and
he didn't acknowledge the fact that I had a handicapped child.
He didn't want anything to do with her. The marriage was a
great friendship. I also loved his mother very dearly. But that all
broke up. Later I met my present husband. He's 18 years older
than me.

Then I started thinking about my birth mother more and more.
The changes in the adoption laws had come in, which meant that
I could trace her – or at least get some identifying information.
Find out who I am. My husband was concerned that I'd be disappointed. He felt that maybe what I had concocted in my mind
wouldn't be what I'd hoped it'd be. But I rang the adoption
workers in Auckland, who were fabulous and very caring. They
conducted all my counselling over the phone. They rang back quite
quickly to say they had a name for me. My birth name. It was
Code. I said, 'You're joking! What an odd name!' Then she said
she had the original birth certificate and sent it to me. So there
it was. I'd got it in front of me. I was Paula Code. I couldn't believe
it. So then I thought, 'What do I do now?' I know who I am. And
there I am. I'm half Scottish. It felt weird. Then I looked in the
phone book. After that I did a search in Wellington which they
said could take weeks, to find out if she married, and I did a ten-
year search on a marriage certificate and a divorce certificate and
a remarriage certificate, thinking she might be like me and married
twice.

It was about a week later when I rang my husband, as I was
working quite late, and asked if there was any mail. He said there
was nothing of any importance. It was winter and when I got home

he had this fire lit for me – and on the table was a letter marked OHMS. I opened it up and there was her marriage certificate! She'd married a year after she gave birth to me. And I thought, 'Oh my God. He's my birth father too.' It was wonderful! So I rang the adoption worker the next day. But in the meantime I'd been very sneaky and found the name in the local phone book with the right initials.

Ron, the adoption worker, said I could make contact in one of three ways. I could approach her personally, write a letter or ring her. He said that approaching her personally at her age could be risking a coronary; a letter she could rip up. A phonecall seemed the best way. I'm sure the advice is designed to protect birth mothers, adopted children and adoptive parents. But if the phonecall didn't work out I would've followed it up with a letter and a photograph – I wouldn't have left it there. I might even have gone knocking on her door selling raffle tickets or something. But I knew I was going to meet her.

Ron had stressed that if I rang her I was to say my name clearly and ask if she was in a position to talk; that it was important not to put her in an awkward situation. He emphasised that I must keep saying my name and where I lived so that she could contact me again if she wished. In the meantime a friend of mine rang her workplace. Yes, it was my birth mother's name – Jean. I knew I'd got the jackpot.

I phoned her that night. She denied it to start with. I said, 'Do you remember the 20th of April?' and she said, 'No.' I told her my name and said I'm not here to hurt you and she said, 'Oh, oh my God'. I then asked her if she was able to talk and she said, 'What do you look like?' Just like that. And we talked for about an hour. She told me about her life, which had been tragic. She'd married a guy who was a chronic alcoholic, not my birth father. He'd spent time in prison for drinking and driving, and was a compulsive gambler and could never hold down a job. But in fact when I met him he turned out to be a delightful chap. He's been so good to me.

She kept putting off the meeting and finally agreed to come round here for lunch on a Saturday, which she did – two hours early! This was about a month later. It was good, actually, as it gave me time to think. Also we talked on the phone a couple of times before we met.

The day of the meeting was amazing. We met halfway down the drive. I went out and there she was! She's lovely – a sweetie.

We talked for hours. It was so good. We looked at all the photographs and she then said 'Look, I'm sorry dear, but you just don't
look like any of my children.' I don't think I look like her either.
She was an old ... young person, was weatherbeaten, had a tragic
life, I thought, had a great sense of humour -and that's about all.
She was really happy to meet me and has told me since I'm a very
big part of her life, and I feel I may be. I may be a snob too, but
I come from a better background than hers. But I wasn't disappointed. I couldn't be disappointed in meeting someone who made
the right choice in giving me up.

I've met her other four daughters and I don't think I look like
them either. Maybe one of them, but it's only the colouring. I
was hoping when I met them that I would've resembled one of
them and even today I still keep asking that question, 'Do I look
like them?' The reason I wanted to find my birth mother was to
find out who I looked like. So that's been disappointing. But I'm
happy she made the right decision and I think she's happy there
are no grudges.

One of the things I really wanted to know about was my birth
father, because I'm a male-orientated person. I'd been advised to
be cautious asking about this because of the emotional upheaval
it can cause the birth mother. So it wasn't such a shock when she
said she didn't know. Then she came out with a name which I
wrote down and she said I'd spelt wrongly. But when I said, 'So
you do remember?', she denied it. I said I understood. I do feel
she may know but I'll leave it unless it comes up again. I wouldn't
want to hurt her in any way.

My adoptive father was very important to me. I lost him when
I was 20. We were very close. He was my best friend. My adoptive
mum and my brother, their natural son, were very close. That
happens in families. I feel maybe I've missed out and that I'm
searching for a father. I've always been attracted to older men,
and I wonder if my birth father was an older man because all Jean's
daughters have married men much older too.

Things in common? Absolutely nothing – apart from telling good
jokes. Otherwise nothing. Nothing. I can't think of one thing. She
hates gardening. She's quite creative, though. She sent me a
beautiful basket she made up when I came home from hospital
recently, with little dogs and things made out of facecloths. She's
very creative in that way.

It's now three years since we've met. She is lovely but our relationship hasn't developed. It's stayed where it was. That could

be partly my fault 'cos I don't ring her very often. But one of the daughters keeps on ringing me. She keeps wanting contact. She's the one who looks on me more as a sister than the other three. I have tried with them all, but they come from a different social background. One half-sister, Yvonne, who's very kind and caring, is involved in the spiritual church like me - and healing. That's one thing I've got in common with Jean – healing. I've often wondered where that came from and now I know. And Yvonne is also very clairvoyant. So yes, that is one thing we've got in common. Apparently Jean's mother was clairvoyant too. But really there's nothing else.

They've popped in a couple of times. One night I had a barbecue, but it was difficult, the conversation didn't flow. You know how you can meet strangers and it can flow … well, it didn't and I really tried hard. Perhaps I tried too hard. But I hope Jean knows I'm there for her if she needs me. I do wonder if she hadn't given me up whether I could've helped her with her difficulties. I'm sure I feel guilty that I might have been able to help her, protect her, if she hadn't given me up. Maybe I can still be of some help to her. Perhaps I should ring her more often, but I think she knows deep down that I am here for her. I hope she knows that – that my door is open to her as it would be to anyone who needed help.

How am I left feeling? She's not my mother. No. I'm quite adamant about that. She's someone who gave birth to a daughter and had her adopted out. I couldn't call her 'Mum'. My mum lives up north and although she encouraged me to find my birth mother, she still won't talk about her. Nor will she talk to me about the daughter I gave up for adoption, even though she's made provision for her in her will. She never coped with my having them. She sent me a 'get well' card in hospital! But I won't talk about it with her either. I can't. I can't talk to anyone about it. Perhaps I'm frightened that if I do, I might be disappointed with her like I was disappointed with Jean. The time will come. I call it the Day of Reckoning, but at least I've got the support of my husband.

She's a difficult woman, my adoptive mother – that's just her personality. I didn't tell her for about a month that I'd met Jean. I've said to her quite openly, 'Thank you for being there,' and in some ways it's brought us closer. But my brother and I have drifted apart since the reunion. He's their natural son. In the early days we were very close … I admire him enormously. He didn't want to discuss it either. All he said was, 'Open subject, close subject,' and that was it. I was hurt. I thought he'd be more caring.

I'm convinced more adopted girls got pregnant. I'm sure I did deliberately. I was in such emotional turmoil at that age. And I'm also convinced I'm a grandmother – and that the family line has carried on in the same way. I feel it psychically. I also think it's about torturing yourself. Your parents love you, they got you for a reason, but you've always been different. There's something deep down that says 'I'm going to be just like the person before me.' I've known other adopted kids who've gone out and got pregnant. I had a good friend who was adopted and at 16 she deliberately got pregnant and told her adoptive mother, who said, 'You're just like your mother,' and she said, 'That's just what I want to be'.

But I'm pleased I know about my birth mother and her family. I just didn't realise it'd be this hard … maybe it's the disappointment that she's not like me … and I still don't feel like anyone.

Pregnancy and Twins

One thing I can remember very clearly is at the solicitor's office, signing the adoption papers. I'll remember that day till I die. If I ever meet him again I'll kill him! I was waiting in the reception area and he gave me these papers to read and said frostily, 'Please read these and I'll see you in ten minutes.' And I was sitting there trying to understand all the legal writing, thinking, 'I'm going to hold myself up high – you bastard!' And I walked into his office, this big room with a big desk and I said, 'Where do you want me to sign?' And he looked at me and said, 'You're a bit cold, aren't you?' When I asked him what he meant he said, 'Other ones I've had in here, they've sat down and they've sobbed and sobbed …' and I said, 'I've done my sobbing.' He then asked, 'How could you give up a twin?' I said, 'I've got friends and a doctor helping me …' He said 'Once you've signed it, you have no rights.' And as a 20-year-old I stood tall and refused to sit down; I remember there was a witness and having to put my hand on the bible …

It was that experience of him that made me put it out of my mind forever. I remember getting a bus home and I thought I'll never talk about it again. I have only one child – very sick and in and out of hospital. I did my best …

I was pregnant when I was 20. It was 1970. I had to go into hospital just before they were born as something seemed to be going wrong … and that's when the humiliation of being unmarried started. I was strapped on to this table to have an X-ray and then the alerts began. I was immediately induced and everyone was alerted to come in. I had to go through the humiliation of being alone. I was crying for my fiancé who'd been killed. I could hear them saying I might need a 'Caesar' and talking about me just outside the room. No one was allowed to see me. I was given an enema and shaved ... it was humiliating.

Then it all started and I was pushing and they were putting a mask over my face. I could hear them shouting, 'This is it!' and, 'Cut her! Cut her!' And then I felt this knife and then this baby coming out – and I was so happy! Then they told me there was something wrong with her – she was screaming and I could see her arms waving about and blood ... and then they said she needed a transfusion. I shouted, 'I'm keeping her! She's mine!' And there were people everywhere. I can still see the theatre with a screened table and people all around her. I thought she was a blue baby. And the next thing was I wanted to keep pushing and they were saying 'Pound, pound.' And I didn't know what the doctor meant. I was calling out, 'What? What?' And they said 'Keep pushing!' And then I saw my daughter just go. Whooosh! Out of the room! And then another baby came ... and I said, 'No, no I've just had her...and I really thought, Sue, it was just a dream. And she was whipped away as well. I didn't know I was having twins. No one had told me. But they knew because of the X-ray. But I had no idea. The next thing was legs up, injections, blood ... I didn't know what was happening.

About three hours later the doctor and nurse in a suit came in and said, 'You've had twins!' I thought it was the placenta. And they said, 'Don't you remember having twins?' Then they said they were going to wheel me down to the nursery and the ambulance was there to transfer Vanessa, my first daughter, to another hospital as they'd diagnosed spina bifida. She had to go to theatre straight away. I was meant to stay with the other one. I said that I was going to have the baby adopted but they thought then to give me the option. They said, 'You've got 24 hours to decide what to do.' The Motherhood of Man was there and involved too. They were the adoption agency involved.

I had no intention of keeping any baby. I decided it was better that way because I was given a good life. The father felt this too. We had agreed that we'd always be there if he or she needed us.

The next morning I decided I wanted to be with both the babies, so I asked if Theresa – the other baby – and I could go to the same hospital that Vanessa had been transferred to, and they said, 'No. What is your decision?' I said, 'I'm leaving here to go to my sick baby.' Also, because Vanessa was first born, to me she was real. The other one was a dream. I think at this stage I still didn't really believe I'd had two babies, even though I'd seen the other one. So I went to my sick baby, but couldn't stay there because they only had accommodation for married couples. And I really wasn't wanted there. So I had to return to the first hospital. She had the best treatment and care, but I was the unwanted mother because of the adoption.

Then everything got screwed up. They didn't know which baby was up for adoption. The adoption agency said they would not take Vanessa as she was handicapped – and that I had to be at hospital with the other one (Theresa). It was very confusing. Also my breasts were very sore and I was filled with injections and given pills. I returned and looked at Theresa and said, 'I love you but I've got to let you go,' and asked them to find a happy family for her as I had to go back to my baby. My daughter. Theresa didn't feel like my daughter. My daughter was the one in theatre who was ill, with drains in her back, who was screaming, her arms waving ... and I had all this milk. I didn't know what to do with it. One of the things I asked when I left the first hospital was whether I could express the milk for Theresa, as they wouldn't let me breastfeed her. I was allowed to do that and gave her her last drink. Then I walked away and the Motherhood of Man was chasing me again out of the hospital and into the ambulance saying, 'Are you quite sure this is what you want?' I remember someone standing there and saying, 'How can you be Solomon?' And that was the first time I'd heard of Solomon. It's a religious story about cutting a baby in half and dividing it and sharing it out. Apparently I played Solomon, putting one part here and one part there. But I did it – and I did it for the right reasons ... I'd made the decision that the second baby was a bloody nuisance and how could God do that to me, what was he trying to prove? And that I had a very sick baby that needed me.

I think there was definitely a connection between rejecting Theresa and not being told I was having twins. Also I'd heard that you have to go through the labour again to expel the placenta and I honestly thought that's what was happening. Then I saw this perfectly formed, tiny child they held and I'd been given this gas and couldn't work out what was happening.

Really, until today Sue, I've never really acknowledged that I had a second child ... I didn't want a second ... and today is the first time I've ever called them the twins.

I guess the natural maternal bond does go to the sick one. Just like when you have kids at home and one gets sick. Surely it's the same thing. And I miss Vanessa so much. I miss her terribly. She was lovely ... She died at eight and a half ... after 37 operations. It's not right that a child should suffer like that.

And now I wonder if I've put my other daughter into a situation of no return. Apparently it was the thing 20 years ago to leave a letter. But I didn't have time to leave a letter. I had a sick child, no father, I had to get fulltime work. My mother was sick – she had a breakdown. I had no family support. Will she understand? Will she?

How do I explain to the one out there? Would she really understand? Could she? That I kept her sister? I mean – I chose. Is she going to go through life like me feeling there's someone out there? They weren't identical, so maybe that'll help ... but apparently I was an identical twin. I found that out from my birth mother. It made sense of so much. I was always aware of someone else there ... there was always my friend.

I remember sharing this with Jean and she said the same thing – that the stillborn came out first – my sister – and I came second ... and she went for a long time telling everyone there was no adoption – only a stillborn ... God, it's tragic isn't it ...

Coming back to what I've got in common with my birth mother, Sue – a hell of a lot, actually! We might have come from different backgrounds but spiritually we're very similar, we've got a great sense of humour together, we've both had children – twins – and both situations were never quite right ... yes, we've got a lot in common!

3 April

April had a child, Dominique, 13 years ago when she was a schoolgirl. She had been sexually abused by her father and the child was his. She managed to care for her daughter until she was three, but without emotional support she was left feeling vulnerable, and her daughter unprotected. The stress caused by her family led her to believe that her daughter would be better off elsewhere.

She met the adoptive parents once. They were white, middle-class friends of the social worker who told her that no same-race, black adoptive family could be found. April has not seen or heard of Dominique for ten years, but understood in the beginning that she would have information about her.

I had Dominique 13 years ago. I had her when I was at school. I was sexually abused as a child. I can't remember a time when I didn't have to have sex with my father. That went on for years and years and years. My only escape was school. I did quite well there, I was quite clever. I didn't have my first period until I was 15. When I had it, I felt total power as I thought he wouldn't risk making me pregnant. I told him he couldn't touch me ever again because I was a woman now. I was also sexually abused by my mother as well. He totally ignored me and didn't agree stop. He went out and got drunk and came back and raped me. So after that first period I was pregnant.

It wasn't talked about in the house, not by either of my parents. I have a younger sister but she didn't know anything about the sexual abuse. They were both violent and used to beat us up all the time. We were very scared of them. We weren't allowed out after 4 o'clock. It was a terrible existence.

I knew straight away I was pregnant, the minute it happened. I went to tell my mum and he followed to stop me and threatened me with violence. So I kept it to myself and carried on going to school. I knew if I told anyone I wouldn't be able to go to school any more, so I blocked it out. I needed help. I was suffering and became very aggressive. My personality changed and I became very introverted. Also I was bullied at school because I felt different from the other kids. This happened from the age of five or six, right through to 15. I was always hounded and followed round the school. I think it was because I was relating on an adult level and all my friends were a lot older than me. I didn't see myself as a child – I hated cartoons, anything to do with childish things like pin-up pop stars. I didn't relate to the same things, so they probably saw me as different. I was very overweight. I used to eat because of my problems and they used to pick on me because of that. Also I was a bit scruffy as I wasn't very well looked after at home.

After I was pregnant he didn't touch me again because I threatened every day that I'd go to the police. He was scared. I had total control of the house from that day. He'd cry and things, but still no one talked about it. I wanted to make him suffer. I never spoke a word to him – just glared and threatened him. He used to beat me up. He knocked me out when I was seven months pregnant. He tried to punch me in the stomach to get rid of it. I didn't ever go to the doctor's. I was like two personalities – one knew I was pregnant and the other wouldn't admit it. That enabled me to cope with school.

I was in the fifth year and it was just coming up to the exams. I was just about to deliver the baby. No one at school knew until the morning my waters broke. We always used to get up at 6 o'clock in the morning and that's when it happened. I knew what it was, or at least I knew it was something to do with me being pregnant, but I still blocked it out. I left for school really early. I was having contractions and I was in pain. There was lots and lots of water. School was about half an hour away. When I got there I decided to tell the teacher. I told my best friend I was pregnant but she wouldn't believe me. I suppose being big I didn't really show, and I'd been doing sports and running round the track the week before. I saw the teacher but I couldn't tell him and muttered something about my period. I was given some sanitary towels and went into the exam. It was French. I sat in the exam in labour and my waters were still coming out – all over the chair and on the floor. The kids behind me could see the water and tried to tell the teacher but I glared at them not to. Then the teacher came up and asked why I was crying. He said it shouldn't be too difficult for me to get through the exam. I managed to get through it and wrote three or four essays and did the practical part as well, which meant I had to talk in French for about half an hour. At the end I was soaking wet and the teacher came up to me and asked me what was wrong. I still couldn't say, so he got a female teacher and when I told her they took me straight to the hospital.

I suppose someone told my parents. I think my mum knew I was pregnant but she was denying it as well. When I got to the hospital I had an examination. The doctor touched my belly and said, 'You're pregnant,' and what did I think the hospital was – a hotel or something where you just came in to drop your babies? But it was horrible, her saying I was pregnant, and I just started screaming because I had to admit it. I think she thought I was about 30 or something, much older than I was. I'd just turned 16. They took me to a room and didn't tell me what they were doing. They put electrodes on the baby's head. I found that out later. As the lady did it she said, 'Come on, you've opened your legs before, it shouldn't be a problem now.' Then this lady came with massive hands and it was really painful. They treated me really badly, like I was a slag.

Then my mum came and she asked me who the baby's father was. I didn't answer her and she asked, 'Is it your dad's?' and started choking me in the bed, trying to frighten me. That was what I expected from her. When I was five my dad tried to have intercourse with me for the first time. She came into the room and caught him and she just called me a slag and walked out. That's the last time I ever remember communicating with her about it at all. I was screaming and screaming for her to come and help me but when she saw what he was doing she turned on me. That's what she was like. I got the doctor to get rid of her as I couldn't cope with it all. It was a really long birth. I didn't have her till the next morning. They gave me an epidural and I didn't know what that was. They injected me in the legs – I didn't understand what was going on.

Just before I had the baby I banned my parents from the hospital because they were shouting the place down. They were so loud and noisy that the hospital staff didn't want them there either. They're like that family in [*the TV Series*] *Boys from the Black Stuff*, always shouting.

Not long after, someone came to see me about contraception, saying I should go on the pill. Sex was the last thing I wanted. That was when I asked to see a social worker.

When I told her about my father she said I mustn't tell anybody else in the world. I should keep it a secret and go back home with my parents or let them look after the baby. She said it would be a big scandal and she was sure I wouldn't want anyone to know about it. She asked me if I wanted to keep the baby and I said I did because I saw her as a victim as well. We were both victims and I thought we should stick together. I'm sure the social worker couldn't handle what I was saying, but she was the first person I'd ever told. She sent me back home and I thought, 'Well, I've told an adult now and that means if they can't help me, no one can.'

At first I thought it was a monster in me. But within three minutes of delivering her my whole feelings changed. She was mine. I took her home. There was constant fighting. And my dad was gloating over the baby, like 'It's my baby.' Everyone assumed I would keep the baby but no one offered me any help. Maybe it was because I seemed quite grown up at the time, I don't know. They knew I'd been raped but they didn't want anything to do with it. No one wanted to talk to me about it.

My sister didn't know what had been going on, although she knew he was abusive. My mum never left her on her own with him and she watched him all the time. But I was like a sacrifice to keep him there all the time. My job in the house was to keep the peace. I worked that out when I was about seven. He'd say things like, 'If you don't do it I'm going to beat your mother up.' He used to beat her badly. The other thing he'd say was, 'I'll get your sister and do the same thing to her.' I didn't want her to feel the pain. I thought when I was little that what men had in their underpants was a hot knife. He'd bring these knives home from work and that's what I thought he had down there. I never looked. I just knew that it was painful. I was in pain all the time he did it. But as a child you don't know. I didn't want her to suffer that as well, so I protected her. I've always protected her – fighting at school and things. No one was going to hurt my sister. She knew when I was at the hospital that dad was the father because mum told her. She wouldn't touch the baby. She refused to hold it. She just felt sick. She couldn't relate to the baby at all ... even though the baby was beautiful.

After I returned home with the baby there was so much trouble. Then our mum burnt the house down to get away from my dad. I think she thought it would be a way of getting us into a home away from him. She took all our clothes out but left the cats in.

I knew she did it. I asked her at the time and she denied it. She still does, but I know when she's lying. She was questioned by the police and apparently she was seen near the house at the time. Also she owed lots of money. She was spending all the rent money on drink. She was a bit of an alcoholic.

Looking back, I think I thought my dad was not all there. But he was very, very clever at the same time. He was into witchcraft and would cook things like pigs' heads with the brains and make us eat it. Then he'd take the eyes out and bury them in the grass and cast spells. He'd have crosses all round the house and garlic. I don't think it's cultural, I think it's just him. One day I took the cross away from the mirror. It's supposed to reflect or something in the mirror and I took it down to look at my school uniform. I forgot to put the cross back and I got beaten really badly for that. I think he was frightened of himself. He used to talk to himself in a funny language I didn't understand. He was a crazy man. You couldn't just bump into him. It would be like he was taking your strength. But maybe what he did to me was his way of showing me love. He had a fixation on me because apparently I reminded him of his mother, I looked like his mother. I don't understand what was going on there because my mum had a similar fixation. They used to argue about whose mother I looked like.

I was quite a spiritual child. My mother couldn't answer my questions, so she sometimes got people in to talk to me. They were spiritualists. I used to get premonitions of my life. I saw all these things that have happened to me. I knew I was going to have a baby. I knew that when I was about eight. That's what helped me to cope. I saw a picture of the baby and she was a little girl. She didn't look exactly as I remembered from the picture I had in my mind, but it was definitely her. I knew I was going to do well in my career. I always knew that. I didn't have any friends. I just had my spiritual comfort. I told everyone outside that I had the best parents in the world and that they loved me.

I begged my mum to have me adopted. She was always ill and tried to kill herself a few times. I used to say to her 'You don't want me, you don't love me – have me adopted.' My mum was white and sometimes she'd say to me, 'You little black bastard. If it weren't for you I wouldn't be stuck in this mess with you two. If you weren't born, all this trouble wouldn't have happened to me.' She felt she'd wasted her life because of me. She was a very intelligent woman. Sometimes I would believe her, but then I used to think she wasn't well. She sexually abused me too, but not like my dad although she started it about the same time as he did. She used to touch me and make me touch her and I didn't want to. I think I was six. I've only just admitted that in the last year. But I knew there was something wrong with both of them.

I went back to school. They had wanted me to be the head girl because I was their best pupil. They helped me a lot and bought everything I needed for the baby – a pram, clothes – I didn't need to buy a thing. The teachers were very shocked. I got on well with them. Every year they bought me Christmas presents, and when they had their babies they'd let me see them. They loved me. They were the only friends I had. I didn't have any schoolfriends except one. She helped me after I had the baby.

I couldn't stay at school because I was being teased all the time and I missed my baby. When I told my mum she was upset because she was going to lose her family allowance. She said if I wasn't going to go to school I should get out. So I walked straight out without anything, and I left the baby there but I was going to go back for her. I knew my dad wasn't around. I remember shouting down the road that I was free of her.

I gradually became very angry with my dad, but I still couldn't tell anyone fully. I told a social worker at the homeless families place where we had to go after the fire and she told the police. I didn't tell her everything, but I signed a statement about the time he raped me and I became pregnant. I couldn't handle talking about the rest. Later I went back and made another statement, which was bad for me because when it got to court they didn't believe me. The judge advised them to disregard the second statement. My mum backed my dad in court and said I was promiscuous from an early age. That was when I really turned against her and didn't speak to her for years. I was only asked about three questions but I had to describe every single detail. It was like being raped again. It ended up with the judge saying he was very sorry, he knew my father was an upstanding citizen of society, and everyone was looking at me like I was a slag. It was like I had tempted him and it was my fault. The judge added that he had committed a crime and he would have to give him two years. The way it was given to him was like, 'I'm really sorry I have to give you this sentence ...'

Eventually we got rehoused. My dad wasn't allowed to come near because of the court case coming up, but she started having him round to stay. We avoided each other completely. Then she asked me to leave, and I did go and leave the baby there. I couldn't see any other way out. I slept rough for a few days, stealing food and trying to work out a way to get Dominique out. Then I went to Social Services and told them everything that had happened and they helped me. Dominique and I went to a mother and baby home, and then they tried to rehouse me in a very rough area which I wouldn't accept. Then I got into college and was rehoused near there.

It was really hard. I was rehoused to a flat with a baby and that was it. I was lonely. I hadn't had time to build up a proper relationship with my daughter because of all the emotional turmoil of the court case and everything. She was a very deep child and was suffering. I had to keep taking her to the hospital. She wouldn't eat at times and always had infections and then dehydration. I felt like a really bad mother. I think it might have been because of all that shouting at home and them pulling her by the legs and screaming, trying to stop me taking her every time I threatened to leave. I think all that disturbed her a bit.

I went to college, but after the court case I flipped. I went mad. I broke a handbasin in the toilets with my bare hand. All the anger I had inside me came out. I felt I didn't count. I wasn't even a human being. I was just a doormat for people to wipe their feet on – what was the point of living? They came and took me away to a mental hospital and the next day they let me go. The doctor saw me counselling some of the patients. I actually got one of the patients who'd been in there a long time to agree to go home. The doctor asked me why I was there and said there was nothing wrong with me. He said I had every right to feel angry and sent me home. But I wasn't well, although I'd convinced him that I was. I went back to college. One of the teachers looked after the baby for a couple of days and gave her back and I was left on my own with her.

I kept on going to college and then met a man who later became my husband. He loved Dominique and was prepared to bring her up. I wasn't concerned about his feelings; all I was concerned about was whether she was getting the best care. I didn't feel a good enough mother. I also used to think about my dream of wanting to be adopted. I'd made a pact with her the day she was born that if I couldn't give her the best life then I'd make sure someone else did, even if it was in five years' time. I was prepared to take that amount of pain and make that sacrifice because I wanted her to have a happy life. Also, I always felt she wasn't safe with my parents around. I was more frightened of what they would do to her than anything I might do. I had to get her away from them. My dad had just come out of prison and was looking for his child. They followed me everywhere. I didn't want him touching her – ever.

One day I went to collect her from nursery and they called me into the office and said she was disturbed. She was violent and aggressive. She was nearly three. It was like an echo in my head. I thought, she's going to be disturbed. I was a bit like that when I was younger. I wasn't a normal child. I was always worried that people would find out about my dad beating me. I was always covering up my bruises and anxious in case anyone asked questions and I'd be bringing trouble back to the house. I saw that what was happening to her was similar. It was unintentional – I didn't mean to give her a bad life but it was coming out. So I thought, 'Right, tomorrow I'm going to Social Services and I'm going to hand her over.'

Social Services listened to what I had to say and then said they could see I'd made my mind up. They didn't try and persuade me not to give her up. Looking back, it wasn't the right response but I don't think they would have changed my mind. I'd made this pact from years before. She went into voluntary care. I had to give them all her toys and clothes and things … and that was the hardest part, just letting go. My emotional side was telling me not to do it but my sensible side was saying I had to. And that's the side I always listen to. I hate that side of myself, but I always do the right thing. It was the most horrible time of my life – the hardest.

They found parents for her very quickly. The social worker had friends who wanted to adopt her and that's how I was going to have some contact. They would give me information but I couldn't give them anything. I went to see her for the last time. She begged me to take her home. She was talking really well – I could see the improvement already. I hadn't seen her while she was in foster care because it would've upset me too much, and I wanted her to be stable. On that last visit she got a heavy toy and threw it in the foster parent's face and said, 'I don't want you. I want to be with my mummy.' It was like she wanted to be on her own with me. Then she asked if she could come home with me. I had to tell her no.

She was a very powerful child. I don't know if she took all my pain but she was a very, very intense child. After I said she wasn't coming home with me she wouldn't speak to me. That was it. She wouldn't give me a kiss or anything. She turned her back on me and let the car drive off. I looked back and she still had her back to me till the car was gone. And that was the last I saw of her on our own.

I felt bad. It was really hard letting her go – especially into a family with a man and a woman. I'd have much preferred her to go to a woman on her own because of my experience. I didn't trust men at all. But that choice wasn't given to me, so I had to listen to my 'sensible' part and take a chance. I met the parents and they seemed to really want her and they seemed nice – sort of *Little House on the Prairie* types. They looked like a couple of farmers. The social worker arranged for me to meet them and then I handed Dominique over. It was really hard. Dominique wouldn't say a word to me. It was like she remembered what I'd done, walking away the last time. She just looked at me as if to say, 'You bitch.'

I felt I'd done the right thing for her. But all the time I kept having a picture of the adoptive father and wondering if he was as nice as he seemed ... worrying whether he'd harm her or hurt her in any way. They were both teachers, never watched television and said there'd be no chance of my ever bumping into them. They were into arts and things like that, which I was into as well – drawing, music and so on. I thought she was quite cold. I didn't get any feelings of warmth from her and that worried me a bit. I couldn't relate to her at all. It wasn't that I didn't like her, and she certainly looked nice and pretty, it was just the lack of warmth. I got that off the father. He was nearly in tears when I handed her over. He seemed to love children, but she was talking technically. But I couldn't change it because it wasn't my decision and it was final. By that time everyone was doing what they wanted to. I wasn't given any options. Those doubts have stayed with me all these years and the doubt about him as well, because of my own experience. How can you ever know? My dad could be the nicest person to people who didn't know him. He could be very warm, was always giving money to charity, he was hardworking. He had two lovely daughters ... and some of my good points I've got from my dad. If he wasn't a monster he'd be a nice person. He had a really good side that was sensitive and caring.

It's ten years since I last saw my daughter. It's been a nightmare, constantly worrying about her. There have been a couple of occasions when I've felt she wasn't happy – I could feel it. It's made me feel helpless. I've tried to get in contact with her, but the social worker's office closed down and after that I couldn't get any help from anyone. I'd had this 'agreement' about getting information about Dominique from the adoptive parents and the social worker as they were friends. It was agreed that I would get photographs whenever I requested them, through the social worker. But because I lost contact with my social worker I couldn't request them and no one believed me because it was a private arrangement. There was nothing on the file. Apparently it wasn't allowed. That's what I was told by quite a few social workers – that contact wasn't allowed.

About 18 months ago I looked in the telephone book to see if there was any organisation that could help me. I saw Post Adoption Services listed, so I made an appointment and they gave me some advice. I spent hours searching through the records at St Catherine's House in London. Eventually I got the adoption certificate, which gave me some names and where they lived. I think that was a mistake and I was given it accidentally. It had been hard work searching because I didn't have their surname, but my daughter had such an unusual first name I eventually found it after going through about 3,000 records. They weren't in any order and I didn't have the date of the adoption. I think I must have blocked it out. I had to go through all the adoptions for that year to find the adoption certificate – 1983.

It was brilliant getting that information. I felt so much closer to her then. That happened this year. I didn't know where she was and I didn't feel I had the right to have another child without knowing that she was happy, even though I'd been married since 1985 when I was 21 – I didn't want anyone to take her place. I'm also scared of having another child because of the circumstances of her birth. It wasn't painful apart from the contractions, but it was a horrible experience delivering a baby. My husband had been disappointed that I gave Dominique up. We met when she was still with me and he wanted to bring her up. He had no say in the matter. I just took her while he was at college. We share everything. He knows about my childhood and has been very supportive. He stood by me and accepted my decision and understood why I had to do it.

Not knowing about Dominique has made me fret a lot, especially on her birthdays. I have nightmares as well, usually around guilt and that she'd hate, me especially if it didn't turn out well for her and she'd been given the wrong parents. That's always been a worry, especially since she's black and gone to a white family. The social worker said at the time that a black family wouldn't

have her at that age and it was dead hard to adopt black children
and these were good parents and I might not get another chance,
otherwise she could end up in permanent foster care. At the time,
I was only 19 and I'd been through the court case and all the
turmoil at the time – I didn't know anything. I did know from
her being in the foster home that whenever a black person came
on the telly she'd be happy. Also they had a black postman that
came round and she never wanted him to leave. I think he was
the only black person in the area. She was there for about three
months and adopted from there.

When I got the information about her I felt much better. I didn't
want to do anything else at that stage; having that information
was enough. Then a good friend moved to Devon and about six
months ago she said she met a girl of the same age with the same
name as my daughter who was having problems. But the surname
didn't check out. Everything else did, including the parents' occu-
pations, and apparently she even looked like me, so I thought that
she was my daughter. I was going to leave it until she was 18, but
after thinking about it for a few months and worrying constantly
because I had a feeling that she wasn't happy, I went there two
weeks ago to see if I could get more information. I rang the house
as well. Thank God I didn't interfere too much because she wasn't
the right child.

I've been having help from the After Adoption Centre for about
a year. I needed to have someone to talk to about how I was feeling
and about my grief. It's been very helpful. There are a lot of
things I don't know or can't remember and they have helped by
explaining everything – especially things about how Dominique
might be feeling. I'm glad they are here because I wouldn't have
gone to Social Services. They didn't have the resources or the time
and they don't have the same experience and expertise. They are
specialists at the centre. I'd like to give back what they've given
me.

I think birth mothers should have more rights. They should be
able to turn down parents they're not happy with and they
shouldn't be badgered in to signing anything before they're ready,
and there should be support systems to help them. Adoption isn't
always a solution like everyone says. When you are young you
believe the adults know best and that it'll be alright.

Looking back, the ideal solution would have been to move to
a different part of the world without the family and with some
support – especially emotional support – somewhere I could go

when I was feeling low, where I could tell the truth about how I was feeling without having my baby taken away from me. I suffered from postnatal depression for about a year after she was born. Sometimes when I looked at her I'd see my dad – and other times I'd see my beautiful daughter. She scared me. I didn't get any counselling with that either. No one offered me any help, and as far as I could see I was a freak and it was an abnormality that shouldn't have happened. I did ask for help but they didn't know how to help me. They did the best they could.

The stigma of losing her is still there. Sometimes people I know come up to me in the street and say things like, 'Bitch! Where's your baby?' It's still happening, but now I just say she's living with another family. I appear tough in front of them and then go away and cry.

I believe she was meant to be born; she's meant to be here. Unfortunately that's the way she was meant to come on to the earth. And that's the pain I was meant to suffer for some reason. I knew from a child she was coming, and that's helped me cope. Now I feel that I could help her. I feel I've got something to offer her. My self-esteem has improved so much. I'll never be 100 per cent and there will always be part of me that feels inferior in some ways – a bit insecure, although I've never admitted that before.

As the years go by it gets harder and harder and I've felt like there's a big gap in my life. Part of me is missing. The last thing on my mind before I died would be her. It's not a happy thought and I feel bitter about that.

We're more family than family because of the circumstances. She's not only my daughter, she's my sister as well, because we share the same father.

The day before April and I had arranged to meet, she received a letter from the social worker involved in arranging her daughter's adoption. She said she had watched Dominique growing up and that she was having problems. Apparently the parents thought about making contact with April two years previously to see if she could help them deal with Dominique's problems, but changed their minds. She is now living in a residential home and is wanting contact. This same social worker, whom April always thought looked familiar, has been playing badminton with her for the last seven years.

Part Two
Reunion

I am grateful to you -
for waiting, yet leaving
messages like pebbles
in fairy tales – this way
through the woods. When he came
You opened your door.

Shirley G. Cochrane, 'To the Birth Mother'

Reunion in the context of adoption can be described as the coming together of an adopted person with his or her birth family for the first time, usually as an adult. All the adoptees in these stories – who grew up in the UK or in New Zealand in the 1960s or early 1970s – knew they were adopted but had little, if any, real knowledge about their origins or the reasons they were relinquished for adoption. Their birth parents in turn knew nothing or very little of the whereabouts of their children while they were growing up, or of the adoptive parents who had the privilege of bringing them up.

All those I have interviewed have experienced a need to know. For adoptees, this is a need to know their origins, their roots, the circumstances of their adoptions, their social and genetic history. This concurs with the findings of a considerable amount of research in this area. By contrast, the needs of birth parents to know what has happened to their children and a correspondingly powerful need for many to meet, see, touch and find out about them – to know them – has been, until recently, ignored. Scanty, subjective and inadequate information like 'a fast girl, wearing too much makeup' was recorded on our files. This reflected a practice that was committed to meeting the needs of infertile couples who were expected to graft the children on to their families as if they were their own, so the less information they had, the easier the task would be for them.

Some birth mothers have managed to initiate contact themselves, some spend years searching, others carry on pretending it never happened. Many sit and wait and hope – seeing no other option. Far fewer birth parents than adoptees have taken advantage of their rights to trace in New Zealand. They often do not want to intrude on their children's privacy or disrupt their families, and fear that their children might not want to know them. Some see reunion as the only way they can begin to heal themselves: many say they feel incomplete, a part of them is missing. (So do adoptees.) All, bar nine, of the 262 respondents to my question-naire want to be found. Two-thirds have tried searching for their lost children or have tried to find out about them, including some who are in their 60s and 70s.

Looking for relinquished children is often the result of pining. This pining or yearning constitutes separation anxiety and is the 'subjective component of the urge to search'.[1] It is not diminished by time or by subsequent children. Many birth mothers, as mentioned previously, say they think about their lost children frequently, some daily; and 136 out of the 262 surveyed said that these thoughts increased over the years, rather than decreased.

The main reasons birth mothers want to make contact with their relinquished children is to be able to explain to them the cir-cumstances of their birth and subsequent adoption; they want to reassure their sons or daughters that they were loved and have not been forgotten. Birth mothers also need reassurance from their children that they are well and happy. Making contact would be the first time that many birth mothers had made a decision about themselves in relation to their children.

Birth fathers too often have a need to know their lost children. They get little mention in this book and elsewhere. In many cases their names do not appear on birth certificates or in files. Many myths surround them: they are the culprits behind unwanted pregnancies, they don't care about the birth mothers or what happens to the children.[2] Nearly one-third of the 262 birth mothers returning the questionnaire had stable relationships with the birth fathers, nearly half of whom wanted to keep their babies. Twenty-three sets of birth parents subsequently married after relinquishing their children and 24 sets who didn't marry are still in touch.

Not all birth mothers or adoptees want to be found. A veto provision was incorporated into the New Zealand Adult Adoption Information Act 1985 to give both parties a choice about whether or not they wanted their identity revealed. The veto expires after ten years unless it is renewed and lapses with the death of the person who placed it. Far fewer adoptees than birth mothers placed vetoes on releasing information: about two per cent of adoptees had done so one year after the Act, compared with about 4.2 per cent of birth mothers. Many adoptees experience a veto as the ultimate rejection. Adoption workers say placing a veto is less to do with preventing information being given out than the result of fear of being approached directly and having no control over the situation. When these birth mothers have been approached, a significant number have been willing to meet their children. Adoptees tend to place vetoes because they do not want contact at the present time but may do in the future. Often they are in their early 20s and already facing many new things in their lives; some have been negatively influenced by their adoptive parents and some have a strong sense of having only one set of 'real' parents.[3]

For adoptive parents, ideas on reunion differ. Some feel betrayed by the New Zealand government at the change in the law; they had been guaranteed secrecy and now see themselves threatened by what they perceive as the possible loss of their children, who 'belong' to them. Differences of opinion centre on the right to privacy and protection, versus the right to know. In fact, studies show that in adulthood adoptees report a greater sense of closeness and attachment to their adoptive parents when they have been able to re-establish contact with their birth relatives.

Other adoptive parents recognise that the genetic link is very powerful and say it makes a nonsense of the idea of bringing up adopted children as if they are your own, no matter how closely matched. This is often the reason why some help in the search for their children's birth family. 'I brought them up and I felt this was the final thing I could do for them – to help give them their identity,' said Noeline, an adoptive parent from New Zealand. 'My daughter is very much restored to her birth family. But she is still our daughter and we are her mum and dad. It has extended our family. The need to know their birth parents has been as great for them as us.'

References

1. Parkes, M. (1972), *Bereavement.* London: Tavistock Publications.
2. Carroll, M.I. (1992), 'Out of Sight, Out of Mind'. *Social Work Review,* vol. nos. 1–2 (November), NZ Association of Social Workers.
3. Howarth, A. (1988), *Reunion: Adoption and the Search for Birth Origins – the New Zealand Story.* Auckland: Penguin.

4 Zoe

Like so many birth mothers, Zoe was assured that adoption was far better for her daughter – and for herself – so much so, it warranted no discussion. Her daughter was going to a good home. In fact there was no home lined up, Zoe discovered many years later. Nor was the home her daughter finally went to a 'good' home. Zoe traced the adoptive father, who admitted they 'weren't fit to adopt'.

There are no real safeguards for a child in the closed system of stranger adoption, only statutory obligations and duties. Adoption is a hit-and-miss affair. When it succeeds, the experience can be positive for the adoptive parents and the child. When it fails there is no one to look out for the child as happens in secure families, no one to connect with, worry about, truly love that child. He or she becomes the responsibility of the state, and is at the mercy of the quality or lack of quality of that system. He or she is vulnerable, may be open to abuse and may have no protection. In Maori terminology, that child becomes a 'non-person'. In traditional times, according to Maori belief, a child given to an absolute stranger could end up being 'food for the oven'. In the Pakeha/European culture our assumption or belief is that the state will provide for and protect the child. As a result, he or she must feel like the child of no one.

My daughter is 26 years old today. In all that time we have spent about 26 days together. I always knew I'd see her again. It's a feeling I've carried with me ever since I first saw her, just after she was born. She stared silently up at me – an hysterical, screaming teenager. I've never forgotten that look, her perfect, beautiful little face. It had such a knowing look. Well, that's how it seemed to me.

I was 17 when I found out I was pregnant. I'd been going out with John for about a year. We were the same age. We had a great passion for each other and were constantly together. We still care

43

very much about each other. It was quite a long time before I realised I was pregnant. I don't think I was really aware that it might happen to me. We didn't know much about conception or birth control – it wasn't an option anyway, not as teenagers. Abortion was illegal, so that wasn't an option either. We didn't know where to turn for help. It was 1964 in a small city in New Zealand's South Island – Dunedin. At the time anything relating to sexual matters was very mysterious and highly charged.

I remember being absolutely terrified when I eventually realised I was pregnant and felt totally helpless and alone. I was terrified of having to tell my parents, especially my father. My mother had always been ill and I was worried about how this would affect her. The idea of telling them paralysed me. It was the worst thing I'd ever done. So I didn't. I couldn't. I don't know what I thought my father would do to me. I still remember lying awake night after night crying quietly for hours, not knowing what to do about it. It felt like my whole world had come to an end. And somehow I'd made it happen.

It was my mother who eventually asked me in front of my father if I'd had a period lately. I was shocked that she'd asked me in front of him, particularly since she'd told me that men didn't know about periods! I remember being stunned for a moment then tearing out of the house and running flat out to the beach. I cried in the sandhills for hours, staring at the sea and wishing I was dead, that it'd all be over. I think I was about five months.

After that everything changed. There was no discussion about it. Nothing. From then on I became severed from everything. Disconnected. I was forbidden to see John. I had to go away. I wasn't allowed to keep the baby or even talk about it. I wasn't allowed to make any decisions myself or be part of any decision about me. It was as if I didn't exist. My father was very much in charge of everything. Somehow it seemed right. I didn't deserve any consideration. I don't know what my mother thought. She never really said.

I was in my first year at teachers' college and John was working in a bank. We still saw a lot of each other. We were very much in love. I'm sure he felt as powerless as me to do anything about it. We talked about getting married, but we weren't old enough and I knew in my heart I couldn't disappoint my father any further. He had plans for me and John wasn't part of them. Also I think I found the idea of marriage rather terrifying. I didn't feel ready for all that.

In some ways I still felt very much a child. I was living at home and didn't have any independent means of support. Looking back, my own terror played into my sense of powerlessness. It paralysed me. What was going to happen to me? Who would take care of me? It was like being frozen in time and it wasn't really happening. I'm sure John was also afraid of going against my father. We were just kids with no options, no choices and I don't think we saw ourselves as having any rights. After all, we weren't in 'the right'. We'd transgressed enough. Maybe complying with my father's wishes was my way of attempting to gain forgiveness.

I didn't dare think about the baby as a baby. My pregnancy represented 'sin', and I'd been branded as wicked – there was no connection with a baby. Nobody else mentioned the word 'baby'. It was as if morality and being seen to do the 'right thing' outweighed anything else. Even a child. And I became part of that mentality too. I colluded with it. So what had been beautiful and loving had suddenly become bad, criminalised by accidentally conceiving a child that no one could bring themselves to mention. And it was all my fault.

My girlfriends were sympathetic and concerned, but were unable to express any feelings about what was happening. Perhaps they didn't know what to say. So nobody said anything. When I think back, there wasn't anyone to talk to, apart from John. I wasn't aware of any agencies. My father arranged everything with the doctor who confirmed the pregnancy and together they decided to send me to a friend of his, in the North Island. Apparently they needed a girl like me [to help around the place].

I didn't know what to expect as I didn't know anyone else who'd got pregnant and wasn't married. But I knew I was being banished because I'd been bad and had brought shame on the family. So I couldn't be seen.

I stayed with the family [in the North Island] for about four months. It was like living in infinity. The only way I could connect with the real world was to mark each day off the calendar in bold red pen. I was so lonely. The days were long and full of emptiness. I'd never been away from home for any length of time before. I'd never been without friends. I'd never really been on my own. The highlight of my day was the post. John used to write huge letters nearly every day. I've still got them. But she [the woman I stayed with] seemed to resent my getting letters. I felt she resented my being there. She hardly ever spoke to me or mentioned my 'condition' and I never felt comfortable with them. I had to do jobs I'd never done before, like carrying coal and taking care of the children. It felt like that was the only reason I was there – to skivvy. I was cheap labour. I recently discovered John had to pay for the privilege of my working for them.

I remember not wanting my child to be born; not wanting to give her up. That way I could stroke her little body surreptitiously, talk to her in a whisper late at night, tell her about her father, her family. She was part of me, sometimes sympathetic to my sadness, nudging me with flailing limbs as if to reassure me. But at other times I lay terrified on my bed, resenting those flailing limbs reminding me of the nightmare I had suddenly been thrust into.

When my waters broke I panicked. I thought I was having the baby there and then on the bedroom carpet and frantically set about mopping up the mess. It was very early in the morning and the house was still. I was too scared to go into their bedroom to tell them. I clutched my bulge and waited. I was terrified. Eventually she drove me to the hospital and just left me there like dumped baggage that had suddenly outlived its usefulness.

My whole experience of giving birth was coloured by the simple fact that I was unmarried, even though they insisted on calling me 'Mrs'. One doctor examined me very roughly, muttering, 'Another young slut.' I had wanted to protest, to say I loved my boyfriend, that we wanted to get married and keep our baby but we weren't allowed. But what was the point? I was made to lie on a high narrow table under bright lights. I was in agony. My legs were pulled apart in stirrups and a sheet draped over my upper body. It was like being raped. I screamed and screamed. I thought I was going to die. No painkillers – not for sluts. I got a slap across the face instead. I think I fainted.

I screamed at the nurses for my baby as they began wheeling her away. That's the only time I saw her. I think I jumped off the table just as they were pushing her through some double doors. Amid all this noise and trauma was this tiny child lying in a cot, just staring at me. Dark hair, pencil eyebrows, blue eyes. She was beautiful. I ached to hold her. My whole body ached for her. Then suddenly they whisked her off. I never saw her again.

I was put in a ward with other mothers. They had their babies and their husbands. They had cards and flowers and visitors. My space was empty. No one spoke to me. No one mentioned my baby. Without a husband I didn't deserve my baby, so adoption seemed like a punishment.

No one discussed the possibility of my looking after my daughter. I just remember not being allowed to see her. I didn't know where she was and I was too afraid to ask.

I didn't stay in hospital for long. I remember wearing my 'Beatles' cardigan, my fawn home made skirt that I could almost do up again and my brown patterned blouse with buttoned-down collar, but I don't remember leaving.

The path led inevitably to adoption. It was never discussed. A social worker came to see me after my daughter was born to ask about my background and John's. She completed Form E 5/81. It took about ten minutes. I now have the original form after asking for all the information I was entitled to under the Adult Adoption Information Act 1985. Having it was confirmation that it really did happen. It wasn't a nightmare. It was there in black and white: a sketch of my life and my family's so that my daughter could be 'matched' to strangers and help create the illusion that she was theirs, grafted on to them – nothing to do with me.

The information was amazingly superficial, as if any attempt to match was not all that important. Even less important was the apparent need for information – for records, for the adoptive parents or our children. So what really was important?

This 'Report on a Child Available for Adoption' was a single foolscap page divided into small sections: health, education, intelligence, personality and family history. I've just noticed 'V.D. test?' squeezed in as well. Each section was less than an inch in depth! It is handwritten, which means the smaller the social worker's handwriting, the more information was recorded. (There was no provision for additional information.) It was followed by a description of me stating my height (wrong), colouring (wrong) and that I am 'an attractive, pleasant girl, well-spoken and intelligent' (which may also be open to doubt). This was dated three days after my baby was born. Did I really seem pleasant? Did the social worker regard this as a competent assessment which would help determine my child's future – all in ten minutes?

The space for information about the father was even smaller. In spite of the officer's comments that 'the parents hope to marry when they are older', there was no discussion about how we might have kept our baby or what options were available.

The report also included a space 'Reasons for desiring adoption: cannot keep the baby'. No explanation. Nothing. The reasons weren't considered important; *we* weren't considered important. Our wishes and feelings were irrelevant. Our future plans were irrelevant. Nothing short of actual marriage guaranteed you could keep your baby, without professionals and others assuming you couldn't. How many of us really 'desired adoption' and wanted to give our babies away to strangers? And how many of us gave proper, informed consent?

Judging by this report, it seems there were no adoptive parents lined up for my baby. The couple who took her were not approved as adopters until 13 days after she was born. It seems they then had *a few days* in which to prepare emotionally and physically for Jane, compared with most couples who have nine months.

I knew nothing about my baby or the family she went to live with. I got the impression they were friends of the doctor and I remember thinking they'd have a lot to offer her – a lot more than I could. But I was never consulted. I remember ringing my father towards the end of my pregnancy and screaming at him that I was going to keep the baby and I didn't care what he said. But in my heart I knew I couldn't manage on my own. Looking back, all those empty weeks were spent waiting to be rescued, hoping my father would relent at the last moment.

Everything changed for me after I went home. I could only stay a short time. I felt I didn't belong there any more. I no longer fitted. The sense of loss I carried with me was numbing. The baby was never mentioned. It was a taboo subject. The effects of what had happened were devastating and it seemed that all the family traumas that followed were a direct result of what I'd done. My mother died not long after. We were very close and I still miss her terribly. For many years it felt like it was my fault.

I often wonder what she thought about giving my baby to strangers. It was their first grandchild. Their own flesh and blood. Why didn't she say something? But then how many of our parents could've taken the focus off the fact that you'd had sex, and exclaimed, 'Never mind that she's not a virgin, who cares! What about the baby?', or, 'Isn't there some other way?' What was everyone so afraid of?

My relationship with John had changed as well. He wanted us to get married. But it wasn't the same. I couldn't deal with the guilt. I didn't care too much about what happened to me after that. I had a motorbike which was quite powerful and used to take enormous risks on it. I returned to teachers' college but left after a short time. Then I left home and bummed around, fruit-picking, casual labour, that sort of thing for a year or so, always moving on.

Eventually I went to university. I must've been pretty determined to get through as I served endless pie and chips and milkshakes for the next three years in the Union caff to support myself. But I still didn't really care what happened to me and continued to take all sorts of risks with myself in an effort to bury all thoughts of my baby.

Although I was close to my friends I also felt set apart from them. We never talked about what happened to me, or later to three other girlfriends who became pregnant and were sent away. It was mentioned once by a friend when she was persuaded to change her mind about us flatting together as her mother (a devout Christian) had said I was a 'bad influence'. I did feel I was bad. Wicked. And they weren't. I don't know if that feeling has ever left me entirely.

It's difficult to know exactly how much having her adopted has shaped my life. I left New Zealand when I was 21. Whenever I went back for visits I would fantasise about seeing or meeting my daughter and they got progressively stronger with each successive visit. I used to fantasise that I was her teacher and wouldn't even need to look at the register for birth dates as we would know each other instinctively. A few years later I'd be scouring the faces of all the teenage girls I saw, looking for family resemblances. As she became a young woman, I'd fantasise about meeting her in a pub and somehow striking up conversation and then asking her birth sign. Although I felt I'd meet her one day, there was always the feeling that she mightn't want to know me.

I remember going to a medium a few years ago. Mr Close. My husband said his first name should've been 'Not so'. He said she was happily married and had a small child, was well off and her adoptive parents were very proud of her. However, she didn't want to know me. She didn't want any upset in her life. Nothing could've been further from the truth. But at the time I was delighted with just knowing she was alive! She was happy! And at 34 I was a grandmother! After the reading I raced down the street to the nearest phonebox to ring my husband. The most important things were that she was well and happy. Not wanting contact was somehow secondary in spite of all my fantasies and my own needs.

And yet I hadn't made myself available for contact in spite of the fact that I wanted to be reunited with her. I wasn't on the national register in New Zealand. Perhaps I was afraid she wouldn't want to know me. After all, I'd been persuaded to give her away. I hadn't fought for her. Could she understand what it was like then? And would it make any difference?

I'm not sure if coming over to England was in reaction to giving her up. I know it was part of it. I'd lost something irretrievably and there was no hope of ever finding it. It was an emptiness that I was leaving behind. A void. I learnt about the proposed changes to the adoption laws from John shortly before they were passed in 1985. It took seven years to get it through Parliament and had tremendous media coverage during this time, but no one wanted to 'worry' me about it.

From that moment on I became obsessed with finding her. I could think of nothing else. It was like being in love – that all-consuming feeling that nothing else matters. As soon as it became law that birth parents could be helped to find their children and vice versa, I wrote to Welfare. The idea of being able to meet her enthralled me. Preoccupied me. I wrote to her! At last I could tell her myself why I couldn't keep her. At last she could know something about me and her father and that we were still in touch. At last she could know who she was and where she came from.

Then I waited. I wrote to Welfare again after a few weeks. And waited. I lived for the postie. Every day I would greet this diminutive figure as he strutted up our path, restraining myself from grabbing the mail. We were living in a cottage in a small village in Gloucestershire. It was nearing Christmas. I would race home at lunchtimes from my job over 40 minutes away down snowy, winding lanes in my clapped-out Citroën just in case. Nothing. Eventually I rang Welfare in Wellington to be greeted with, 'We've had thousands of enquiries,' and no luck apart from an acknowledgement and a request to take part in some research on reunions. I'd have agreed to anything.

That same day my brother rang me. He was staying in Bristol on sabbatical.

Had I heard from my daughter? 'Well, she has just rung Auntie P. in Dunedin.'

I was absolutely stunned.

'No, she didn't catch her name. No, she couldn't quite catch where she was living – up north somewhere.'

'What *did* she catch?'

'Better not ring her now,' my brother said. 'She's had a shock.'

I rang her anyway. I'd hardly had any contact with her for 20 years. Her impaired hearing hadn't affected her ability to talk and I was excited and happy to shout 12,000 miles down the phone.

'I didn't know you'd had a daughter!' she said. 'Why didn't anyone tell me?'

My brother was right. She didn't catch her name or where she was living. Apparently my daughter had said she was a friend of mine and had lost my address.

'After I gave it to her she broke down and said she was your daughter!' my aunt said. 'And that she'd been in care since she was seven.'

I remember everything stopped. Silence. It was like telling me she'd died. And that I had killed her. I felt sick. And then I was.

For a while nothing much affected me after that. I felt numb. I felt tremendously sad. I felt very guilty. Horrified. Angry. Outraged. But most of all I felt responsible. Everyone kept saying it wasn't my fault. How was I to know?

I became paralysed with guilt and grief. I was convinced she wouldn't want to know me, but nurtured the hope that, like me, she'd have some measure of curiosity in her nature. I rang Welfare again and heard the confirmation like a death knell down the phone. Yes, she had been in care since she was seven, but she has great spirit, she's a survivor, a beautiful, intelligent girl. The social workers that knew her weren't available at the moment. That was the ultimate irony, since I'd been a social worker for years only to find out my own child had spent over half her childhood in care. They offered to trace her for me. They were very kind and caring.

Now the postie assumed an even greater importance in my life. Jane was constantly in my thoughts, my conversations. Every time the phone went I was sure it was her. I became a complete and utter bore.

Then she rang. It was 6.45 am on a very cold winter's morning. The whole family leapt out of bed simultaneously and hung around on the stairs while I answered.

Her first words to me were 'Hello. It's Jane ... do you know who's speaking?'

'Of course I do,' I cried. 'I've been waiting 22 years for you to call.'

Then we both cried. Then we both laughed at each other crying. And sounding exactly the same. She was keen to know everything about me, what I looked like, where her curly hair had come from, her nose, her warped sense of humour … all about her sisters. We talked for over an hour. Collect.

'I've waited a long time to have my own name,' Jane said. 'Thanks for giving me such a posh one, ma.' Then she whispered, 'Thank God you're still alive.'

One of the things that struck me was that she used the same words and phrases as me, the same expressions. 'My heart sank when I found out you lived in England ma,' which was exactly the same remark I'd made to my husband: 'Her heart will sink when she finds out I live in England.' That mirroring has continued – our thinking, feeling, values, passion, creativity, use of language. We even do the same things at the same time. As Jane says, 'Ma, it's spooky being your daughter!'

A week after our first phonecall her letter arrived. In spite of all the Christmas kiwi mail the little postie seemed to know this was it and waved it mischievously in the air as he came up the front path. I leapt up, rushed out, grabbed it and tore back inside. I remember sitting down at the kitchen table and staring at the envelope, touching it, sniffing it, scrutinising the extremely neat writing, the address, her name on the back. A stranger's name. My daughter's.

After a while I opened it. Inside there was a fat letter and some photos. I can still remember feeling almost too afraid to look at them, as if by doing so she would, after all, become real. I know I let out a howl – a long, loud, piercing, primitive howl that came deep from within my being. It was 22 years of grief that I'd never been in touch with, never really knew was there. Twenty-two years of silent, forbidden grieving for my baby. Now here was the woman my baby had become. She looked very familiar. She looked just like me.

My other two daughters were at home. Anna, who was 13 at the time and had known about her sister since she was nine, raced downstairs, clutched the photos, then me, failing to hide a look of intense sadness. Little Sophie cried in sympathy.

I don't know how long it took me to read her letter. Scrawled along the top 'Read this one first – letter No. 2' and a smiley face, just like I'd have done. But the smiley face hid the reality of her life. Reading what had happened to her, how she'd been abandoned at the age of seven, three days before Christmas, was like the ultimate betrayal. The ultimate deception. I had been assured that she would go to a good home, to a couple that could give her all the things I couldn't. How could I be so selfish wanting to keep her? Surely if I loved her, the least I could do was give her up? What complete abuse of trust. What complete abuse. Of both of us.

Reunion

We met at Christchurch Airport within a few weeks of making contact. It seemed the natural response to having finally made contact and to meet as soon as possible, in spite of people's comments about waiting or 'how brave' I was. I told everyone. I showed them her photo I carried around with me. I even told the stranger sitting next to me on the plane. I could think of nothing else. It was only when we shuffled through customs that I was overwhelmed with anxiety. What say she didn't like me – or I didn't like her? What if we didn't get on or she couldn't forgive me for giving her away to strangers?

In spite of a huge crowd I saw her straight away. She stood out from everyone else, looking beautiful in a long, jade silk dress, holding a bunch of 'English' flowers. She was all the women in our family rolled into one. One of us. We clung to each other. I could've stayed like that forever, holding her for the very first time, touching her. I wanted to squeeze her to bits. I wanted to stare and stare at her and take in every inch of her. I wanted to touch her wonderful curls that matched my youngest daughter's, stroke her face, ask her forgiveness, explain that I was only a child myself – that I had no choice. Instead she squeezed me, saying, 'What a little mother I've got,' and gently frogmarched me out into the sunlight.

We sat under the shade of a solitary pine tree in front of the airport holding hands that were identical, giggled in the same self-conscious way, her smile my mirror-image right down to the same crooked front tooth. 'I always wondered where I got my nose from,' she laughed, sounding just like me, 'and my warped sense of humour, mother.'

I have since found out that Welfare got in touch with my father nearly two years after Jane's adoption had broken down and her parents had abandoned her. I now have the original social worker's report, which states:

1. I have interviewed Jane's natural grandfather.
2. He informed me that the natural mother is married and living in England though they are intending to return within the next two years. *Perhaps the most important point is that Jane's mother did not marry the natural father* [emphasis added] and the grandfather doubts that his son-in-law knows of the existence of Jane. There is one recent child born to the marriage.
3. The fact that Jane's natural parents did not marry coupled with the natural mother's absence in Britain leads me to doubt the usefulness of pursuing the line of contacting Jane's mother. I feel there is little to commend such action and would suggest that you consider alternatives.
4. Despite not being able to offer any suggestions regarding Jane, the grandfather expressed an interest in her future and I would be grateful if, within reason, you would keep me informed of developments regarding her future.

My father died two years later. He told me nothing about it.

This information has also been hard to bear. Once again he and others were making decisions about me and my daughter. Once again I was excluded. Invisible. Why? I was 26 years old! I'd hitchhiked round the world, had a degree, a driver's licence, was *married*, had another child! Did I still need to be 'protected'? Or did they assume that I wanted to erase myself completely from my daughter's life and for her to leave no trace on mine?

'Perhaps the most important point', to use the words of the social worker, is not that I didn't marry the natural father, which was barely noteworthy at the time and yet assumes enormous significance a few years later. 'Perhaps the most important point' isn't that my (ex) husband was ignorant of my daughter's existence, having known about her long before we married and has now met her. 'Perhaps the most important point' is that I was not consulted directly, that I was not given the opportunity to care for my daughter – to have her restored to me. I feel I was, at the very least, entitled to that. And so was she.

'The past has got to take a back seat, mother,' Jane said rather sternly some time after we met. 'You must forgive your father. I have.' Is it simply a question of blame or reparation? These aspects feel like part of a process I've been going through as a birth mother – an unconscious process – a cycle of self-healing which began with contact with my daughter. It amazed me that after the initial joy, came the grieving. All those feelings associated with grief: regret, inner emptiness, guilt and anger that had been buried for years; alongside the anticipation of reunion, the excitement, apprehension, disappointments, joy.

It's also been important to fill in the gaps, however painful, to gather together the details of what happened, to be able to make sense of it all; to come to terms with it; to be grounded in it; to reclaim it as mine. I'm getting there but the process is not yet complete, in terms of resolving things and accepting what has happened to my daughter and me and being able to integrate it all into my life.

The hardest part has been to make sense of the secrecy – or should we call it confidentiality? Hardest because of the damage it's done. That my daughter should have had to grow up in care and not be allowed to know who she was or where she came from, or have the chance to be restored to her own mother, because it was confidential. Secrecy overrode all other human values! Why? We didn't beg for it. It was part of the adoption package. We were made to swear on the bible never to make contact, because our children no longer 'belonged' to us but their adoptive parents. How else could ownership of them be confirmed by their adoptive parents? In law my daughter 'belonged' to her adoptive parents long after they didn't want or need her any more. She then became the property of the state. Legally I didn't exist. It must've seemed to her that she was the child of no one.

I spoke to her social worker about it. I also spoke to Pam, her former educational psychologist, about it. She and her family befriended my daughter from her early teenage years. Pam had known my name. But what could she do? She found a photo of my grandfather in a history book and left it lying around, making absurd remarks about family likenesses!

So much rhetoric goes into 'protecting' birth mothers' privacy etc., but who cared about us at the time? Social workers were only interested in solving the problems of childless couples and we provided a neat solution. They weren't interested in helping us. We didn't count. Or our feelings. So we simply acquiesced. Otherwise the whole edifice would've fallen apart. That's how adoption works – if one can say that it works. There's a lot of research to show it doesn't – especially with teenagers.

I managed to trace Jane's adoptive father, 18 years after he
abandoned her. I needed to find out directly from him what had
happened with my daughter in the same way an adopted person
needs to find out from their natural parents the circumstances of
their birth etc.

I decided to simply knock on his door as it'd be less easy to refuse
to see me. I took a girlfriend. A woman let us into the kitchen
where he was fixing something. He was short and seemed to be
draped in gold mayoral-looking chains. I announced myself.

'I may or may not look familiar to you,' I said. 'I am Jane's
mother.'

I was greeted as though I'd just popped in for tea. He asked his
lady friend to put the jug on and wasted no time telling me what
had happened.

'We never should have adopted,' he said. 'We weren't fit to adopt
... but of course they didn't know that. We'd have been better
off getting a dog. A red setter actually. I never wanted to adopt
Jane in the first place. But the wife was bored – our two children
were growing up, we had this big house and I was away on
business a lot and having the odd affair ...'

I was deeply shocked. Stunned. I certainly didn't want him to
see the tears that filled my eyes and began plopping on to my lap.
I held my friend's hand under the table.

> I never liked Jane. I never wanted to adopt. She was there
> for the wife. And she spoilt her rotten! Always had her
> dressed beautifully. She was a pretty little thing, mind ...
> lovely skin. But what a handful. Oh yes, she gave us a hard
> time! ... Well, I didn't have much to do with her. I wasn't
> there a lot. But she was hard work and very bright. Then
> the wife got bored. Well, I didn't blame her ... she went
> off on a cruise and met this sailor. Well, he wasn't an
> ordinary sailor, he was an officer and earned good money.
> And that was it. The boy went to boarding school and the
> girl followed her mother a year later to England and I
> haven't seen either of them since.

I couldn't speak, I was so staggered by his insensitivity. Then
I tried to empathise with his position at the time, being left with
Jane.

> I suppose some people thought she was callous leaving like
> that but I quite admired her really, following her inclina-

tions. No, we didn't think of the birth mother in those days. But I did know quite a bit about you, I suppose ... that you were from Dunedin, a student, I think I can still remember your name. But I wasn't going to tell her anything. I thought she might make trouble.

Naturally I had to take her back to Welfare ... I didn't like the child! And I certainly didn't want to take responsibility for her. Yes, I saw her once or twice after that, but she played me up so badly in a restaurant, that was that. I wasn't going to put up with that again. I know she wrote to the wife a few times but she never replied. I don't know where she is. New York I think.

Jane called round on me when she was about 17 ... hasn't changed. Actually it's funny you should call today because I am just in the process of cutting her out of my will.

Why was I so bloody nice to him – and his ex-wife? I'd written to her by registered letter and enclosed some photos of Jane not long after we met, acknowledging what a difficult decision it must've been for her and asking for information about Jane's childhood. It was returned. Perhaps I was still feeling I didn't have a right to a relationship with my daughter.

I can never make up for the emotional damage done to her. 'The system has failed your daughter', wrote her social worker after we all met. 'Her history is tragic, it reflects her drive for identity, acceptance and self-worth ... I believe your daughter is special.'

It's hard not be sad thinking about her childhood and what we might have had. I can never not feel raw inside whenever I read the reports from Welfare on my daughter as just another case, moved from pillar to post. I am only beginning to emerge from accepting that I am not responsible for what happened to her. I gave her up because I loved her. I wanted the best for her.

I used to get confused about my role. I like it when she rings me for a chat or just wants me to listen when she's feeling down. 'Don't go getting upset on me, ma. You're no use to me all upset.' And often she'll say, 'I can't get over how well you seem to know me!'

The physical distance between us makes it hard to get close, but we're in touch lots and she sees the family and her father's. She's better at keeping in touch than I am, but she's always on my mind. I have been out there twice and twice I've had to leave her behind – again.

But she's been brilliant in helping me come to terms with what has happened; helping me to forgive myself. And her whole life has changed dramatically for the better, now that she knows who she is and where she comes from. In fact she is the proudest member of our family heritage. When we first met, my friends wept at the sight of us together, we're so alike. She is my daughter, yet I haven't been her mother. Now, at last, I have another chance – to be there for her in a different phase of our lives. An honest, open, healthier phase – without secrets.

5 Fern

Fern and I went to high school together in Dunedin, New Zealand and have kept in touch since then. When I think of Fern I see her wonderfully bright, red hair. When I think of our lives, I see the daughters we gave up for adoption, like a dark bond. Neither of us had spoken to each other about the experience in any depth until this interview. It was followed later by separate inverviews with her daughter Gail and Gail's birth father, Ross. Fern and Ross married a few years after Gail's adoption, but subsequently divorced.

I was 17 when I met Ross, who's the father of my daughter. I was still at school. We'd known each other about six months before we started sleeping together. I was about to go to university. I didn't get my period. Then I started to get anxious. Fearful. I talked to various people and managed to get some quinine tablets from somewhere, tried them, hot baths, etc. On the one hand I was trying to pretend nothing was happening, and on the other hand I was terrifically frantic. Ross was planning to go to Sydney on a three-year catering course. It was assumed he'd go – we both just assumed that, and I assumed that I'd carry the can for whatever happened.

We were on holiday with a group of friends, tobacco-picking. Ross and I went to a doctor, which was awful. He called me a slut and gave me a terrifically bad examination and told me I was pregnant. Looking back on it, I was so full of shame. The whole area of sexuality was so overloaded and emotional that I couldn't look at it with my rational part. I was also very upset that I was pregnant. I hadn't had any sickness or anything, apart from my breasts getting bigger and from then on I started fainting and having these blackouts.

I went to another doctor to try and get some kind of abortion, which was another horrible experience, and every doctor I saw, including the one who was supposed to deliver me, was an absolute bastard, apart from one. They just made me feel like a piece of shit. I can still remember that.

I was so terrified of telling mum and dad that I just let the developments of my going to university take their place ... letting them buy my books etc. I was in this terrific dilemma of being too frightened to tell them and yet time going by.

I went to another doctor when I returned home to Dunedin and he laid out what I had to do: it was too late for an abortion, that I'd have to have the baby and that I'd have to tell my parents. Also, he wouldn't do anything until I told them. But he was quite kind. My recollections are very hazy. When I remember it, it's not the details but the feelings, the way I felt, it was a horrible choking feeling, and not being able to speak to anyone about it either ... The feelings got worse because there was nobody to talk to about it. I didn't really share it with my friends ... I'm not sure why at the time. It was to do with shame ...

In the end I had to tell my parents. I remember going to tell them. They were in the kitchen preserving fruit. Pears. I couldn't think about this memory for about ten years afterwards. It was the worst thing that had ever happened to me in my whole life – by far! The actual telling them was the worst thing – worse than the birth or anything else. I was breaking every code – and quite unconsciously. I didn't do it deliberately to wreck their lives or anything. Telling them was as awful as I'd expected it to be. By telling them I'd passed the control of the whole thing into their hands. From then on, I was there – but I wasn't making any kinds of decisions ... it was completely out of my hands. The reality of the situation had nothing to do with me any more. I still tried to pretend it wasn't happening. I had no idea how they felt. I was so immersed in the process of it ... things were never said in our family, never talked about. So if they weren't talked about they weren't happening, even though you knew instinctively that they were.

My parents had great expectations of me and I endeavoured to do my best, being the oldest, and to be a good girl. It was very much to do with being good. I was groomed to be clever and going to university was part of that.

I had no idea what was going to happen. I was a kid. Today, 17- and 18-year olds have a much better understanding of life ... I was so overprotected.

We had a meeting with Ross's parents. They were mortified because Ross had gone off and left me. It wasn't until years later when I thought about it that I suppose it wasn't a very gentle-manly thing to do – but on the other hand that was the way it was – that the man should do his thing ... there was no reason for him not to go and get his education. It was me that had to face it. And I was madly in love with him.

I wondered why they were involving me at this meeting, as all the decisions had been made – it was all completely out of my hands. It was just the way it was. I didn't feel as if I had any right to speak. I think it was to do with guilt and shame. There was also some discussion at the meeting about keeping the baby, but I knew there was no way my mother would have wanted that. She'd had her babies and she didn't want any more. But it was basically to do with her not wanting me in the house with a baby. I think that's what it was all about. I couldn't have gone against my mother. Life would've been unbearable!

Also it had a lot to do with morality ... and Presbyterianism. They didn't tell anyone and I don't remember my brother and sisters knowing at the time. It was never discussed. I don't know what they told them. Later my sister was delighted I'd had a baby, which was an utterly spontaneous reaction and yet I couldn't handle it at all. It was the last thing I wanted to hear. Then she went out and had a baby the next year.

We [birth mothers] were all so isolated – why didn't we speak to each other? There were three of us then. We had no social skills, it was before women's liberation. It was a taboo subject. No one really acknowledged what was happening. I came home halfway through my pregnancy – and had a party. And no one really said anything.

I had a wonderful relationship with Ross's mother – and I still do. She accepted the fact that I was pregnant without any kind of judgement. She gave me little presents to go away with – a nightie and toiletbag ... it was really nice and important to me. I knew she loved me and it didn't matter what I'd done. There were no conditions attached. Not like my own mother. I didn't feel like a leper. She organised a place for me to stay with some friends of hers on a farm in the high country. It was very isolated. The couple was young. I was very busy on the farm and enjoyed being there. They were very kind people. Ross wrote all the time. We were in love.

Mum had a book on natural childbirth and I was determined to have a natural birth. I had no access to any other information.

So I did have a textbook about how I would like it to be, which was good. But I learnt nothing in high school.

I remember the labour very clearly. Joan, the lady I was staying with, had given me information as well and came with me and sat with me the whole time. She rubbed my back and helped me with my breathing. She was great. I couldn't have done it without her. The doctor didn't even bother to turn up. I was just a hunk of meat on a plate. But he didn't get his fee, apparently!

The nurses were OK but I was in stirrups, ugh ... but as soon as the baby was born they took her away. I wasn't shown her or anything. I had her and she was gone. I was taken back to my room. But I can still remember the exaltation; I was so high ... so happy and proud and pleased with myself ... even though I had nothing to show for it. And I wrote Ross screeds and screeds! I don't think I've ever been that high! It was just amazing.

And then the bad things happened. I was literally in coventry – nobody spoke to me. I was in a room by myself for four or five days. I was absolutely terrified and ashamed. People came in and tended to me. I didn't know where the baby was. I didn't know where I was. I was too scared to go out of the room. I was just terrified. And I was just left. My parents came to take me home and my sister was really pleased to see me.

What I'd been plotting was that I was going to see my baby before I left. My parents took my bags out to the car and I raced all over the place lookng for her – and I found her. I was under pressure because I didn't want them to know that I was looking for my baby. I don't know why I left it till then. I don't know ... I think I was numb. I do remember being numb. But this was my last chance.

I found her. She had red hair. She was so sweet. I just looked at her. She was all bundled up. Swaddled. I had a very intense time with her. I just wanted to memorise her. I can't imagine what it would've been like if I'd never seen her. Unbearable. There was no staff around. It was all so covert – it was fear. It was just awful. It was like a concentration camp – a human reduced to that inhuman state ... and all the controls were operating from inside myself. I mean what could they have done to me - behaving in such a natural way? I learnt my lessons very well.

Then I got into the car and returned home. I had been tightly bound and given those pills they now say can be carcinogenic. That was pretty painful. I continued at university. I thrust myself into learning. The baby was never spoken about. The next year my mother came into my bedroom late one night and told me my sister was pregnant and she was being sent away and not to say anything to anybody. Nothing was ever spoken about. It would've been wonderful if they'd been able to talk about it – but they weren't like that. It was as if nothing had happened. And then my parents had a lot of trouble when my sister didn't want to give up her baby. I couldn't handle it. I couldn't deal with it emotionally.

Ross returned and we got engaged, with conditions attached – like finishing uni. I'd been a bad girl and wronged them, so I had to be good. And there were very strict controls on us. I missed out on a lot of socialising because I was working so hard. Also things between my parents were not good. At the end of my second year, I was able to persuade my parents to let me go to Australia with some girlfriends. Ross was still there. Then I wrote to dad and said I'm not coming back. We're getting married! He said we should get married at home and that I had to finish my degree. So I stayed with Ross for a year in Australia and came back and finished my degree.

Then we got married and two years later, when I was 23, my son was born - Gail's full brother. I was devastated when I discovered I was pregnant and went almost crazy. I didn't want to be pregnant. We'd booked our passage to Canada. I was on the pill and still having periods, although they were light. So by the time I discovered I was pregnant it was too late for an abortion. When I found this out, I went a bit mad. I became crazy – just one night ... the sane part of myself went. The lid came off the feelings inside me ... I don't remember a lot, but I think I got hysterical and was hyperventilating ... kind of crazy. It was horrible. I didn't know who I was or anything. This pregnancy had a lot to do with the whole previous experience and it wasn't particularly happy ... in fact it was very unhappy. The labour was horrible – they gave me pethidine even though I told them I didn't want it.

After I had my second child it really affected my sexual relationship with Ross. I'm sure it was all linked with the first baby. It wasn't until I had my third child 14 years later, when *I* decided to have a baby, that I was able to do it my way and it was an incredibly healing experience. I had a very experienced midwife who was a homoeopath and naturopath. In my labour I kept starting and stopping and she was convinced that it was to do with my past – and that I was delaying it because of deep emotions relating to my first pregnancy. I had thought this as well, but she verbalised it. I knew she was right. I was in quite heavy labour but the cervix wouldn't dilate. She slept with me every night from the Tuesday when my waters broke. Then I had to go to hospital for an induction on the Friday. Being there was a nightmare. I was terrified. I didn't want to go. I was a home-birth patient. I think they're pretty wary of home-birth patients as the midwives have quite a lot of control, political control. I said I didn't want any drugs, that I was doing it my way. I think they were quite impressed! A male doctor said later, 'We didn't think you'd do it.' It's much fiercer having an induction as there's no rest between the contractions. After she was born on the Friday, I had her with me every minute and didn't let her out of my sight. Two hours after she was born, I went home. It was a very healing experience ... knowing what I was feeling. I called her Phoenix – which means rising out of the ashes. She was born on my sister's birthday. The one that committed suicide.

Joan, my midwife, was waiting for me. She put me in the bath with baby immediately! It was wonderful! I was as high as a kite and had heaps of energy!

My second child, Damon, and I are emotionally very inhibited – we can't touch. We love each other and he's great. We enjoy each other's company. But I didn't really bond with him. He had his own room and we were separate right from the start. I was alienated from him. I slept the whole day after he was born because of the pethidine – I just couldn't connect with him. I loved him though. But there was no way I would have had him in my bed, like Phoenix, my little girl. She slept in our bed. That was partly to do with her father being Maori. His ideas were completely different from mine. And I liked them, they felt absolutely right. He would have had her in the bed anyway, regardless! I feel as though I was carrying on the family pattern with my son and I've broken that with my daughter.

There's illegitimacy in the family history and I feel we were carrying that – some kind of cultural inheritance, and I feel as if I've helped to break that link – and it's to do with morality, religious beliefs [Presbyterianism] and sexuality. And it's to do with women taking the blame and the shame and the guilt – and motherhood. But with the help of my generation and our concerns, we've broken through something – in the way women value themselves and feel about themselves and the link with motherhood.

I feel that my life is very firmly placed in a social context, that what happened to me as an individual, all that suffering and pain, that I wasn't alone. It's very important that as individuals we do the best we can because we're changing our culture as we do it ... it's the value of the women and the kids.

The fact that you're interviewing all these other people is the fabric that you're part of – the work is part of it somehow. There's so many of us! So many horror stories... all part of this monstrous value system that has to be changed. But it's a very slow process, changing. We have to break so many generations. Women have been brutalised for generations.

I was a classic victim! I went along with it! But some women kept their babies. They stood up against the same kind of forces. Yet they kept their babies. But I went along with it. I chose to be a victim. But children don't have that many choices. I didn't know what my options were. But when I look back in a way I would say, 'I regret nothing.' I'm glad I had my education. You have to. In an ideal world I should have been able to do it all. In an ideal world an extended family that supports and sustains the life force ... I mean if children aren't valued – what sort of society are we going to have? We don't value children – or motherhood.

I think that by rebelling – and losing our virginity – it was our way of becoming an adult. It was the only way of becoming an adult that wasn't controlled. I didn't think about the repercussions – didn't know. The only information I had was a book mum had given me about chickens! She'd told me about periods, but it was full of shame and horror and I didn't want to know.

I see myself as a victim of social forces that were too great for me to overcome at that time. I don't like to think of myself as a victim, but that's the way I see and think about myself right now. It makes me want to bring up my daughter, in particular, so that she has more control over those forces. I want her to have more control – and responsibility that comes from her.

Having her in terms of a healing process is about knowing what I'm feeling. I don't think I knew what I was feeling. What would I have said? I didn't have the language. Women's Lib. brought about the idea of women talking to each other in groups. Before that we didn't know how to do it. I wasn't in touch with the feelings.

Reunion

I feel utterly alienated from Gail. When I went down to meet her for the first time I had assumed we would make direct contact ...

like I had with my other children. A connection. I thought I
would just look at her and love her. When I met her I didn't feel
anything – nothing. I had no feeling – it was like I was ice. We
talked but there was no connection. But there is a connection with
Ross. A bond. And that's what I thought would happen with us.
It was very unnerving for me because she looks the spitting image
of Damon, her brother. A female version of him but slighter,
shorter. It really upset me. I came back and just felt dreadful. I
don't know if its something that will grow – or not. I try to be
optimistic but my feelings about our future aren't very hopeful.
I keep saying 'Time' – we have to get to know each other and we
need the circumstances that will allow that. That's what I say to
myself. But I feel the severing has been irrevocable. Certainly we'll
never, ever have what we should have had as mother and daughter.
Never. You can never make up or recompense what has been taken
away. The umbilical cord has been cut. And that's that.

I knew I had to find her and I always knew that I would. There
were periods of time when she was growing up that she'd be very
near me. In dreams particularly. There was some kind of
connection.

As it turned out it was her adoptive parents that were stopping
the link. I thought it was Social Welfare, but it wasn't. I had
written to Social Welfare to keep on reminding them I was here,
that I'd like contact. I wrote regularly over the years – they'd write
back with a little bit more each time of physical information.

I think it was largely because of consciousness-raising groups that
I started talking about my past. I couldn't have thought about it
before but it was very healing. Then I started making contact with
Social Welfare - not just for myself, but for my sister after she died.
We were concerned that the child she gave up for adoption knew
his mother was dead and that we were here for him. We didn't know
whether Social Welfare had told him or what. I went through [the
support group] Jigsaw as well. They were fantastic. I still have links
with them. My mother tried to find him as well and I guess I felt
angry about that. I felt she was doing it for her own needs. She hadn't
helped me with the whole process at all. Nor really with my other
two children ... not in the way I think is appropriate anyway ...

The adoptive parents never told Gail that I was available. Social
Welfare had passed on all my letters and would've made me
available. The adoptive mother told me that. I understand how
she felt, although I didn't like it. She told me that when they got
Gail she was terrified of even leaving the pram outside the shop

– for years she feared I'd change my mind. It was a real fear for a long time. About a year before the law changed, when it was obvious that it was going to change, I wrote again and the parents did pass it on. Gail was 20 by this time. Then she and her mother wrote separately to me with their address and their letters arrived together.

Before we met, I had long sessions with Jigsaw and they were very helpful. They gave me practical advice – like it was very important that we meet by ourselves in a place where we both felt safe – as well as emotional sustenance.

But it didn't work out like that. Her mother was at the flat when we met. And that made things really difficult. I just wanted to see Gail on my own. She has been up here to stay and has met her brother and half-sister. That was much more relaxed, but I'm not sure what she thought about our lifestyle. It's so different from what she's used to.

We keep in touch by letter and she sees Ross and has a good relationship with him, so that's good. I hope we can get to know each other in time, but I'm not very optimistic.

Ross

Ross is a naturopath in his mid-40s and lives in a house on an almost deserted beach outside Dunedin, a city in the southern part of New Zealand's South Island. I have known him since our school days.

When we think of the parent of a child for adoption, we think of the mother. When we think of the grief experienced through that loss, we think of the mother. Even the term 'birth parent' suggests the mother. But if birth mothers are the silent side of the adoption triangle, then birth fathers are a mere shadow. They don't exist. It is almost as if we managed it all by ourselves. They were barely mentioned; and often banned by parents. Although information for 'matching' purposes was required on the adoption report, their names were not required on the birth certificates. While birth mothers were not 'allowed' to feel anything for their babies, birth fathers experienced a double denial: emotional and cultural. Permission to grieve was even less likely to be accorded to the birth father, since he may well have been the focus of blame by both sets of parents and, as a result, denied any responsibility, bar possibly a financial one.

I am 44 and was 19 when Fern was pregnant. I can remember her telling me very clearly. We were sitting on the steps of Nelson Cathedral. I was actually on my way to do a three-year course in Australia. I was shocked and horrified and didn't know what to do. I also felt extremely guilty. The worst thing about it was that I just let Fern do everything ... I certainly felt extremely responsible; at the same time I don't think I seriously thought I could see myself as raising a child ... as far as I was concerned I was still a boy.

We'd been together about a year at that stage and I was very committed to her and intended marrying her later on. We did use contraception most of the time. But when she became pregnant I had no idea what to do or where to start. And she was terrified of telling her parents. So we were open to the possibility of an abortion. We had no moral or spiritual climate on that at the time. However, it wasn't possible.

This business of 'going away' – again, because I wasn't there I didn't feel I had any say or control in the matter. I wasn't there – and I still feel guilty about that. I didn't know what to do – so all I could do was to continue to support her and write to her all the time. I felt helpless and that I'd opted out by going away. At the same time I couldn't see what I could do by being there. I know I didn't feel guilty about having brought a child into the world – or even about the adoption. I think I felt mainly guilty about not being there to support Fern. All I could do was write – about three times a week. I felt pretty low in Australia, isolated, although maybe I wasn't aware of it and most of my emotional energy was spent worrying about Fern. I didn't think too much about the baby. Also one certainly didn't talk about feelings. I suppose it was a reflection of the times. I could talk about the actual event, but not feelings. But I was very mixed up in my feelings ... about the baby – I never saw her or had any contact with her. She wasn't very real to me. Fern described her to me ... but she never had the emotional impact on me that she had on Fern. Often over the years I've wondered where she is and what she was doing, but there was never a strong emotional pull ... my main concern again was how it had affected Fern.

I guess I had the belief that career was all-important at that stage and I was in no position to offer any familial support or anything like that. I just wasn't very 'compis' when I think about it. Adoption was just what happened. But there were certainly a lot of stirred up feelings in later years. I went through them again and had some important counselling. It was about four or five years ago ... at least I've managed to sort things out emotionally – a lot of NZ males don't. It was a lot to do with sadness – sadness that I'd never consciously experienced at the time, sadness at never having known this daughter. It was like never having grieved for her.

I know that having Gail made me more determined than ever to do the right thing by Fern and stay committed to her. The adoption was almost a separate issue – we made a mistake and that's how you dealt with it. Having our second child made things a lot better – we had a child together we could keep. We were in control of the situation, although he wasn't planned. She was on the pill. In some ways it was a kind of redemption having him. So from that point of view I always felt very good about him. Perhaps adoption made him a bit more special than he'd otherwise have been.

I had a vasectomy when I was 28. We had duplicated ourselves and it wasn't appropriate to bring any more children into the world. We'd brought Gail into the world. I had to take responsibility for that and she was a very important factor in that decision. There was definitely a connection there.

I consider it an amazing bonus that Fern and I have remained friends so that we could plan to meet Gail again.

Reunion

My first impression was that I was totally struck by her resemblance to Damon! Looking at her, you could never not say they were brother and sister. I had had visions of another redhead. But she was Damon's clone in everything. I remember shaking at the time when she opened the door. I thought it must be her – it was so obvious! We went in and sat down and started talking. I knew from what Fern had said that she was pretty guarded as far as feelings go. So I didn't really open up much on that level at all. We started talking about our lives and then got on to spiritual growth and self-growth and things of that nature: and she'd never talked on this level before – she'd never heard of it before and she opened up. I couldn't have picked a more pertinent subject and she became very excited. And we clicked! It was wonderful! We talked for a few hours and by that time felt really good with each other. It wasn't a deep, emotional level, that wasn't appropriate at that stage. But there was a solid feeling there.

It didn't really matter what we had talked about but that it had been established.

It was one of the special evenings in my life and I remember it very clearly; but I did feel she was pretty closed off. I felt that what we'd done was appropriate and I didn't pursue things too much. We wrote a couple of times and then she went overseas for a couple of years.

But one of the things we had in common was rock climbing and mountain climbing. That was very interesting for us both. Also she likes drawing, like her brother. No one else in her family does ... I think it comes from my side of the family. And both Gail and Damon love skiing, so they've done that together which was really good. But they don't have a lot to talk about as they've had such a different life.

When Gail returned from overseas we went rock climbing together – it was a magical day ... doing something we both love doing together as well as that degree of depending on each other for your life ... but just doing something like that – and in each other's company. It was great. We were also able to share our current relationship problems, which we were both having and we've written a few times since that day too. It's been really good! I feel as though something very valuable has come out of all this and I'm very happy about that.

It's not so much like father and daughter – we're more like friends.

Meeting the Adoptive Parents

I met them with my mother. We'd arranged to meet them at midday at their home. There was a howling gale all the way there. It was as if we were fighting to get there. It felt like the very elements were conspiring against us! When we eventually got there, the father, to put it bluntly, was rude. He started interviewing me – as if I was asking for his daughter's hand and as if I had nothing going for me at all. I realised almost immediately that they were both very defensive, so I just talked to him in a friendly way as if we were all normal people having a perfectly normal conversation and after about half an hour it was fine. But he asked me questions like, 'What do you call yourself?' (meaning my profession), and, 'Do you make enough money to support yourself?', as if I was on the dole or something like that.

The mother's way of coping with this was to talk non-stop. He was talking to me and she was talking to mum and me. I gave up even trying to reply to her. You couldn't get a word in. Then he went back to his butcher shop and she took us for a trip round [a small country town] ... this is where Gail fell over in the gutter, this is where ... and saved the biggest thing till last ... she wanted to take us to go and watch her husband slaughter the pigs! I said, 'No thanks, we've got to go.' I hadn't dared look at mum ... who said, 'Good God!'

But they're country people, fairly simple, and regarded me as a threat. I was going to take their daughter away. I didn't basically give them anything to worry about. They just felt fear. Fear that I was going to contaminate her or take her away or something like that. I was extremely suspect from the start. They had to look up what I did – naturopath – in the dictionary. They hadn't heard of it. So that didn't help.

I'd like to maintain my friendship with her, and although geographically we're apart I'm sure that when we get together it'll be easy, especially since we've now established a number of things in common. I'm sure we'll enjoy each other's company. There's not just the climbing. She's also very interested in the work I do, so maybe I've been able to establish more rapport with Gail at this point than Fern, and in a way that doesn't feel right. After all, she put in all the hard work and this feels like it's fallen on to my plate. But the communication is easy and I'm very happy to share it with Fern.

Both the kids have a quirky sense of humour, even though Gail was brought up in a different environment. There must be things there [inherited] because we can talk to each other very easily and on a profound level and psychologically it feels good – and it might never have happened. I don't have any high expectations, but I do have a strong feeling that when we see each other we'll relate well. In her last letter she says she's coming down here with her boyfriend. She gets on very well with my mother too. But she feels more like a friend than part of the family.

Gail and Damon have had totally different life experiences. Damon lived with us in a commune, very different from family life. But they get on quite well. They both acknowledge they don't have a lot in common but, I think, enjoy each other's company, in a guarded kind of way.

I feel that a lot of healing has taken place. There's still regrets about the past and that'll never change and I just have to accept

that, but what's happening with Gail and me now is very healing
... it feels like the best things have happened. She was brought
up in a way that she feels very good about and I don't think we
could have provided that at that stage. My main regret in all of
this is not in relationship to her, but Fern – that I wasn't there to
support her.

After we were married we hardly talked about what had
happened. It came up on a superficial level occasionally... for me
it was a way of avoiding talking about feelings. They weren't part
of my existence. In a way it amazes me now, but that's how it
was. It's only the last few years I've been able to talk about it.

Gail

*Meeting Gail was a shock. She was the spitting image of her brother.
Not only that, she was very like her parents in so many subtle ways –
the tone of her voice and mannerisms were so like her mother's. I knew
her parents so well. She hardly knew them at all. Gail saw herself as
the meeting point of the two families. But as the focal point of that
union she lacked ease, and felt responsible for her adoptive parents'
feelings. Like many adopted children she had never questioned her
adoptive status. She 'belonged' to them.*

I'm 24. I always knew I was adopted. They used to say I was
special and adopted and mum used to tell me I got those two words
muddled up. I didn't really think about it much as a kid. I was
just part of the family with my brother and sisters. The only
thing I ever thought was I wondered what my birth mother looks
like. But that was the only thing. I didn't really think about it much.
People used to say we looked alike as children. We didn't really,
but people used to say we did. There were some similarities – dad
was deaf in one ear and I used to have ear trouble. Also the dentist
used to say my brother's teeth and mine were the same.

I didn't ever think deeply about it until mum told me Fern had
been in touch several times through Social Welfare as I was
growing up and was looking for me. She told me that when I was
21. It was a year before the law changed, 1985. That was the first
time I started thinking about it. My immediate reaction was, 'I'd
better put her out of her misery and write to her!'

When I was about 15 or 16 my mother told me a bit about
my birth parents – that my birth mother had been to university.

That was a push they'd always had for me ... so they'd be offering just as much as the other mother, or whatever ... I think she knew Ross was a chef. But I never asked anything. When she told me I was quite interested .... I didn't think too much about it really.

I think it was probably appropriate when it happened ... being 21. I hadn't thought about it much beforehand ... I suppose I had everything in my own family ... I never really felt any different from my brother and sisters. I never thought about having other brothers or sisters and a natural family ... the only thing was what she looked like.

When she told me, I wanted to meet her. It's hard to know how I'd have felt if I'd been told when I was younger. I think I would still have had the same reaction, and wanted to meet her.

After my mum told me I went down to Social Welfare and got her address. They gave it to me because they said they knew the law was going to change anyway. So I wrote to her and sent her a whole lot of photos – that was quite fun!

I haven't really had any fantasies about my birth mother although I had a dream once that she was quite short and fat! My adoptive mum is tall and quite big boned – not slim. I was the shortest in the family – the oldest but the shortest.

I quite enjoyed the whole process of finding Fern. I was excited. Social Welfare had told me that Fern had two other children, Damon and Phoenix, so I already knew that before we met. It was quite a surprise to know I had a full brother and also that my father and Fern had married! I did it all with mum ... I wanted her with me. Fern sent me back a whole lot of photos – her children and parents and brother and sisters – that was really interesting to think there's a whole big family there! And an extended family to learn about as well!

It was really weird seeing myself in someone else, especially Damon! I was like a female version of him! I can see likenesses between Fern and Ross and me too. It was weird 'cos you know he's not a stranger but you've never met him before ... I couldn't explain it – there was nothing written down in books ... but it did feel like a bond there.

It was also weird that Ross had taken up rock climbing and I had got into it at the same time! That was amazing. It makes you wonder if there is a tie there. And when mum and I met Fern mum noticed that Fern had a really determined personality and recognised that in me!

Reunion with Fern

Fern came round to my flat in Christchurch. I opened the door
to her. We hugged and I remember sitting out on the porch and
just talking – and having cups of tea ...

I don't know if I look much like her. Perhaps in the shape of
the face ... I thought her hair was amazing, the colour! It was a
funny sort of time because mum was there as well. I think Fern
was more interested in just meeting me, so mum felt a bit left out,
but I wanted her there. I thought of it as a time for family to meet
family. I think part of the problem was to do with where we met.
It was my flat rather than my home. And it wasn't Fern's home
either. I think mum was a bit disappointed; it wasn't that good
a feeling.

My idea was that it was like two families meeting, but it wasn't
really like that. Perhaps it should've been just Fern and I from the
start ... or she could've come to our home. But that would've been
really hard on her ... I can see her point of view as well. I think
mum was keen to be there and I think she felt a bit left out. She
went down to the shop at one stage.

I haven't really felt a bond with Fern. It's hard to say why. She
lives so far away. I haven't seen her much. I think I've only seen
her twice. I stayed with her in Auckland for one weekend and that
was really good. At least that means one of you is on your own
ground and relaxed and things. I really enjoyed that weekend. It
was great.

I was very interested in her life and also her lifestyle and
interests, especially astrology. I don't know much about it but
thought it was fascinating. I haven't seen that much of her, so I
haven't been able to develop that much of a relationship with
her. I probably feel more of a bond with Damon, and also Ross,
as I've seen him more.

Reunion with Ross

He came to Christchurch as well. I think I felt more relaxed in
Ross's company. I come from a conservative background and he
seemed to be more on that level. Fern seemed very radical to me.
Far out! So that was quite difficult to come to terms with. I don't
think I found that as hard as my parents, especially dad. He
didn't want to talk about it to start with ... the reunion, I mean.
He felt he'd been betrayed by the law. The conditions that they

had a child was that they'd never, ever meet the other party . But
at times I think it's wonderful and everyone can see that's the way
it is – and it's a good thing – and a natural thing – that you can
be open about it.

I think its been good for me because I've made some more friends!
Ross has come up and I get letters from Fern – and there's more
people around. Its a bonus being adopted because I've got two
families!

It's been good in other ways too, coming from a conservative
background and seeing other people's lifestyles. I think it's made
me a more balanced person; I've had trouble deciding on my career,
so it's given me different options, different things to think about.
I'm very interested in alternative health that Ross is in to ... that's
something I'd like to think about more. Emotionally, it's quite
good to be able to see both points of view. Initially I felt I was in
the middle, in between the two families. It was hard to start with,
feeling as if you're in the middle, joining the two. It felt like a
responsibility, especially for mum's feelings.

Finding out who you are gives you more options as to who you
can be ... having different role models. So many things change
you at this age, like getting away from home, going to varsity –
its an ongoing process. I think its all related. I also think I'm quite
adaptable. I stayed with Ross in Dunedin and then with Fern in
Auckland and that was quite different from what I'm used to. I
fitted in with all that and had a good time! I enjoyed the experiences. It has been a learning process.

I don't know how it would have been if I'd known them as I
was growing up. With them living in different parts of the country,
perhaps it would have been just the same – them coming and
visiting me and me going to them. They both live so far away ...
as it happened it's worked out OK finding out about myself and
where I come from. It's been quite a smooth transition, meeting
the family and so on ...

I'm glad I've met my birth family. It's helped me in terms of
growing up and learning more about myself – and I've made
some more friends. Before reunion I didn't really have any question
marks or gaps. As you get older, it does become more of a question.

6 Raylene

Raylene is a New Zealander. She had two children adopted, a boy and a girl. Both are now in their 20s. She had no counselling before she placed a veto on the birth registration to stop them getting any identifying information about her. But they found her anyway.

We met at an adoption conference in Wellington, where her 'admission' to using the veto caused quite a stir over the issue of adopted people's basic human right to have identifying information about themselves. The UK White Paper on adoption has recommended the same right of veto.

I am 44. I was first pregnant at 16 in 1964 and have had two children adopted. At the time I was living in a small town in central Otago, in the South Island of New Zealand. I became pregnant with my second child, Joy, after being raped.

The first child was by my boyfriend, who wanted me to have an abortion. I was very much against it. It wasn't what I wanted at all. I was probably about five months pregnant. I hadn't let on to anyone at that stage. Mum and dad thought I should go away, but Gary was born six weeks early so I was still home. I had him in the hospital and he was adopted straight away.

My parents said there was no way I was keeping him. I had a sister who was only two months old so they felt they had enough babies living at home. There were four of us. I was living at home at the weekends.

I wanted to keep him. But it was impossible if they weren't going to support me. So I had no choice. I had to go through with it.

I stayed at home, but I wasn't very big. My parents weren't very pleased about me being there. But if people came, they came. I didn't really want anyone to know either. Nor did I want any more to do with the father. My parents thought we should marry, but I thought if we can't agree about that, there's not going to be much else we'll agree about. I didn't think that was the reason we should get married either.

Gary was only three months old when I was raped and got pregnant with Joy. That was just the pits ... it was terrible! At the time I knew he wasn't a New Zealander as he had a very heavy accent. After he raped me I knew I was pregnant! I just knew. So I made him tell me his name. He said it was Steve but I didn't believe him. I still don't ... his age and job ... I knew I had to have information like that if I was pregnant and this baby was going to be adopted. I still don't know how I'd have coped – keeping her with what her father had done, although I did try and work out ways I could keep her, probably more so that I did with Gary. But there was just no way I could financially. My parents wrote to me saying they didn't want me at home. I was fairly nearby in Christchurch, but after the baby was born I was allowed to go back home.

I'd forgotten all the information I had about him except his name – and I felt terrible about that when I met Joy. I'd blocked it out. I had to get the file and see what was on it from the social worker. Her father was Italian. The social worker said they had a terrible time adopting her in Christchurch, because she was mixed-parentage having Italian blood. But they managed to get them adopted together in the one family, so they have grown up as brother and sister.

They said they'd always known they were adopted, but I don't think they did. Friends have told me they were 15 and 16 when they found out they were adopted. Their mother died when they were ten and eleven – she had cancer, Gary said, for 5 years. Joy said she couldn't remember how long she'd been sick. I felt terrible when I heard that. And the father remarried three years later and they made Gary a state ward. He ran away from home, as he couldn't stand it any longer, and went to Nelson, which is a long way from his home. He was a big boy and passed himself off as 16. The school realised he was missing and he was found and put in a boys' home. That was the wrong place. He should've gone to a church home, he wasn't breaking the law. But he was put in this place with other 'bad' boys, so that's what he became. I think he has quite a list of offences ... I don't know.

Joy left home when she was 16. She couldn't stand it any longer either. The stepmother had three daughters of her own and I guess she could do without them – especially a 14-year-old boy. Gary has no time for his father or stepmother. He gets on with one of his stepsisters, that's all. Now they are both in Australia and don't have any contact with their adoptive family at all. But they get on very well with their grandmother, their mother's mother. She's been very good to them. But she's 90 now and they don't want her to know they've met me. They think it'll upset her. I don't know if it would, but I respect their wishes. She's in an old people's home here in Dunedin.

No one ever talked about them after they were born, except just once my mother mentioned Gary when I was holding my baby sister and said, 'I wonder how the other baby is getting on.' He'd have been about three months old.

And yet now they are quite delighted with their first grandchildren. But I feel it's kind of false ... their attitude. My mother said to Joy if they hadn't been able to be adopted they would have taken them. But they never told me that. So I don't really believe it.

Both my parents were brought up in families where the illegitimate children had stayed in the family, but neither of them thought it was right, partly because there were too many 'mothers'. My aunties on both sides had had babies out of wedlock. My mother was one of eight girls, and her sister had a son who was part of the family. I don't think he was ever adopted, he was just there. And he eventually inherited everything! He was the only male. My father's sister had a son and he had far more than the others ever had as children. He recently told the other children of that family that he was actually their half-brother, as they had always thought he was their uncle.

Veto

When the law changed, I placed a veto to stop information being given out so they wouldn't be able to find me. My other two children didn't know about them and they were taking their exams. I thought they had enough to cope with. It took me a long time to decide whether to do it or not. I decided on the golf course. I was a really keen golfer and had had this excellent round in single figures which I thought was an impossible dream. It was after that I thought I had to make a decision about them and the veto. Sounds daft, doesn't it? And I haven't had a decent game of golf since, might I add!

The law was coming into effect in the September ('86) and I thought if they were looking for me it would've coincided with my other children's exams. I didn't think it was fair on them. I hadn't told them for lots of reasons. I didn't want them to think I wasn't as good as they thought I was. From a parent's perspective, you don't want your children to think badly of you. Also my husband's mother and father had found out just before we married that I'd had a baby – not two – and they wanted the marriage called off. I guess that was society's attitude then and it made me feel pretty low. My husband said it was our business and we went ahead. My mother-in-law was ridiculing our having a white wedding, which we didn't have anyway, but I didn't tell her that. So as a result I didn't have the relationship I should've had with them. Apart from that, his mother was quite a nice lady, although I never got on with his father.

I wasn't so much worried they would turn up. It was more that I was worried about the other kids and how they'd cope with it.

I hoped Gary and Joy were in a good family. I'd given them up because I'd been told they were going to be much better looked after than I could ever do. We were told that. You don't think that they're not going to be in a good family. And I'd have hated to hurt the adoptive parents or made them unhappy because the children were trying to contact me. I knew quite a lot of adoptive parents and many of them were really worried about the change in the law and they felt they were going to lose their children. I realise now that's a lot of rubbish. If they've been good parents it's not going to happen anyway. But that's something I have come to realise.

I think with the veto being on and the fact that they still wanted to find me, meant that they really did want to know me. I didn't think they would want to know me. I didn't think I was important in anybody's life. And I never really thought how the veto might affect them. I know I consciously avoided anything that was written about it, very consciously avoided it, and now I think it's a great pity really that other birth mothers are like me – because society's attitude at that time gave them all these hangups and you really couldn't believe that things had changed; it was only people saying that it had.

I always felt I wasn't good enough. I was inferior. 'How stupid could you be?' and that sort of comment. But they found me anyway. Even with the veto. As far as I'm concerned, having the veto on and the fact that they found me anyway means they really did want to know me!

Reunion

Joy wrote me a letter and very basically outlined where they'd lived and so on and that they'd been adopted together. It was the first time I knew that. I was very, very grateful to know that they were together. But if I'd known that, it would've helped me, knowing they had each other. It has been really important to them, especially with the life they've had.

They are obviously very close. But when Gary became a state ward they weren't allowed free contact – the only contact they had was at school over the fence. She said she got loads of detentions for that. They were only allowed contact at weekends. But she didn't tell me anything about the problems Gary had had in her letter. That all came later. She told me she'd been working in a wool shop, which amazed me as I'm a spinner and weaver.

Getting Joy's letter was like going to hell and back! It brings it all back. I was also worried about what people might think. I thought if I meet them and it works out I'll have to tell them. I'd never talked about it to anyone, apart from one friend. And she only knew about Gary.

I was worried about whether they would like me – and would I like them. Up until then I guess I'd just locked all my feelings away. I thought I would 'Forget about it … it never happened dear.' That's what you were told. As one birth mother I know put it, 'It's like a piece of your heart is locked on ice and then when you know, the ice starts to melt.'

Joy went on to say there was another letter and photos with the social worker in Dunedin. So I arranged to go down there and pick them up. That made it really real! They were real people to me then.

I was quite amazed when I saw the photos. They are really nice-looking kids. I could see Gary was tall, like my family. So I was pleased about that. There was a really lovely photo of Joy. She's so much like my other daughter – and Gary and Joy look like brother and sister. She doesn't look very Italian (she didn't know that, by the way). I could tell from the photos that Gary had tattoos on his hand and was wearing a leather jacket. But that didn't matter. I knew they were my children and I loved them and that was it. But perhaps there was some fear about what he was like and how much it had come from the adoptive parents or what.

But having put this veto on and them finding me meant they must have really wanted to know me. They would have got their birth certificates, but without my name on it to identify me. But they found me anyway. They'd found photos of me in the paper taken in 1963 when I was in the Queen Carnival. So there must have been something about that in the non-identifying information they'd been given. They've never really told me how they found me. 'That's ours to know', they say.

I thought it'd be better to see them on neutral territory, so I decided to meet them at the social worker's office. My husband came with me for support (and 'cos he's nosy!). He would've had me arrive half an hour early, because he didn't want us to meet on the stairs going up. We arrived about ten minutes early and talked with the social worker, especially about telling my other children, as I hadn't told them at this stage. Also if there wasn't going to be any relationship afterwards I couldn't see any point in upsetting them.

I kept wondering what I was going to say when I first met them. But they came in and I just gave them both a hug. We sat and chatted for a while. I had actually rung them before I met them, after getting the letters. The social worker had never had any contact with Gary, so she didn't know what he wanted out of the relationship. I wanted to know what his feelings were before we met. So I decided to ring him. When you're talking on the phone you can tell a lot from their voices. I had two or three brandies and then I rang Joy. There were tears and yes, she would love to meet me! She was going to arrange it all. After I put the phone down I realised I'd forgotten to ask for Gary's phone number. I thought I couldn't bear to ring her again that night so I rang again the next night and got it. I rang Gary several times and couldn't get him and by the time I did I'd had about six brandies! His wife answered the phone and I just asked for Gary. But Joy had been in touch, so they were waiting for me. Gary said two of his friends had rung and his wife had just put the receiver straight back down again 'cos she knew I was going to ring!

We had a long talk and he obviously wanted to meet me just as much as Joy did. It was great! I suggested he think of somewhere for us to have lunch after we met at Social Welfare and he said his local hotel. My husband said, 'He obviously accepted you 'cos he wouldn't be taking you where his friends could see him.' Gary said afterwards his boss was freaking out about him meeting his mother and although we were to meet at 12 o'clock they had to go to the pub at 11 as neither of them could cope with it any longer! We were only there five minutes and his boss walks in with his pay packet!

Our relationship with them has gone very well, although Gary's marriage has broken up. Finding me may have put a strain on them, although she had been very insistent that we meet, especially after they found the veto and couldn't get any information. He was quite happy to know who I was and said, 'I knew where you were and I'd have kept tabs on you for the rest of your life and if I ever needed you I'd have been able to find you.' But Joy was really wanting to meet me. And Gary's wife wanted it too. Her mother said it was Pandora's box they were opening ... which is true. You don't know what's going to come out. I think his wife was expecting that I wouldn't amount to much. After all, I'd had two children. On top of that, this photo they found of me in the paper looked like I had a big birthmark across my face! But she was very nice when we met that first night and had cooked tea for us.

There haven't been difficulties as such. I feel really awful about his marriage breaking up, but there were other problems. But it hasn't helped. He's now moved to Australia.

We told our children separately. My daughter Michelle was delighted to have a big brother and sister but added, 'You're not such a goody-goody after all!' My son was also delighted and said, 'I've always wanted a big brother!', although he was very upset that I'd been raped. They responded quite differently from the way I'd expected. I think that comes out time and time again – that the siblings are so pleased and that very few of them are jealous. They are adults and not going to be taking over or on your doorstep ... they are pleased to accept them into the family. In fact my daughter Michelle is living with Gary in Australia at the moment. They get on very well. The sisters do too.

People at the adoption conference were quite thrown to hear about the veto I'd placed. I was able to say I had changed my ideas about it. But the thing is I don't know how you educate other birth mothers into accepting that it isn't going to be as bad as they think it is, because if they are like me they don't want to know – they don't want to be hurt again. There's been too much hurt already. I think it's not so much not wanting to meet the child as the effect it might have on you. And also that you're not going to measure up.

I'm now the co-ordinator of our local Adoption Support Group. It's been really good for me going there and I just wish more birth mothers would go to groups and find out they're not the only ones ... that we all share similar feelings. We have a fair mixture of adoptees and quite a few adoptive parents. It helps you to realise that everyone has all these fears and that helps them to cope with it. I feel that I needed it at the time and I like to think I can now help them. I started going to the support group after I met my

children on the advice of a friend who strongly suggested I should
have some counselling. I've learnt a lot and it's been very good
for me.

My husband has been very supportive and really likes them.
He says it's hard not to, especially Joy as she's so like our own
daughter in personality and the things they do. When we first
met, within a few minutes of our meeting we asked Joy something
and she said, 'It doesn't matter me.' My husband said, 'Did you
hear that?' My other two kids use the same expression! And
there's an awful lot of things they do the same – their expressions,
the way they do things, their mannerisms. They also have a lot
of the same interests, especially sports, and are all very good at
that. It's something that other people notice too. My husband also
has a lot in common with Gary, as they both have an interest in
cars and so does my other son.

They call me Raylene. Gary says, 'One day I'll call you "mum"
and that'll blow the socks off you!' I don't know if Joy would or
not. But it was a nice thought.

I feel really good about knowing them and the fact that we get
on so well. I've had lots of things that other birth mothers haven't,
because they have treasured me as their family and I'm pleased
that I was able to support Gary through the breakup of his
marriage. It was his second and he's only 26. The first was to a
social worker. He went off to Oz to marry her at 18, but that didn't
last very long. She was 23.

Adoption today is so different. It's a last resort, whereas for us
there wasn't the same choice. And they haven't got other people
making that decision for them.

It would've helped me a lot to have had information about them
as they were growing up. The social worker who was involved said
I could write for information if I wanted. But at least I got to see
them. I was so upset at not being allowed to see Gary after he was
born and the grumpiest nurse, or so I thought, came along and
said, 'If you stop crying I'll bring your baby to you 'cos you're not
going to be any more upset from seeing him.' And she brought
him to me and said, 'He's yours for now.' And that was really neat.
And very precious. With Joy they wouldn't let me see her. And I
said, 'But I saw my other baby; why can't I see her?' There were
about eight other single girls there with babies up for adoption,
so if I'd seen mine they'd have wanted to see theirs, wouldn't they?
As I was getting dressed to leave they said, 'Your baby's up there

for you to have a look at but don't dare wake her up. We've just got her off to sleep.' Today I'd have just picked her up anyway, but then I was so surprised. I didn't think I was ever going to see her. So at least I saw them and that was good. I know it was good to have seen them. And I was lucky. A lot didn't.

I felt terrible having to walk out ... but I knew there was no choice. I just had to accept it. I never thought I'd see them again. I didn't think they'd want to know me.

I see our future as really good. I was a bit concerned I was going to lose them when they moved to Australia. But Gary says, 'You're not going to lose us. We're not going away. You're our family.'

7 Caroline

I got to know Caroline when she set up a branch of the Natural Parents Support Group in Bristol, where we both live. She advertised the group on local television and with the initial help of the national coordinators is successfully running a regular support group. She is also a member of NORCAP and Enjoys listening to and sharing experiences with adopted people so they can appreciate and understand the birth mothers' perspective and vice versa. Her friend Angela, who runs the NORCAP group, is also a birth mother and they recently discovered that the adoptive families of their relinquished children are the best of friends.

I was brought up in a very strict Catholic family where I didn't have any kind of relationship with my own mother. I was very close to my father. I left school at 16 and went on a nursery nurses' course. I grew up in a white area of Solihull where there weren't any black people. The first time I integrated into a mixed society was when I went to college. I became very friendly with an Indian girl whose boyfriend was West Indian. We went out together one night and she introduced me to reggae music which was wonderful and so different from what I knew. Eventually I met her boyfriend's brother, who was twelve years older than me and seemed extremely nice. I didn't know much about him. The next thing I knew I was in bed with him. Six weeks later I discovered I was pregnant – something I hadn't even thought of before. I was 18 and I suppose I was quite sexually naive as well. I told my supervisor first and then I had to tell my parents. She came with me.

My mother's first reaction was that I should have an abortion. My father didn't say anything. It was the first time my mother ever hit me. I had a black eye. She told me I had to get out. I told my boyfriend and he said I should move in with him and that I shouldn't get rid of the baby. I didn't know at that time he had five children living with him. It turned out he had nine children altogether. The youngest of these five was four and the oldest was

eleven. When I moved in I thought they belonged to the man
who lived there too. I never even asked any questions, I was so
naive! So at 18 I became the instant mother of five children. I used
to witness him hitting them but I never felt strong enough to go
against him. Looking back, it was an awful time. But up until I
had Lawrence in January 1969 he was OK towards me. After
Lawrence was born he changed completely and totally took me
over. I became his property. He used to beat the children more
and more and I was too weak to get out of it. I did leave on several
occasions, but he always found me and dragged me back. I
couldn't go back to my parents because they would have had the
attitude 'I told you so.' But at that age and in that situation it was
impossible. These children used to go to school with marks on
them and nobody ever questioned them. He regularly raped me.

In 1971 [almost two years later] I got pregnant again. I did
actually have some pregnancies in between – in fact I had seven,
mostly miscarriages because of the beatings he used to give me.
When I was five months pregnant with Tyrone – or Paul as he is
now – he beat me so badly I ended up in hospital, unable to walk.
It was touch and go whether Tyrone would be born and, if so,
what he would be like. I spent the last four months of my
pregnancy in hospital as they wouldn't allow me to leave. During
that time Lawrence was still with his father. Social workers and
the NSPCC all tried at various times to get Lawrence out, but he
was with his father and there was no way they could get him away
from there, even though he had done those things to me.

On February 1st I gave birth to Tyrone, who was 100 per cent
OK. I had to go back to the house to get Lawrence. We stayed there
for six weeks until I could get out. I left quickly with them and
the clothes I was wearing and Tyrone's baby basket and a handful
of their clothes. I went to Social Services. The only place they could
find for us was a hostel. When I got there I discovered it was a
place for people who'd come out of mental homes. There were
women in there who'd been to Rampton for years and years. I
was there with Lawrence, who was two and a half, and Tyrone,
who was eight weeks old. I had one room and one bed. Tyrone
had a cradle. It was absolutely horrific. They used to bang on the
doors all the time. I couldn't go out in case the baby's father saw
me, or someone told him they'd seen me. I contacted his sister
and she came and saw us, but I also remembered that she'd done
nothing to help when I lived with her brother for four years and
she knew what was going on.

While I was there, my mother contacted a church organisation who offered us accommodation in Bristol where I would be a live-in housekeeper and could have the children there too. I did that and ended up with a divorcée with two children. Everything went well to start with and I got Lawrence into a nursery. But gradually she put more and more on me so that eventually I became totally responsible for her children and was babysitting every night. I contacted the church lady again and she thought it would be nice if I met another girl who had mixed-race children. She put me in touch with a girl called Trudy who was a New Zealander. We became good friends. Trudy was concerned about our accommodation and suggested I speak to her social worker, who thought it would be a good idea if I put the children into foster care to make it easier for me to find accommodation. I was so thick and weak and young at that age. But I didn't want to be parted from them – especially Tyrone. I would never let anyone hold him. I was overprotective of him. He was lucky to be born and he was *my* child and extremely precious to me. So I decided to get a flat on my own.

I found a flat, but I didn't tell the landlord I had children. For the first time since Tyrone was born I left him and Lawrence with Trudy overnight and moved into this flat in Clifton Wood. The next day I collected the boys and moved them in with me. From that day on the landlord made our lives absolute hell. He even changed the locks on the door so we couldn't get in. I should have told him I had children, he said. I'm sure he persuaded the other tenants to complain about the children. I'd got Lawrence in a nursery all day and I usually went out with Tyrone to see Trudy, so they weren't a nuisance. But the harassment continued and I became extremely depressed. The social worker again suggested that I should find somewhere else and put the children in foster care temporarily, on a voluntarily basis. She assured me it wouldn't be difficult. So I did. I took them down to Social Services and that was the last time I saw Tyrone.

They decided it would be better that Tyrone didn't see me because he'd get upset. I could see Lawrence, who was then three. Thinking back on it, Lawrence would be the one to be more upset – or certainly as upset. They were placed with different foster parents, I don't know why, and I was too weak, too inadequate at that time to do anything else. After a couple of weeks I got a letter from Social Services asking if I would go and see them. I went down and saw the head of Fostering and Adoption, whose name keeps coming up with other birth mothers I now know. This woman said to me that she had a family who would very much like to adopt Tyrone. I remember saying quite clearly, 'I don't want him adopted,' and explained that I was still trying to find somewhere to live. You couldn't automatically get council accommodation. I was obviously too weak and made to feel totally inadequate. I was told life would be a lot easier for me with one child, and that should be Lawrence because he was that much older. Tyrone was 13 months old.

I can't recall signing any papers or when it happened, even to this day, but that is how Tyrone came to be adopted. Ironically, seven or eight weeks after that I found a flat. Lawrence came straight back. I thought Tyrone had been adopted straight away. I didn't know about the months it takes. I didn't know anything. That time is still blocked out. I was on tablets I was so depressed.

Lawrence went back to the same nursery and everything carried on as normal. I just didn't have the baby. I don't remember much of how I felt then. I do remember I burnt nearly all the photos of Tyrone, everything that reminded me of him. It was awful. Unimaginable.

I met another man who was West Indian. I became friendly with him and again I became pregnant. Adam was born in February 1974, exactly two years after Tyrone was born. I'm sure Adam was born to replace Tyrone. A few months before Adam's birth, I married his father. During all this time I hardly saw my parents. They lived quite near but my mother never visited. My father did sometimes. I was extremely close to him. He is the only person out of everyone I knew that I would allow to hold Tyrone, and yet I couldn't go to him. I couldn't tell him what was going on. According to my mother years later, it broke my father's heart losing Tyrone. She didn't mention how it affected her. I couldn't tell them, I was too weak. They didn't know at the time that the children were in foster care. I wasn't seeing them then. My mother was so unapproachable.

After I had Adam, I discovered my husband had numerous other women. A couple of months after I had Adam I actually found him in our bed with another woman. I was also petrified of him because he could be violent as well, although not as bad as the boys' father. In September 1975 I had my daughter Leah and then in 1976 I divorced him, but he still didn't leave me alone. I did a secret council house swap overnight and two days later he found me. I'd just taken the children to school and he drove up in the car. I was on the ground, he was dragging me across the road. Nobody came to my aid. For the first time in my life I found the strength to fight back, and somebody called the police. With that he sped off. From that day on I didn't have any more problems with him.

I became quite friendly with a social worker called Alva who was around at that time. Alva was wonderful. Everybody says so to this day. I used to talk to her about problems I was having with my husband. I can't remember how we met, but she knew all about Tyrone's adoption. We used to talk about him. I wanted to send him birthday and Christmas cards, and she suggested I send them and she would make sure they went to the right place. So every year from that time up until he was 18 I sent cards, letters, photographs. I don't know if I knew they were being sent to him or not. I think I thought they were. I would write and tell him everything, what was happening in my life and Lawrence's. I also sent presents for a few years, but stopped doing that after a while because I didn't know what he liked. I don't know what happened to them, but I discovered when I had counselling shortly before we met that all the letters and photos were on his file. Looking back, I knew nothing about adoption. I didn't know he wasn't adopted straight away, that I had any rights to him.

The few details I had about the adoptive parents were actually correct. I knew their jobs and that they had adopted another mixed-race child. Unfortunately, they were not given the correct information about me. They certainly didn't know I had another child who was Tyrone's full brother. I also now know that what was written down as the reason for the adoption was bad housing.

As the years went by, there was not a day when I didn't think about him. Lawrence has completely blocked out the memory of his baby brother, even though they spent more than a year together. He can remember when I was in hospital with tubes sticking out of me, but nothing else, even to this day. Over the years I was always going to find the 'right' time to tell him. But how on earth do you tell a child he has a brother? A full brother would have meant a lot to him, as he often described Adam and Leah as his half-brother and -sister. Also Max [my husband] treated him quite badly and he resented him. But that made it all the more difficult.

In 1981 I met Martin, who is English and white. We fell in love and married in December 1983. He became an instant father to the three children. I told him about Tyrone, but we didn't really talk about it. If something came on the television I could feel him looking at me. If I was sitting with other women they would say things like, 'How could anyone give up a child for adoption?' I couldn't tell them. I couldn't tell anybody. Nobody knew I'd had a child adopted. I felt so ashamed. I felt it was my fault, that I had brought it all on myself. I felt that was what my mother thought but he was never, ever spoken about. My father died in 1979 and although he visited, he never mentioned Tyrone either. It was as if he never existed.

In 1990 I had a nervous breakdown. I couldn't cope with anything, kept thinking of Tyrone and crying all the time. I took off for a couple of weeks with Leah, made sure the other two were alright, and left a note for Martin explaining about Tyrone and how it was affecting me. He managed to find me through a travel agent – I'd gone to Majorca. He told me he'd told Lawrence about Tyrone, as he felt he had to say why I'd disappeared. I was quite relieved about that.

When I returned Martin suggested I go to the doctor, who referred me to a psychiatrist. I saw him three times and he was useless. He did nothing whatsoever. He knew nothing about adoption or any organisation that could help me. I just sat there and cried from the beginning to the end of each session. After the third one I got in touch with Alva, the social worker, who suggested I rang another social worker who might be able to help. She suggested I contact NORCAP. The local coordinator was a woman called Angela and it was wonderful just to talk to another birth mother. She suggested I went to the next meeting. We sat round a table – birth mothers and adopted people – and it was the first time I'd been able to talk about Tyrone in that way. I cried and so did some of the others. I showed them photos of my son.

A few weeks before Tyrone's eighteenth birthday, around Christmas, which is always an awful emotional time, I rang the social worker who'd referred me to NORCAP. She worked in the office where Tyrone's file was held and where he'd make contact if he was searching for me. She said there was no news and in any case he wasn't yet 18. She rang me a few weeks later to say she'd like to see me. Angela came with me and we spent about three hours there, during which time she produced Tyrone's file. In it were the letters and photos and cards that I'd sent over the years. I wasn't surprised to see them there and I suppose I was relieved that they'd arrived at the right place. She asked me to go through them and tippex out any identifying information so he wouldn't go hurtling after me before having his counselling, which he needed before he could get his birth certificate. I did as I was told but kept in one surname that she hadn't picked out beforehand, so she must have missed it. At the end of all that she told me that Paul – as he had been renamed – had been sitting in the chair I'd been sitting in yesterday. He'd come asking about his records. She had told him to come back in two weeks' time when he was 18.

Two weeks before his birthday on February 1st I had a phonecall from her. She said he'd been in to see her, and she'd shown him all the photos and letters and he had been very upset. He was very shocked to learn he had a brother. That was about 4 o'clock. About half an hour later I had another phonecall. I was in the shop [where I worked]. It was quite busy and I was on my own. A voice said, 'Can I speak to Caroline please?', and I just knew as soon as he spoke who it was. I was half expecting it anyway. I was in an awful state. He said he wanted to meet me and of course I wanted to meet him too. He said the social worker had told him he had to wait two weeks before he went back, but he couldn't wait that long. I said I had to see him as well. So we arranged to meet at a friend's farm that night!

I rang Angela; I rang my husband. He said someone had rung saying he was from Littlewoods catalogue and he did wonder afterwards if that was right. Angela drove me over there – there was no way I could drive – and we arrived half an hour early, determined to be first. But he'd already been there for ages. I walked into this room and sitting in front of me was somebody who didn't look at all like the baby in the photograph I had, didn't look like Lawrence – really a total stranger. The other thing was he didn't even have his own name. It had been changed to Paul, which came as a great shock. To this day that has hurt most, changing his name, because he was 19 months old when they adopted him. He'd been baptised as Tyrone, all my letters over the years had been to Tyrone, and I was looking at my son – who was Paul.

It was the first time I hadn't cried. I sat down by him and he didn't cry either. He kept his head on one side; he didn't really look at me. I was looking at him and trying to imagine him as the baby. It was really strange. Some time during the conversation he said, 'We could have managed, you know,' and that's always stuck in my mind. I talked to him about his brother, which was strange, and he talked about his family, which I didn't like much. I didn't really want to hear about his family at that stage. Anyway we talked for about four hours. At midnight my friend came in and gently suggested it was time to leave.

Angela and I dropped Paul off and shortly afterwards I was physically sick. I was very upset. Everything hit me afterwards. I went home and couldn't sleep that night. We'd arranged for him to come into the shop the next day and he turned up before opening time and stayed all day. That intense relationship, from 10 o'clock in the morning until 10 o'clock at night, went on for quite a few weeks.

The day after we'd met I arranged for him to meet the other three children in the pub. Adam was quite laid back about finding out he had another brother, and Leah was over the moon. She finally worked out who the baby was in the photograph I had of him at home. So there we all were together – me and my four children for the first time. I was really proud to have them sitting there together, but on the other hand it was so sad. Lawrence and Paul sat next to each other and Paul was looking out of the corner of his eye at Lawrence, who kept his head down. They didn't seem to know what to say to each other, and that was so sad because they were brothers and seemed to have nothing in common. They sat there like complete strangers and I felt so sad.

Since then they have seen each other and bumped into each other when Paul has come to visit me, but as Paul said yesterday, 'He's my real brother but we haven't really got any kind of relationship.' I don't think Paul liked Lawrence's friends and that's partly because he has an identity problem, being mixed-race and brought up in a white, adoptive family. Of course, 20 years ago adoptive parents weren't encouraged to think in terms of a multiracial society, but having mixed-race children you have to encourage them to relate to both cultures. But Paul didn't have any of that. He considers himself as white, but unfortunately he's not. When he met his brother's friends he didn't fit in, couldn't understand what they were saying if they spoke patois. Lawrence has been to Paul's home and stayed overnight, but he felt totally different to him.

In the Easter of 1991 Paul brought a video of his family. Apparently his father discovered it was missing, and when Paul said he'd shown it to me they were very, very upset. His mother's initial reaction was to tell him to 'get out' or 'go to her', so I decided to write her a letter telling her I wasn't trying to take him away from them; that I was very pleased that he'd found me – it was what I'd always wanted; the circumstances relating to his adoption, because all that had been written in his file as reason for adoption was 'bad housing'; and the fact that he had a full brother. I had a very nice letter back saying she was pleased I'd written to her and that she'd always been very grateful to the girls who had given up their babies, enabling her to have four children. She invited me for lunch on neutral territory. I was so nervous before meeting them. I had about four cigarettes on the 2-mile journey. They were extremely nice; you couldn't fault them. But again I felt very inadequate. Sitting with them made me realise how terribly middle-class they are. I gave them some flowers in the car park just before we left, and she gave me a kiss. She sent me a note afterwards to say how pleased she was to have met and that now Paul could be in contact with Lawrence. She hoped he had found what he was looking for and said that there would always be a place in their lives for him. His father promised me some photos of Paul as a child, but I still haven't got them. That was three years ago and I would really love to have them. I've rung her a couple of times and once she rang me to see if Paul was with me, but that's it. I know they must have worried about him, as he'd been in quite a bit of trouble and was drinking too much. But I think it all became too much for him.

He rang me really drunk one night at midnight. He said he wanted to come over and that he'd hitch. He got here at 2 o'clock in the morning. He just came in and cried. We hugged each other for a couple of hours – without saying anything. That's been our most intense, emotional time. It was a couple of weeks after we met.

We've spent a lot of time together, but for various reasons we haven't talked very much – usually because I'm in the shop. People would come in and see him sitting there and ask about him and I could say at last, 'This is Paul – my other son.' Then I'd be telling them he'd been adopted! It was really strange. And they'd say, 'Oh, yes, isn't he like you!' It was wonderful. Before that I used to say I only had three children, and now I say four whenever I'm asked.

I take each visit as it comes. I hope he's going to stay around. I would hate it if anything happened and I was to lose him again. I couldn't bear that. The others all accept him. I know Paul would like to be closer to Lawrence. Adam's quite laid back and treats him as he does his other brother and sister, and Leah loves him. She loves talking to him and thinks he's wonderful. He bought her a birthday present yesterday and she was really pleased. She

jokes around with him and says things like, 'That's hereditary –
you got that from mum.' They just have normal conversations
really.

I had no contact whatsoever with Paul's father's side of the family
for years, except with one of his half-brothers, Keith. Shortly
after I left the family the children were taken into care because I
notified the NSPCC. They were so very ill-treated and abused.

Several years after I left them I took Lawrence up to Birmingham,
as he was asking about them. I remember being very nervous in
case I met his father. Also I hadn't told any of them about Tyrone
being adopted – except Keith. I don't know why I didn't tell
them. Lawrence was overjoyed to have all these brothers and sisters,
so I encouraged them to keep in contact. Only the oldest daughter
remembered Tyrone.

Just after Christmas 1991 Paul wanted to go up to Birmingham
to meet his family. I told Paul's aunt that we only wanted to meet
her and her five daughters. She was all over him, which aroused
all sorts of old feelings in me. You can't help thinking back and
remembering things like the fact that no one was there for us.
All of a sudden there was a knock at the door and in he walked.
That was a huge shock to Paul. He was OK. He sat and talked to
him. I could see him nodding and saying 'Yes' or 'No', just as I
had done 20 years ago.

In the West Indian community you don't have children adopted.
Grandma will often look after the child, who stays in the family.
So I don't suppose it was easy for them either.

On our return journey Paul said he didn't want to see him again,
and we didn't speak for the whole of the rest of the journey. He
was angry but I'm not sure who with. It was awful. But we've
managed to sort it out. He's been back to Birmingham once since,
which worries me as they are a very unhealthy family.

My experience of the particular black people I knew at the
time Paul was adopted was pretty negative, so when I was told
he was going to be adopted by a white family I was pleased. Also
I'm white, so that made sense too as if he had stayed with me
he'd have been brought up in a white family. But my ideas have
changed over the years. It would've been better for him if he'd
been brought up by a mixed-race family. It would have helped
him with his identity and helped him to communicate with
black people. He sees himself as white – that's how he's been
brought up, and that's not right. All my children are classed as
black, and I'm very proud of them because of that. But Paul

hasn't had the multiracial upbringing they've had – all their extended family.

I don't think I've ever come to terms with what's happened. In later years NORCAP has been invaluable and also the Natural Parents Support Group, which I set up in Bristol as there wasn't a branch here. Some birth mothers like to come to every meeting, others until such time as they've traced, and some continue after they've been reunited. I enjoy going to NORCAP meetings too, to hear how adoptees are getting on in their search and also to help them understand what it's like for birth mothers.

The one thing I don't think I'll ever come to terms with is the fact they changed his name. I have found that very difficult. Paul said once he was glad he didn't have Tyrone as a name, so I told him the reason he was called that was because he was so lucky to be born so normal and strong – it made me think of Tyrone Power. Through all those years that's what I called him, and now I call him Paul and part of me feels he's not mine because of that. If this issue comes up on the adoption panel that I am part of – and the adoptive parents want to change the child's name – I always give my point of view. It means the child loses part of its identity – the adoptive parents are then wanting it to lose part of its identity, particularly where the child has already been called by that name, as mine had.

The worst thing over all these years has been not knowing how he is – if he's alive or dead. To have had some information, a letter occasionally. Mine wasn't a 'typical' adoption in that I'd had him for over a year and I feel he was stolen from me by Social Services. I don't think I've ever been in touch with those feelings of anger, not really. I still stay in contact with Alva, who's told me this was the worst case of manipulation she's ever witnessed. The policy then was to find babies for all the adoptive parents. That was 1973.

I hope my relationship with Paul continues to grow and get stronger. I know it can't be a mother-and-son relationship, but I'd like it to be as near to that as it can possibly be.

Paul

I asked Paul's birth mother, Caroline, whether she thought her son might be willing to talk to me about his experiences of adoption. She suggested I ring him, and seemed optimistic as he had spoken about his experience recently when they both went to a discussion group in Nottingham. Paul's

experience has the added dimension of being a black child brought up
in a white family who lived in a town that had no other black population.
Paul is 21 years old. He and his mother were searching for each other
at the same time.

Due to my colour I obviously knew I was adopted, because my
adoptive parents are white. They told me I was adopted from as
young as I can remember. I was also told that my mum was a nurse
and my dad an engineer and that I was born in Birmingham. That
was all I knew. My parents were always quite open – they answered
any questions as honestly as possible. They are both teachers and
I am the youngest of four children. We are all adopted. My
younger sister and I are mixed-race; my older brother and sister
are white. We were all adopted from different families.

The town we lived in had no black people at all and there weren't
any black kids at my first school in the three years I was there,
apart from my sister and two Vietnamese refugees. Up until then
I can't say my colour wasn't a problem, but I didn't realise there
was any difference between black and white people.

There was a point when I was about nine or ten when I had
my first black friend. He was a bit of a troublemaker but we
became quite close friends. I remember telling my parents he was
different from the rest and I could get on with him easier. My mum
asked me if I wished I'd been brought up in a black family and I
said, 'Yes.' You don't realise at nine that that might've hurt. But
she understood what I was feeling.

I'm not sure really whether I see myself as black or not. It's
difficult to say, having grown up in a white family. There are so
many differences between black and white families – the structure
of the family and the different roles within it. In this respect I see
myself more as white, but I also know what it's like to be black.
Sometimes I go to places and feel an outcast – lots of places
actually where you feel your colour is very apparent – when
you're younger, it's things like starting school or joining clubs.
A lot of black people I know just accept they'll be ridiculed at times,
but I won't 'cos I'm not as conciliatory; also it's about having a
foot in both camps – for me it's more in the white camp because
of my upbringing. I find it easier to get on with white people. I
sometimes get uneasy with black people – but then if you talk to
black people they'll understand what you're on about. Racism is
only apparent to many people when it's obvious – like being called

a nigger. But it also operates on a more subtle level too, especially among middle-class whites.

I used to get teased a bit when I was five or six about being adopted and having white parents, but that sorted itself out. It was different when I moved schools at eight. There were a few black and Indian children. But somehow it was worse, like being excluded from games other kids organised because you were a 'coon'. I found the verbal abuse hard to take and didn't fight back. I think I would've found it easier to relate to black people if I'd been brought up in a black family. That 'block' is still there now.

Because of this block it's been quite difficult for me meeting my father's family and all my half-brothers and -sisters. I've worked quite hard on it. When I found out about my birth mother and that I had two brothers I was hoping they'd be black. I always wanted an older black brother when I was younger.

I first tried to trace Caroline, my birth mother, through the Salvation Army when I was 16. But I was told I had to be 18. I later contacted Social Services and had some counselling. All the time I was looking for her I always knew I'd find her and that she wanted to see me. The picture I had in my mind of what she looked like and how she was is pretty much how she is. I'd never seen a photo of her and didn't know anything about her. The only things I was wrong about were that I thought she'd wear glasses and wouldn't have any other children – that she'd be living on her own.

As a child, I was told the reason I was adopted was that she was unmarried and so I just accepted that. It was only when I was older that I started to question everything. It seemed that just being unmarried wasn't enough, as lots of people have kids and aren't married. From the age of about 14 onwards, I tried to find out more about my natural parents and asked my parents loads of questions. I was the only one out of the four of us who asked questions. Naturally they are curious, but I'm the only one who has traced. In some ways I wished I'd waited, as it has had quite an effect on my life. I've been in a real spin for the last couple of years since I found them. I think it's just being young. Since I've left school I haven't really settled at anything – lots of jobs, but I wish I'd been more settled. I'm now at college and hope to go to university next year, so I wish I'd waited until I'd done all that. But that's my nature – I'm spontaneous and tend not to think about the consequences. I think I was too emotionally immature to handle it. But looking back, although I just accepted things the way they were, I've always needed to know.

I went to counselling sessions a couple of times just before I turned 18 and found out that Caroline was also having counselling from the same lady. I was given a load of letters and birthday cards that she had sent into the agency, which I never got. They are for most of my birthdays. I lived with Caroline until I was about a year old, I think. In her last letter she said it would be the last one and that she hoped one day I'd look for her. I think in some respects it's not fair that you're not given the opportunity to see what's been sent to you. From the adoptive parents' point of view it would've been hard. All her letters had things blanked out – like her surname. I was going to see her anyway, so it seemed a bit stupid, censoring them like that, especially since I was looking for her – and it was only two weeks until I was 18 and had a right to the information. But the fact that they'd blanked out her handwriting really upset me. The nearest I got to meeting her at that stage was touching a letter she'd written, so I felt that was a real intrusion and an insult to her.

Although I wanted to know about her as a kid, I think it would have been exasperating getting those letters and not knowing her. Things like, 'I can't wait to meet you,' would have been hard, knowing I couldn't trace her till I was 18 – especially when you're, say ten, it would seem like a lifetime.

But on one letter they'd missed censoring her husband's name. I had a surname! I was told she worked in a video shop so I rang Directory Enquiries and found it. I rang up and spoke to her husband. I'll never forget what I said. I said I was Mr James from Littlewoods catalogue about an order. I had to think up something quickly. So he gave me her phonenumber. I rang her up at her shop. The counsellor told me to wait two weeks, but I couldn't. We met that night. There's no way I could've waited another two weeks. I wouldn't have slept!

Meeting her has had a big effect on me – it's made me quiet. I think I've been completely lost for words. Today was the first time in three years we'd sat down and had a really relaxed conversation. Before that I used to go up to her shop but not talk, just sit there beside her watching TV, then go and come back a couple of days later.

The first night I met her at her friend's house I didn't know what to say. I just could not believe that I'd finally met her. I couldn't believe it! There were thousands of questions I could've asked her, but I just sat there. After I met her the person I wanted to meet next was my full brother. He's my first proper brother. He's three years older. I only found that out when I went to the counselling sessions. At first they didn't tell me anything. I don't think they wanted to tell me anything until they found out whether she wanted to meet me. I think that's how they operate, anyway. On my second session I sat down on the chair and the counsellor told me that my mum had just been sitting there. It was really weird, but I just knew everything was going to go all right.

The reason she couldn't keep me was because she had a hard time with my birth father in Birmingham and she also had my brother to look after. We stayed there for my first few weeks and then moved down south. She had to move around a lot. I think mixed marriages were really frowned upon then and being a single mother with coloured children was a double burden, so it was very hard to find a place to live. She had to keep moving. Lawrence and I were taken into foster care while she sorted out a place to live and when she came to collect us they told her it would be better if she just took Lawrence and not me because I was so young. I went to foster parents and then I was adopted.

I did have feelings about 'Why me and not my brother?' in the beginning especially when I discovered Caroline had had two more children after me, but that was gut-reaction. I expect her circumstances changed after I was adopted. Perhaps it helped her as well, easing the pain of giving me away. But I've had a good upbringing and they've had a hard one, so from that point of view I'm very grateful ... thankful to my adoptive parents. I've been very lucky. It would have been different if Caroline had become a millionaire and I'd had to live with poverty-stricken adoptive parents! The only time I'm jealous or upset, I suppose, is when they talk about family things that didn't involve me – but it's just one of those things. I do have good parents.

I'd like to see more of Lawrence, but we have our own separate lives. The other two, Adam and Leah, accepted me. He's a year younger than me and quite laid back and Leah, who is 18, was quite shy. They have a different father from me and Lawrence.

I talked with my parents about searching for Caroline years before I did it, but not at the time. My counsellor asked me if I'd told my parents I was searching and kept urging me to. But I don't always find it that easy to talk to them, even though they're very good listeners. It's easier now than when I was a kid. Mum can get very emotional and I find that difficult. I told them the day after I met her, when I was on my way out the door to visit her in the shop. That was unfair of me, I know. They took it very well. I thought they might ask a load of questions, but they didn't. I got the feeling that my dad wasn't that happy, which turns out not to have been the case. They've been fine about it really.

They all met up a few months afterwards, which was really good. I told Caroline they wanted to take her out to lunch and I told them she wanted to take them out. But they had both expressed a desire to meet each other. I felt it was important they met and wouldn't have to keep asking questions about the other. And it went very well partly because of this American-style waitress who said, 'Hi. My name is ...', so we spent a fair bit of time taking the mickey out of her. I think that helped. Also Lawrence came too and he usually has quite a bit to say. I just concentrated on sinking as many pints as I could. I think I was pretty nervous. That's the only time they've met. I'm quite surprised they haven't met again, but maybe they both felt a bit embarrassed or uneasy. But I'm glad they've met and hope they meet again. I didn't expect them to become great friends or anything. Also my life with Caroline is separate from my life with them. But it did make me think how it'd be if I got married! Having Caroline there, my parents, all my brothers and sisters, as well as some on my father's side of the family ...

My older adopted brother was quite curious when I made contact, but neither of my sisters said a lot. My younger sister has never mentioned it. Sometimes I might say something about my birth family and then feel a bit uneasy for having done so. I wouldn't want to see mum hurt. I do mention them to her, but I don't think my dad is that interested although I wish he was. If not I'd rather he just said so.

Meeting my birth father was a shock. It wasn't the way I planned it. I went to Birmingham to meet my aunt. She's the 'head' of the family – no one dares argue with her. I also met a sister, an uncle and three cousins. I didn't want to meet my dad, but my aunt decided it was best I did, so halfway through meeting her I was told he'd turned up, which I was very annoyed about. He arrived and I just sat there. It was difficult to understand what he was saying. He speaks broad Jamaican. There were loads of people in the room, but he didn't suggest we went somewhere else for privacy. It was just after Christmas and there were loads of kids running about. I was quite shocked by it all. I think my mum probably knew he was going to be there; that's the impression

I got. When I say 'my mum' I mean Caroline. I felt like walking out. I'd told Caroline I didn't want to meet him – and that I'd do it my own way. No one there thought it was anything out of the ordinary, except a cousin's white boyfriend who said he felt sorry for me, which didn't really help.

I've only seen him once since then. I went up to Birmingham around June or July to see my half-brother and my aunt whom I dare not see! I sat in the car outside his barber shop for about two and a half hours just watching him. Then I went in and had my hair cut by him and he didn't recognise me. I suppose he's got so many kids, although he recognises all the others. We were having a pleasant conversation, although it was difficult at times to understand him. I thought he must've recognised me. At the end I mentioned his sister and it obviously dawned on him who I was ... so I got a free haircut. Anyway, he sat me down and was OK. He wanted to take me round to see my grandfather, but I didn't feel easy about meeting anyone else in the family. However, he took me to meet some other relatives and they played dominoes while I just sat there as I don't know how to play. We left after about half an hour.

My brother Lawrence goes to Birmingham once or twice a year. I expect I'll go again, but it's depressing there. All the kids have had such a hard life, moving from home to home, being in care. I haven't met them all yet. I don't feel any connection with them, although I get on well with Anthony, a half-brother, and I really like Keith, who lives in Germany. But generally I don't feel I have much in common with them. They've had such a hard upbringing and I feel I'm nothing like them. I don't look like them either – I look like my mum, not my dad. I guess Lawrence has more in common with them than I do.

Physical difference or sameness is not that important by itself. If Caroline and I didn't look like each other it wouldn't make any difference. But with my father's family it's having nothing in common at all, having a completely different upbringing plus not looking like each other – they could be anyone. But eventually I'm sure I'll get round to meeting the rest of them. They are all so mixed up because of their upbringing. I wish it had just been me and Lawrence. I find it difficult coming from a family that's supportive and close when they feel so unsupported and uncared for. Their mother lives in Canada.

Although I haven't found what I was hoping for, it has satisfied my curiosity. I wish it was a different story, especially hearing how

my birth father has abused his kids – really sick stories that some
people confirm and others deny. That was part of the reason
Caroline was in hospital for five months before having me,
because he used to beat her. I used to worry much more about
the fact that I might have inherited some of his characteristics.
It's not nice knowing your dad's like that. It's really scary. I got
really unnerved about it when I first knew about him.

I'm much more like Caroline. She is very outgoing and I used
to be much more like that too. But after meeting her I've gone
into quite a shell. It's affected me – not just when I'm with her
but in my everyday life. It's really weird. It's only now that I'm
trying to make a really conscious effort to be a bit more outgoing.
I suppose other people haven't noticed because I change my
moods anyway and can be a bit unpredictable. The impact of all
this has been quite profound. I've always been slightly unsettled
and it's not a bad thing that I am quieter. I suppose I used to be
a bit of a lad. I think it's more about getting on with people. I
don't find it as easy as I used to. I don't know why. It's like being
in a kind of shock. But now I'm recovering from it. It's unbelievable
that after three years it can affect you that much. Perhaps that's
why I'd like to have been more settled in my life before searching,
because it might've made it easier. But then again I'm glad I've
done it. There's no way I could've waited any longer.

I didn't benefit at the time from counselling, I was so confident
everything would go well. But looking back I would've benefited
from it after I met Caroline and everyone. That still applies now,
but not with the same counsellor. She might say, 'I told you so.'
But it would be useful to talk about feelings about my birth father
and help me make some sense of it. Maybe I'm too proud to go
and ask for it. I do talk to my best friend, but it probably annoys
him 'cos I'm always going on about it.

I don't think secrecy is right. I think an open style of adoption
would be easier. At least with fostering, the parents continue to
see the child. The kids I know who have been fostered call their
natural parents their parents and their foster parents their foster
parents. But I call my adoptive parents my parents as they brought
me up, and I call my mother Caroline. She's my mum but she's
not my parent. To know who your natural parents are – and to
see them or write to them or whatever, knowing who they are,
is something I could handle, but only if I was fostered, because
they would still be my legal parents. Otherwise it might be hard
on the adoptive parents. But from the child's point of view it's

better to keep the links with his natural family. As it is, I've had to search for my natural family to find my roots, to know where I come from. It's been hard trying to identify with my black roots as I've grown up in a white family. It would have helped a lot to have had one black parent and one white parent to help me identify with the two cultures I am a part of. I'm glad I've found my family – not just to satisfy my curiosity, but as family I am committed to and want to see regularly.

Part Three
Semi-open Adoption

I am the one who is not there
the absent one, that particular
ache inside you, half knowledge
of something lost that was never
quite answered.

Jeni Couzyn, 'Song of the Almost Remembered'

The stories in the second half of this book – birth mothers mainly of the 1980s in the UK and in New Zealand – are different from those in the first half. No longer is a 'clean break' of the child from his or her birth family – a policy rigidly followed in the UK in the late 1970s and early 1980s – seen as necessary or desirable to give the adopted child 'a fresh start in life'; instead, maintaining links with the birth family – particularly for older children – came to be seen as important for their sense of identity and emotional well-being. Thus the harsh and punitive attitudes towards birth parents began to change, making them visible at last.

Semi-open adoption, as it is sometimes known, refers to the limited contact between the birth family and the adoptive family while the child is growing up. This contact is controlled by the adoption agency or social worker. The birth mother is usually involved in the selection of the prospective adopters by indicating her preference from anonymous profiles passed to her by the agency. She is probably unlikely to have requested contact outright.

The contact can vary from a single meeting, usually before the placement has been finalised, to the limited exchange of letters and photos via the agency. The agreement to maintain future contact – often once or twice a year, but it varies – is only a verbal one given by the adopters, usually in response to the agency's policy; while many prospective adopters favour some openness, it may be perceived by some as conditional upon their getting the child, or they might change their minds after the adoption order has been made. The birth mother has no legal right to enforce the agreement should the adoptive parents renege; nor does the child.

This form of minimum contact challenges the tradition of secrecy in adoption. It is the very least a birth parent can expect in New Zealand, or in some states in the USA and Australia, but it is not the norm in the UK, although it is relatively common.

Knowing about each other helps to alleviate potential difficulties for all the parties in preparation for their possibly meeting again as adults. An exchange of information helps to lessen the anxiety for a birth mother when her relinquished child reaches 18 and the emotional turmoil that ensues should they be reunited; even limited contact gives some reality to the child's existence instead of the birth mother having an image of her child 'frozen' in time. It offers her some reassurance about the child's welfare by giving her an idea of the family her child is living in, and how much he or she is part of that family, helping to dispel any fears or fantasies she may have. By participating in a limited way in her child's life, she is able to take some responsibilty for her child's future; this in turn may enhance her self-esteem and enable her to accept more easily the loss of her child than if she knew nothing.

Contact also helps to lessen her sense of loss.[1] Nevertheless, the intensity of the grief does not diminish noticeably for at least the first two years after signing consent, and it may continue unresolved for years:[2] this includes frequent (daily) thoughts of the child, anxieties about him or her, and regret. Given the same circumstances today, most of the 262 birth mothers who responded to my questionnaire would decide against adoption because of the deep and longlasting effects. Instead, some suggested better use of fostering, guardianship and extended families. Of those who would still consider adoption, almost all would opt to continue to maintain some form of contact, with ongoing, regular information and photos.

There is considerably more research when it comes to the benefit of openness for adopted children, especially in terms of enhancing their sense of identity and self-esteem. Some adoptees say that, in the absence of contact, they experience a sense of rejection, no matter what the circumstances of their adoption; no matter how many lifestory books and photos they may have of their birth families, the information is secondhand; there is still mystery and missing pieces. These feelings are greatly reduced where there is contact; in such instances too adoptees can talk more easily with their adoptive parents about their origins and will feel less inhibited about re-establishing contact with their birth relatives, rather than searching in secrecy for fear of upsetting the adoptive parents, as often happens. According to the Post Adoption Centre in London, providing information to transracially adopted children can reduce their sense of isolation within the adoptive family; most adults the Centre has counselled were extremely vague about their origins and some people of mixed parentage did not even know which parent had been black, or what their racial origins were.[3]

Traditionally, adoptive parents have been seen as the ones with the least to gain from continuing contact in adoption: fears that the birth parents might interfere or deprive them of close attachment to the children, or that the children would become confused or love them less. Contact might discourage prospective adopters. Current research from the USA, New Zealand and the UK largely supports openness – where it is well managed – as being much healthier than secrecy. Where some form of contact is maintained, the attachment is more successful.[4] Adoptive parents feel they have been approved by the birth parents and therefore more comfortable and confident in their role; as a result, their sense of entitlement to the child is enhanced rather than diminished.

Practical advantages include being able to answer more easily children's questions about their origins and always having access to information that might help them better to understand their children's behaviour. Their children in turn are very clear about who their parents are – they are the ones who bring them up. They can cope with different emotional allegiances at the same time without becoming confused, in the same way that many thousands of children living in reconstituted families do, especially where divorced parents have an amicable relationship.

But while it is generally acceptable in the UK that family links are maintained when a child is in foster or longterm care, this may be contestable when the child is adopted. The law requires that where a child is deemed to be in need of care and protection, a view should be taken of individual welfare,[5] giving room for debate over whether or not the interests of children are separable from those of their birth families, or inextricably linked. This applies particularly to children who have been removed from their parents through the courts because of abuse or neglect and then placed for adoption. Such adoptions – often contested by the birth parents – form an increasingly large percentage of placements nowadays as baby adoptions have rapidly declined since the mid-1970s. A two-tier system exists, with social workers deciding on 'deserving' and 'undeserving' birth parents. By contrast, a 'successful' adoption in New Zealand would not usually be one that incurred the alienation of the birth family, in case they chose not to participate in an open adoption.

The lifelong benefits of at least some contact between the two families while the child is growing up could also apply more readily than happens now to birth parents who have lost their children through the care system. In some ways, there is a greater rather than a lesser need for it in such circumstances.[6] The guilt, anger and shame that many must feel at the loss of the children they have abused could be eased by at least some information, some reassurance; occasional updating could also benefit the adoptive family and help them to form a more positive image of the birth family, especially if reassurance by way of information can help them to make some positive changes in their lives.

References

1. Field, J. (1991), *Views of New Zealand Birth Mothers on Search and Reunion* in Mullender, A. (ed.), *Open Adoption: the Philosophy and Practice*. London: BAAF series no. 19.
2. Dominick, C. (1988), *Early Contact in Adoption: Contact between Birth Mothers and Adoptive Parents at the Time of and after Adoption*. Research Series 10, Wellington, Dept. of Social Welfare.
3. Sawbridge, P. (1991), *On Behalf of Birth Parents*, in Mullender, A. (ed.), *Open Adoption: the Philosophy and Practice*. London: BAAF 1991.
4. Thorburn, J. (1989), *Success and Failure in Permanent Placement*. Aldershot: Gower.
5. Ryburn, M. (1994), *Open Adoption: Research, Theory and Practice*. Aldershot: Gower.
6. Sawbridge, *On Behalf of Birth Parents*.

8 Chris

I met Chris through the contacts I made with Social Welfare adoption workers in central Auckland, New Zealand. They generously put me in touch with birth mothers, adoptees and adoptive parents and their office was an open door.

I understand that Chris is now chair of a newly established group, Movement out of Adoption (MOA), which aims to lobby for changes in adoption law, notably alternative options to adoption by which carers of children can assume the legal rights and responsibilities necessary for effective care without changing the child's genealogy and birth status.

I'm 34. When I left school I went to university. During my second year I'd been going out with a guy for some time – in fact we'd split up. But we had a one-night stand sometime later and that's when I got pregnant. I had been on contraceptives while we were going out, but this was a drunken one-night stand. You never expect it'll happen to you – especially just one night. I was 19. It was 1976.

I was quite lucky during my pregnancy in that Roger, the birth father, was quite supportive. He assisted me financially, took me out once or twice a week. My parents were supportive and his were as well. I was flatting in Hamilton. Neither set of parents wanted to have Simon adopted. They wanted him to remain in the families somewhere, my mother in particular. I didn't want to marry Roger and I was quite clear about that. We were great mates and I think he was quite hurt when we split up.

His family had said they'd be happy for Simon to be adopted by one of the brothers – and mum said she'd like to take care of him. But I said no to both options because if I couldn't have him then no one else was going to. Also I didn't want him going to my mother. She's OK, but my father is an alcoholic so I didn't want my child brought up in a situation where alcohol was

109

involved. They didn't get on that well and I didn't want him brought up in that environment.

Another reason was I could not look upon my own son as my brother, which adoption would have created. I think I was pretty young and naive at that time, that I assumed it'd have to stay hidden that he was my brother ... I mean son. I was a bit confused about that.

Social Welfare didn't talk about other options. I saw adoption or keeping him as the only options I had.

The reason why I couldn't parent Simon myself was that I was going through a crisis myself about my sexual identity. I knew instinctively that the only way to deal with it was to leave the country and if I was parenting Simon I knew I'd punish him because he would stop me doing that. I wouldn't have been able to save any money or take him with me. So in the end I decided on adoption and went ahead with it. The social worker was quite elderly and was really nice, but presented no options other than me keeping him or adoption. We did discuss my parents having him, but I said I didn't want that.

However, she was quite advanced for the time [1976] and asked me if I'd like to meet the adoptive parents. Both Roger and I said we wanted to. That was the first birth father they'd had who'd been interested. But the adoptive parents were very hesitant and didn't want to meet, as they thought we'd take one look at them and not let them have Simon.

However, we did meet them. She convinced them to meet. I knew he was an accountant and she had been in secretarial work. I also knew that they were were unable to have children and after a series of operations they had a son who was stillborn and badly deformed. They were told never to try and have children again. That was in the March when their son was born and they got Simon six months later in the September. I found out later they had never dealt with the grief.

There was never discussion on another option like guardianship, which I think in hindsight I'd have been interested in – although it may be coloured by my maturity now. But I'm sure I would have considered it if I'd been told that someone like my mum could parent him under the Order for six months to a year or whatever, or someone else close to me that I trusted – and then I could've taken over when I was ready. But no one ever talked about that type of option. It would have meant that someone like my mum could have had legal custody of Simon but I am still the mother and I'd remain the mother and have rights of contact etc. But it protects the parents because they are guardians under the law – they are entitled to all the law affords, like they would get family benefits. But I don't forfeit any rights although they have all the rights as parents. Fostering could've been another option that should've been offered.

Looking back, I was extremely frightened and no one talked to me about how I felt or what all the issues were for me and how I was feeling about myself. The social worker at the hospital wasn't for adopting children and I think she discussed the issue of my parenting him myself. Ultimately the decision was mine but it was made with only certain facts. So it wasn't really a true informed decision.

I did have support from my family. I wasn't thrown out by them or sent off to an unmarried mothers' home. I didn't have that. I went out with my mother, everyone knew I was pregnant. It wasn't hidden.

Although the Domestic Purposes Benefit (single parent's benefit) had come in three years previously, there was still stigma attached to being a solo mother. I remember we talked about it at the antenatal classes. I had my own views about that and I didn't want to be labelled as one of them either. I think people assumed I was married, since I was sticking out at the front! But I didn't feel stigmatised.

I had made the decision to adopt before he was born, and I met the adoptive parents about five or six days after he was born. We all met in the social worker's office. I had written him a letter explaining why he was adopted and that was given to them. It went OK. We didn't exchange names and addresses – it wasn't that progressive, but basically it was a chance to look at each other and I think they said 'Thanks very much'. I have quite a hazy recollection of the meeting. I was feeling fairly strange at the time; a mixture of emotions. I was also a bit withdrawn, standing back, trying to dissociate myself from it … keep it at arm's length. It didn't really feel real. I remember thinking they looked all right, that the husband looked a bit like a schoolteacher I knew, and he was nice. They appeared to be quite ordinary. But I perceived them as being better than I was anyway. He was going to something better than I could offer … financially he'd be better off and they could give him more than me. Also, he was going to a two-parent family, which I thought at the time was better than one. They did say if I ever needed to know anything to get in contact through the social worker and they would be happy to send me a photograph.

Later I did get to have some sort of contact. I got a letter from them – and that stopped after he was a year old. I didn't hear any more. My mother didn't cope with the fact that Simon had been adopted. She'd seen him in the hospital. They encouraged that, asked if I'd like to hold him, feed him. But I didn't because I knew instinctively that if I did, that'd be it. But I watched him and looked at him a lot.

The birth was good, but it would've been nice to have had someone there with me. Roger had taken me in but gone back to work. I think it was quite hard on him. But he saw the baby. I'd been to classes, so I had no drugs etc. and it was a quick labour. I had him with me for an hour or so after he was born and then he went to the nursery. The staff all knew he was going to be adopted and everyone treated me OK. My only complaint was the Sister – I heard that she apparently hit women during labour. So I was very keen not to upset her in the slightest. But for some crazy reason she gave me an episiotomy without telling me what she was doing. I was starting a contraction and nearly leapt off the table and said, 'For fuck's sake! What do you think you're doing!' It wasn't necessary. It was just pure laziness. But other than that it was OK. I went home after four days, I didn't really want to stay any longer. Then the adoptive mother was taught how to care for him and stayed with him in the hospital.

I didn't return to uni. I travelled around a bit with Roger, got into drugs quite heavily that generally acted as a blocking mechanism to avoid dealing with my own issues. Then I went overseas. I was away for a couple of years.

I'd been told I'd forget all about it. I blocked it out for a while. When I was in England I managed to come to terms with my sexuality and feeling OK about saying I was a lesbian. So that felt really good for me and felt quite freeing. I felt I could now get on with things.

I returned when he was four. That's when I started thinking about where he might be, would I bump into him in the street, and I tried to remember what the adoptive parents looked like and would look out for them, not consciously going out looking for them but if I saw women and children down the street of a similar age I would look. So I went through all that and then I started going through this guilt thing, that he's got to get on with his life and so on.

It got to the point when he was eight that I made the decision that I had to find him. That's when the search started. I needed to know how he was and I needed to talk to him about why he was adopted. I wanted to resolve that with him because I didn't want him feeling bitter about that. And I had this fairytale thing in my head about how the adoptive parents would welcome contact again. They were in contact in the beginning, via Social Welfare, but my mother wanted to be in contact all the time and in the end I was told she couldn't. So I told her I wouldn't speak to her again if she did. It was her first grandchild. So contact stopped, but I thought I'd be able to make contact with them again.

I was working as a probation officer. So I enquired and managed to get some more background information about the parents. I also found that if the child is outside your district, it has to be the responsibility of the district he's living in – and Hamilton wouldn't do it. They said there was nothing on the file to show there was to be continuous contact – and there was nothing to show there had been contact. Apparently the social worker had been doing it from home. Obviously it wasn't department policy, so what she'd been doing was organising it but not letting the department know. I was really frustrated that I couldn't get any information etc., so I decided to look for the old social worker. She'd retired. I wrote to her. This was 1987. The new Act meant that Welfare would help birth parents trace children over 20.

I was doing a social work diploma. She asked me what information I had and gave me the name and address of the couple she thought it was. She then rang them and that's when my problems started. I wasn't in control of the situation. The control was taken away from me. They were excited I'd made contact and thought of me often and Simon was doing well, etc. I was very excited too. She was told there was lots of information from me on the file at Welfare in Hamilton.

I had always thought of them as taking care of my son. Even though he was elsewhere, he was never not my son. I instinctively felt that I had a perfect right to be in contact – and they'd welcome that – because I was the mother. But they didn't see it that way in the end! I always had this image that I was still his mother in spite of the strange feelings I had around the time of the adoption.

I waited weeks for some response to the information that I thought had been sent on. Apparently it had been overlooked at Welfare. The adoptive mother had rung them to ask for it. So I thought I'd ring her to let her know that I was told the information was now on its way. She asked to ring me back, which I wasn't expecting, and we spoke for about two hours. She talked a lot about Simon, what he was like and so on and it all felt quite good. She asked me what I'd like and I said photos, and she offered to write down a social history. She also said she'd like to meet me again. She said she wasn't sure about me meeting Simon. I got a letter a few days later and photos from when he was little right up to the age he was then, which was ten. Also lots of history about him. It was like total disbelief it was even him! I had no idea of what he was going to look like. I had to sit back from it for a while. I kept looking and looking at them. He looks like me. And he had become more real. He had a history. A personality. I'd never clung to the baby thing, I'd always known he was growing up.

But at the end of her letter she said she'd talked to others and reckoned this would be all I'd need and there was no need for a meeting. I nearly dropped dead! I couldn't believe it! Here I was on a high and suddenly the carpet was pulled out from under my feet. At least I had the support of the birth mothers' group, which was great. Letters went back and forth and telephone calls and they got more and more entrenched. They said that I wasn't allowed to send him any presents – I could send a card and that was it. So six months would pass before a letter was exchanged.

They said I should honour the contract that I'd signed and became more entrenched in their fears. I think it was more him. She told me he'd said, 'The kids aren't really ours, are they?' So they hadn't even dealt with that aspect, assuming that they'd been born to them. So in the end things got so bad that I decided to visit. I'd sent photos, so she knew who I was but they weren't sharing any of this with Simon. She said Simon wasn't ready to have any contact. It wasn't till later they did say things to him, as there'd been an article in a magazine and the newspapers as well as my photo to do with my involvement in a birth mothers' group. So I kept popping up out of the woodwork. Here I am again! A friend of hers from up the road had brought the article down to show her! She didn't know anything about me, only that Simon was adopted. She said 'Is this Simon's birth mother? She looks so much like your Simon!' That really went down like a lead brick!

I called when Simon was at school as I deliberately didn't want to involve him. I didn't think it was fair on him. Birth mothers are always so considerate, thinking what might be best for them and the adoptive parents and they couldn't care less about you.

I took a friend, Karen, from the group with me. The adoptive mother didn't stop talking! She's like that every time. She doesn't want to hear what you have to say because she just doesn't want to have to deal with it. She's got an adopted daughter two years younger. She reckoned she put the birth mothers up on a pedestal, but once I made contact, I fell off because I'd become real. She talked about how she fantasised about how she'd given birth to Simon. It was nauseous. I thought I was going to throw up! But she was honest. She was so possessive of him, she wept when he returned after a week's holiday. It was the first time he'd been away from home!

The interesting thing is that Simon is his own person, it seems. One of the things that we've talked quite a lot about is that kids who are adopted signal that they're different from kids born to their natural families by doing something. It may be at a later age they're heavily into drugs and alcohol, end up in welfare, get into criminal activities, truanting. I see loads of them in my job. Apparently Simon is a loner, doesn't mix with other kids very well, spends most of his time on his computer after school. He's an exceptionally bright child, but he doesn't fit with other kids. Every year he has a new teacher, she apparently gets a call from the school to come and talk about his anti-social behaviour.

At the age of two he stopped eating meat, fruit and most vegetables. And he's never touched them since. He went through puberty really early. I saw him that day I visited as she kept us talking so long at the gate. He ran past us. But I'd seen him before that. I found out where their batch [holiday home] was and camped near there. They were refusing me any contact whatsoever and I had a desperate need to see him. I didn't want to have to put Simon in an awkward position in front of them, but I needed to see him.

I don't know to this day whether he knows he's got photos and family history stored at his house. She told me that when she saw my photo she just burst into tears – I looked so much like Simon. It made me real. I was like this mystical birth mother with a wand who came down and dropped the baby in their lap and they were forever thankful, but that I'd never show up 'cos I wasn't real. All this sneaking around on my part was because I couldn't stand not actually seeing him. I was determined I was going to see him although I wasn't going to involve him necessarily.

It was really weird seeing him on the beach. It was kind of like a movie that I was watching. I had no concept of time whatsoever.

I may have sat there for two minutes or half an hour. I took lots of photos of him. I just looked at him. He looked at me and smiled. Inside all of me was screaming, 'I just want to say this!' But I couldn't. His father was there and might've asked him who he was talking to, and I didn't want to have to put him in the position of choosing to lie or to tell the truth, knowing how they obviously feel about the situation. He knows I've been in contact 'cos when the social worker phoned he was in the room at the time and asked who she was talking to about him. So apparently she told him. But as far as anything else goes, I don't know.

I had been down to where they lived and checked out their place some time before. I'd also met up with another birth mother who belonged to the same adoption group as Simon's adoptive mother and hoped she'd put in a good word for me. But once I came on the scene she pulled out of the group. I expect she didn't want to be challenged about why she wasn't meeting the birth mother and so on. So I was able to find out about them, but through devious means.

The time I did see her, her husband came home and said, 'If we'd known all this was going to happen, we'd never have adopted the kids.' I was shell-shocked. Thankfully, Karen was able to pick up the conversation. She kept saying why couldn't I have waited till the law allowed, when he was 20 … and 'We've told them we'll help them and tell them when they're 20.' She suggested, when we were trying to make a contract, that friends had said once every two years should be sufficient. I said I didn't think that was very fair and wanted contact at least every six months and photos. In the end we decided to leave it for a while and get back to each other. So that was OK. But then I didn't hear from her for a year or so and it was coming up to Simon's birthday, so I rang her and spoke politely and she ranted on for ages and ages on my phonebill. I couldn't speak. She said they'd talked to him about his 'situation' and he's not interested. Then she said he was going to send you a tape. So I said, 'That's great! I haven't received it.' Then she went dead silent and changed the subject. But I thought no kid would want to send a tape saying they're not interested. If anything, they'd write. I suspect they wouldn't let him. I'd been sending him letters too, always through them, which I discovered they'd been reading as she let something slip. I was very upset and tearful and couldn't take any more so I shouted, 'I'm sick of you shitting on me!' and slammed the phone down. I haven't spoken to her since. I refuse to have any contact with her again and any contact

I do have with Simon will be directly with him. I'll have to decide when it takes place. It'll have to be at the school or somewhere.

I've been left feeling pretty upset and angry and thinking why me? I'd done everything by the book. I'd helped lots of other people find their children and everything had always gone fine. I just needed to talk to Simon, have contact with him. There's things I need to talk to him about. I'm really worried about his development. He's obviously screwed up in some ways and they're not prepared to acknowledge it or see where it's coming from.

It's difficult to know whether a proper contract would've worked, because if they were presented with a contract that actually bound them to some sort of continuing contact, I don't think they would've been able to cope. Or else they would've dropped out. One of the things she asked me was why I'd left it so long. And it was like it was my fault again.

I think having contact with him in some shape or form has been really important for me and at least I've got some photos of him, I know what he looks like and other people don't even have that. What I think is criminal is that people like that are allowed to take other people's children. Surely parenting means giving them skills to run their own lives and that means letting them go, letting them be free. But I think with a lot of adoptive families they get so possessive they are unable to let them go.

I feel distressed about what will happen to him in the future. I feel he's either going to become a social introvert or heading for some sort of trouble. I have made a decision about what I'm going to do and that's to go through the school counsellor and see him at school. It reinforces for me that children shouldn't be parented by either sets of parents in secret situations – that it just breeds unhealthiness for all parties concerned. I'd certainly never do the same again. Not now – put my son with strangers. In fact I'd keep him in the family. I've regretted he's gone outside the family, that I was unable at the time to work the issues through to a point where I could parent Simon.

I think it's affected me in lots of ways. It has meant I've gone into a profession where I'm helping others, that I've needed to put things right by helping them to sort out their lives and that has in a way helped me. I can see myself in a parallel situation where my life wasn't sorted out. Also, it was when I joined the probation service that I was able to make the first step to contact him.

I'm sure subconsciously its affected me too, like I have periods when I put on weight and I'm not eating any more. I'm sure it's psychological and about protecting myself. I've also had periods when I've drunk a lot to block it out and keep the emotional pain away. Also the drugs.

Also I've found in relationships I've had that I've had difficulty in sustaining close relationships. Maybe that's partly my family background too. I'm a relationship addict and a very good co-dependent. I've been doing a lot of work on these lately. A lot of it's about trust. I also cling on to people, in case I lose them or they go away – the same as Simon did. It's fear of loss. But I don't think I'll ever resolve my loss of him until I can work these things out with him. That's one of my driving forces; to see him so that I can work some of the stuff through and also allow him the opportunity to do that too. It's obviously affected his life in spite of what his adoptive parents think.

Aotearoa Birth Mothers' Group

It started around 1983 or 1984 and came about as a lot of women were uneasy about what they were hearing at the adoption meetings in terms of judgements of birth mothers etc. So a few got together and started meeting in each other's homes. Its primary function still is support for birth mothers. It just got bigger and we became involved in the political work looking for law change and helping women to find their children. A lot felt powerless and that they had no right to find their children. We were getting referrals from all over. We were finding that women felt uncomfortable at the mixed meetings, sharing some of their stuff in front of adoptive parents who've always been in a controlling situation, and adoptees too who probably didn't understand that level of pain.

We were getting bigger and bigger and operating from a broom cupboard in the centre of town. We had four voluntary workers almost fulltime, a newsletter operating that went all round the country and overseas as well. So we had to get bigger premises, which we've done. I was working fulltime for a while, then had one day off a week .

We found women coming through the door in tremendous pain. We were working with the adoption team and Welfare and getting written requests to do interviews. Adoptees were asking us to help search. It was a fulltime operation and still is. It was a social service without proper funding. People came in off the street. It was important to be separate from Social Welfare, although we now have their support, which is important. I think they eventually saw that we were a credible organisation, that we handled things sensitively, were important to women as a means of support and being able to help them with their grief and contacting their children. We've been involved with research, setting up other groups, a manual on starter groups and how to get funds, the media. My role was to set up the international links and encourage other women to set up birth mother groups at home.

Unfortunately, workers got burnt out. They were working five days a week, as well as phonecalls at night from women wanting support. They weren't able to pass their expertise on to train others, and it was unfair really as the same thing would happen to them. So this is why we're looking at joining forces with the other two groups, to share all that and give us more credibility, especially for funding. We're still seen as those naughty women who had those children, sluts etc.

We have managed to make people aware of birth mothers' needs. That's why the adoption teams work so much in consultation with us. It wasn't like that to start with. They were threatened, and would come to meetings armed with their manuals. But eventually they started working alongside us. I do a lot of work with kids under 20 wanting to find out information about their natural families. Legally they shouldn't be given identifying information until they reach 20, but practice can vary and people have always been given the odd hint to help them trace. I see a lot through the schools' guidance counsellors. We usually contact Social Welfare first to get the file. They trust us and the way we work and they don't get any backlash. We encourage the kids to do their own contact if that's what they want and give them all the options as to how they can go about it, but we'll be intermediaries as a last resort. Almost all of the contacts have turned out really well. Birth parents have, in the main, always expected contact at some time.

I think its important to say that the Adult Adoption Information Act does not mean that you can only trace once you are 20. Legally you can search at any time. There's nothing in the Adoption Act that says you can't trace. All the Information Act did was to enable those who couldn't get information to get more information when they turned 20. It's really for those who haven't been able to trace and it's helped them to do that.

Also birth mothers have a perfect right to know who the adoptive parents are at the time of consent if they ask. There's nothing in the law that says you can't know. It was just Social Welfare's interpretation of the law and their policy that's determined how it's been. But it says in their manual that if the birth mother wants to know the adoptive parents' name and address at the time of consent, they have to give it to you. But no one ever told you that.

The take-up rate seems quite low under the Act, but a lot of people will have already traced themselves. It often happens that when one starts to trace, the other is searching as well. It's strange. But it happens a lot.

9 Cathie

I made contact with Cathie through the Post-adoption Centre in London. Quite a number of birth mothers involved with the Centre had passed their names on to me as a gesture of support and a means of reaching out to other birth mothers through the sharing of their stories. 'Here are the names of [15] women willing to be interviewed', wrote one of the birth mothers. 'I feel they must really trust you to have agreed to give their names – probably because you are a birth mother too.'

I'm 26. My child will be four in December. When I found out I was pregnant, I wasn't particularly surprised but I didn't know what to do. I wasn't involved with the father – it was a one-off relationship. As I'd been brought up in the church, which was a big part of my life, I contacted my minister, who is also a good friend. He saw me straight away and was very shocked. He discussed the options. I didn't know about keeping the child but I knew I couldn't have an abortion. He also mentioned adoption. And telling my parents. I'd been living away from home since I was 18 in an adolescent hostel, so it was quite a major thing to go back and say I was pregnant.

He had already arranged for me to see a counsellor from Life. So I went and saw her and it didn't then seem like the end of the world. She was very nice. She talked about the possibilities of keeping the child, having support and perhaps staying with a family who could offer that. I didn't feel very happy about that, losing my independence. She also mentioned abortion, but I didn't want that. Then she talked about adoption. In some ways I thought I should do it, but then I thought there's no way I can be pregnant for nine months and give away a baby. She mentioned an adoption agency that would work with me ... all the niceties about how they'd do it, like sending me a photograph of the baby, that sort of thing. I went away and thought about it and saw her the following week when I decided I would give the baby for adoption. I weighed it up and thought I didn't really want to see myself in a council flat like a friend of mine, with no money and a baby and wreck my career. I was going to go off to university that year and do social work training and already had a place.

She arranged for this guy from an adoption agency in Croydon to come and see me. A Reverend somebody. I spoke to him and it all sounded very, very nice. I'd give the child for adoption and they'd take him straight from birth and they'd send me a big photograph to keep in a frame. But what I really wanted was to select the family for my child, to give the criteria that I wanted in a family and to look after my child for the first week instead of him being directly placed. I could then get to know my child and go through the bereavement process – so that I'd have somebody I knew a bit of, that was really important. I'd been in therapy for quite a long time, as I had a lot of problems when I was younger and was in voluntary care when I was a teenager. My therapist didn't advise me but it helped me to work out what I really wanted. And that was important.

At that stage I hadn't heard about birth mothers choosing the family for their child, I just knew I wanted to do it. I wasn't going to give my baby away to someone who wanted it for a status symbol, a token child with the big house and car and so on. I also wanted him to go to a family that had already adopted a child. That was really important. And a couple that couldn't have children. I didn't want my child wasted on a couple that could. That's how I saw it. My child was special and I'm special and I wanted him to be important to them. The other thing I really wanted was to be able to hand my child over to that family. Everybody was against this, apart from the social worker. But by doing that physically I was letting go and saying goodbye and I could say to him in years to come that I handed him over to his mum and dad and I met them. It was a very painful thing, but I knew I needed to do it. I need to go through the painful things to get the good out of the other side.

I saw this guy from the adoption agency but I didn't feel particularly good about him, although he was saying all the right things. It seemed all very nice and we're going to get your baby from you and you'll go away and be sorted out and we'll come and see you a couple of times afterwards … Also I was living in Southampton and it's a long way from Croydon.

Fortunately I'd been given some good advice about getting in touch with the National Children's Home. Their social worker was amazing! He sat with me for five hours while I talked. I'd just been kicked out of my flat as my landlady found out I was pregnant and that I wasn't having an abortion. She thought I was a disgrace to her household. There was a lot of pressure on me to have an abortion, including Social Services. Some people felt really strongly.

The social worker listened to what I wanted. I said if I can't get what I want, then I'm not going through with this. So he said that was fine, that he hadn't done it like this before but we'd go ahead. He returned a couple of weeks later and talked to me again and took notes about the sort of family I wanted for my child. That included their having a Christian belief, another adopted child, that money didn't matter and that they wanted to meet me. If they didn't, that was it. Also that I could hand him over to them. He was going to give me a list of five families for me to look at and then he phoned and said he had the perfect family. They had adopted a child three years before and had actually met his mother. And they were quite happy to meet me.

I also wanted him to meet the father of my child. He was threatening to go to court for custody. I was really scared by that. So he saw him and helped him work things out. I think it was to do with his anger towards me and what I was doing. A lot of people from my church were very negative towards me and that was difficult. They said, 'You'll never go through with it.' So I felt very unsupported. But I still go to that church.

Telling my family was hard. My parents are separated, and I went to tell my mum and took my auntie. Mum said, 'You've got to have this child adopted.' But we did talk about other options. She suggested I could go back home to live with the baby. But that wouldn't have worked. We didn't get on that well, I'd have lost my independence and the stigma meant I couldn't have coped. But then she wouldn't let me go home any more. She didn't want anyone to see me pregnant. She didn't tell my brother. He still doesn't know. Nor do other relatives. I wanted them to know. It was important. I felt that people were protecting me, but I didn't want to be protected. The women I was living with at the time were very supportive. It wasn't till I sobbed my heart out that they knew I was really going to go through with it. I went through a lot of the bereavement process before I gave my son for adoption.

The other things I found difficult were that a lot of people clearly thought I was doing the wrong thing and that adoption was wrong. Also, being with other mothers-to-be at the antenatal classes. They'd be talking about when their babies were due and

I couldn't say I was giving mine for adoption. Every time I got to
see the doctor I'd cry. Then they'd say, 'You don't want to go
through with this, do you?', and they'd phone the hospital social
worker who'd come over and say, 'Stop messing me about.' They'd
ring her automatically. I was crying because it was part of the grief
– and also the pain of knowing I was going to give birth to a baby
that I wasn't going to keep. It should've been a really joyous
occasion and some of it was during my pregnancy. The medical
staff would treat me as if it was a joyous occasion until they
found out I was giving the child for adoption and then they were
really negative. I just felt like a one-woman band. The doctors were
very dismissive of me and the nurses kept saying, 'Can't you
keep the baby?' and, 'Are you really going to go through with this?'
and, 'Why can't you get help from Social Security?' But I had a
very good midwife.

I remember my mother phoned me up during the pregnancy
and said, 'I really think mothers ought to get money for their
babies.' I thought that was horrific and knocks everything I
believe in. What sort of person would that attract? Maybe she'd
seen something on the telly. But I see the child as a gift.

Mum wanted to be there with me in labour. I didn't want her
to come in and I was upset about it. But I didn't feel able to say
that to her. I got one of the nurses that I lived with to come instead
and asked her to phone mum after the baby was born. It was a
difficult labour and I was sick all the way through because of the
pethidine. The baby was very distressed. They wouldn't give me
an epidural for ages and I wanted one because the pain was so
bad. Also I wasn't getting anything at the end of it. After he was
born his heartbeat was causing concern. It'd been irregular during
the birth, so he was whipped off to the special care unit. My friend
was worried but I thought, 'If he dies, what the heck …' A nurse
brought him back after a short time and asked if I wanted to hold
him. So I said I was going to look after him for the first week. She
gave Matthew to me quite reluctantly and washed me and put
me in a clean bed with him in my arms and that was the best
moment, being wheeled through the wards and having him in
my arms and thinking, 'Nobody knows he's going,' and, 'I'm a
mother and I've got my baby.' I was on a real high. He felt like
my baby and it was wonderful! I was put in an eight-bedded
ward. I was high all night and kept pinching myself and looking
at him. They'd wanted to put him in the nursery that night but
I said no, that I wanted to spend every minute with him.

I wouldn't breastfeed as I felt it was wrong because of bonding. I'd be breaking away from that bond, like the mother's smell, and that would affect him emotionally. Also they wanted to send Matthew away to another hospital and keep me there because he was going to be adopted. They said they did that with everybody else. So I had to put up a big protest, even though my social worker had been in to let them know what was happening. The next day, after all my family had been in to see me, I was really down. It was the day before Christmas and they were clearing out the ward, getting as many home as possible. So husbands were coming in with flowers and things and I just burst out crying. The ward was slowly clearing and all the other mums were saying, 'It'll be great when you get home,' and when I said I was having him adopted they didn't talk to me after that. They couldn't cope with it. And I found that all the way along. People couldn't cope with talking about adoption, so they ignored me and that was really very painful.

I was crying and this nurse came along and said, 'Why don't you keep him?' I said, 'I can't. I haven't got any money, I can't keep him, I can't look after him properly, I can't give him what he needs.'

I felt very ambivalent after he was born – and while I was pregnant too. I know that other women have changed their minds once they'd had their babies. I felt so torn, being pulled in two different directions. If I let him go, he's gone.

I put on a brave face when visitors came and would cry my eyes out when they left. The social worker came in on Boxing Day and I was crying on the bed. I said, 'I can't give him up. I can't. I want to keep him.' Then I looked at Matthew and he was asleep in his cot and looked really happy and peaceful and I thought, 'I've got to let him go – for him. I can't keep him for me. It's got to be for him. He needs that family.' Later the minister came up and he did a little dedication service, and that was really sensitive, and then he said, 'You've got to let go of him.' He didn't think it was a good idea for me to hand him over to the family, but I said I was going to.

The next day the couple who were going to have Matthew came to meet me. Bob [the social worker] came in first and talked to me. He said they were very nervous as well, which I knew they would be. They came in and sat down and went through a few formalities and chatted and things, and I found it very difficult. I was sitting in my nightshirt clutching Matthew, but in the end

I thought I've got to overcome this so I said to Chris, the father, 'Do you want to hold him?', and I could've killed him at that point because I thought, 'He's got my baby in his arms,' and I felt incredibly angry towards them both. They were very nice, but they had all that joy and happiness that I should have been having. I found it really difficult. They stayed about half an hour or more, and both had a hold of him and said he was lovely and I looked just as they imagined and talked about their son and that was quite good.

My social worker strongly suggested I go home and have a break after five days there. I said I couldn't leave Matthew, but he insisted. So I did. In the meantime Paul, his father, met him. I wanted him to be able to grieve Matthew. Bob brought him in and he spent ages with Matthew and held him and fed him and changed him. Bob took photos of him with his son. And he knew about the family he was going to.

I wanted the adoption to be cleared up by the end of the year so I could start the new year afresh. It worked out really well, as Bob was going to pick me up on the 31st and I was going to meet the family again and hand Matthew over. I was expecting it to be quick and out of the way. So we turned up at the hospital, and the adoptive parents had their son with them and he said, 'Mummy, who's that woman?', and she answered, 'She's Matthew's mother.' That was very significant to me, that she was so honest and open with him. It also confirmed that what I was doing was right. Bob took me into the room where Matthew was and asked if I'd like to change him and feed him. I wasn't expecting to see much of him. So I spent about half an hour with him. Bob took some photos of us together. So I said my goodbyes there. It was really painful. Then they came up with the Sister, who was lovely, and I handed him over to them in the corridor. I was crying and so was she and I said, 'I'm only giving him away because I love him and I want the best for him.' And she said, 'We'll look after him and we'll always think of you on his birthday. We'll always think of our son's mother on his birthday.'

Then we went down to the car park, and the Sister was holding him wrapped in their shawl. I thought I'd never hold him again, and the Sister handed him to me and said, 'Do you want to hand him over?' So I did. And they drove off and we waved goodbye.

After they'd gone I had to walk round holding a hot-water bottle against my tummy all the time just so that I coud have something warm next to me … to sleep with it. I just felt such a tremendous loss, it was horrendous. It was much more than I thought it would be. There was this tremendous gap in my life and I thought, 'I'm never going to get over this.' It was like a really big bereavement. But people didn't recognise that. It was, 'Well, the baby's gone now. Put the photographs away and forget him.'

I wanted to talk about him all the time, but no one else did. Bob came to see me a lot and I spent a lot of the time crying. I still feel bereaved. The worst bit was probably the first six months or so. I was in a total daze and I had this really responsible job. I don't know how I managed it, as I wasn't well and thought I was going to have a breakdown.

I wanted Matthew to know about me and I was glad Bob took a lot of photos of us together and that Matthew has copies. He'll know what I look like. Bob wrote a profile letter telling Matthew about me – the good and not so good things about me, my family background, my interests, what I'm like. Also about his father. I think the family has got it for him when he's ready to read it. I know that when he has that letter he can always get back to the adoption agency to see what's on his file. There's an article I wrote in a magazine that's there, although it took a lot of persuading to have it put on file.

It's hard to know how I'll feel about tracing when the time comes. I've been married for a couple of years now and my husband always says that Matthew is our first child. Our (joint) child will be our second. That's how I feel as well and I'd always tell my children too, that Matthew is their brother. I feel he has a right to know me, but I've let him go so I don't think I've got any rights over him. I'd want the contact to be his choice and I'd never want to impinge upon him. I want him to live his life as he wants. But I'd love to know about his life, whether he's happy, what he's doing. If he chooses not to find me then that's his right. It'd be really painful, but I'd have to come to terms with that.

It's been really important to me to have information about him. The photographs particularly. I've got them all over our flat. They're there and they're staying there. And knowing that he's quite like me in some ways, the things he's got up to … also gives me a picture of him in my mind and so that he doesn't just stay as a little baby in my mind, but he's growing up and he's doing things, like he's at home on his own now that his brother's started school. It's helped me to grow and develop and it means I'm not living in the past. It's a reality and it's ongoing and I can accept it. It's made it a lot easier. It hasn't been easy, but it's easier than someone who's had no contact and doesn't know anything. But it's painful when I get the photographs.

I felt that with that first agency the idea of sending me photographs was a kind of 'package deal'. You give us your baby and we'll give you this big portrait you can put on your wall ... you do what we want and you'll get that photograph. I felt he didn't listen to what I wanted. But I didn't feel that with the second agency. I wasn't made any false promises. I was told that I'd probably get a photograph on his first birthday and maybe the next year but there was no guarantee. The letters just happened.

I do feel I made the right decision for me and definitely for Matthew. But it's still painful. In some ways I regret I got pregnant, but I wouldn't be who I am now if I hadn't been through that. It's helped me mature a lot and opened a whole new spectrum of my life. Also, I feel I'm special because I've given my child for adoption, I'm a birth mother. I can identify with people, feel for people. And I've learnt a lot about bereavement.

If Matthew's adoptive parents did stop sending me photos and letters I'd just have to accept that, although I know I'd be very upset. I do see every one as a bonus. And I know I'll want to know more and I know it will affect me when I have my second child. I'll always want to know how he is.

10 Margaret S.

I wrote to Margaret at a London psychiatric hospital after reading an article about her and two other women in the Guardian, *entitled 'Three Tales of Ordinary Madness'. Margaret has a son of 19 and two daughters aged nine and seven. Her daughters were removed from her care six years ago because of her neglect. She was an alcoholic. Her older daughter, Ann, had also been sexually abused by Margaret's partner, Ann's father. They were returned to her later, but she was unable to care for them adequately and the older child was sexually abused again. Margaret contested the care orders and lost. They have been with prospective adoptive parents for over three years. Margaret became suicidal after the trauma of access visits and seriously harmed herself on numerous occasions. As a result, she has chosen not to see her daughters. Communication between them is now via Social Services, though at the time of the interview it appeared to have broken down because information was not passed on directly to Margaret, causing great distress.*

My first daughter, Ann, was born in 1984 and the second, Maria, 18 months later. I was a bit shocked at having more children as there was ten years' difference between Ann and my son. Ann was a surprise, but I was very, very happy to have her. I was divorced at the time and living with their father. He was pleased too, and was at the birth. When she was born I was scared. I was an alcoholic but I wouldn't admit it. I started drinking about 18 years ago when my son was born. My husband forced me to drink and hit me if I didn't. Then I got addicted to it. By the time Ann was born I was worried I wouldn't be able to cope. I started drinking very heavily, then got valium from the doctor. After a while he refused to prescribe them.

The drinking went on and then I discovered my children had been sexually abused. My son came to me when he was 14 and told me I had to get rid of Alan, the girls' father, as he'd abused him when he was eight and again recently. I couldn't believe it.

I was angry and hurt. I contacted the social worker straight away. She came round and spoke to me and then to Alan. My son made his own decision to return to live with his father. He refused to come back as long as Alan was there.

Three months later I had a phonecall from the nursery that Ann attended. She told them her bottom was hurting and bleeding and that her father had done it. We took her to the hospital. I asked to have my younger daughter examined as well and she was OK. She was about 18 months old. Then I had to watch Ann from behind a two-way mirror while the experts discussed the abuse with her. It was horrible. I didn't want to believe this was happening – I still trusted the man. I thought he was so gentle and loving. He had protected my son and me from my husband, who used to beat us up, which was why I left him.

I started drinking more heavily. I didn't want to believe it. To me he was an angel, he was good to me and very caring. I found out much later that he'd been sexually abused as a child. The police wanted me to charge him, but I wouldn't. I just wanted to forget and get on with my life.

At that stage I was living at home with my two daughters. Alan wanted to come back and make a fresh start. I told him to get out of my life. I didn't want him near me. Then the neighbours started to get abusive. They probably overheard me shouting at him when I was drunk: 'You bastard! You've interfered with my kids!' They knew it was him. I was tortured after that. They put letters through the door saying things like, 'You drunken bum, living with a sex abuser.' I asked the council for a move. I went to the police. They knew what had happened from the records. Alan had been told not to come near my place, but he did. And I didn't want to believe that he'd abused my daughter. I wondered whether it might've been other friends who used to take the girls out.

I felt sorry for him and started to see him again. The social workers suggested that we all go and live at the assessment centre for a year. But after six months we had to leave, as he abused Ann again. There were strict rules governing bath times. We were supposed to bathe the children together as a couple. I wasn't around on this particular day, so he decided to take Ann and bathe her on his own. She started screaming, 'Daddy hurt me up the bum!' Alan said she was putting toys inside herself. She was three! Ann told the staff and they told me. That was when I really believed he had done something. I didn't want him near us any more. I haven't seen him since, except accidentally.

I began drinking really heavily again, and then the social worker told me the children were going into care from the assessment centre. I went to hospital to dry out. I wanted to get off the drink. I'd lost my children and I wanted help. I was only there for two weeks and they reckoned I was alright and discharged me. I came out but I was scared to go back to my flat because of the neighbours' accusations. A friend, Janice, said I could stay with her and her mother for a few days. She's a lay preacher and had been trying to help me. I stayed for about three weeks and started drinking again whenever I went out. I'd return in a real state. They couldn't handle it and kindly asked me to leave.

I hadn't seen the children during this time because I was so ill. I was worried that I might upset them or frighten them. I was allowed to see them about a month later with Alan. He was still in the picture because his solicitor said he had a right to see his own children. The social workers then felt it was best we saw them as a couple because that was how they remembered us. I hated every minute. I wanted to see them on my own. I'm sure it must have been very confusing for them. I just wanted to knife him. This went on for about three months. The social workers said that if I improved I could have the children back. But I just kept drinking. I wanted to hide.

While all this was going on, I was raped. The man got five years. It set me back so much. It happened three and half years ago and took nearly a year to get to court. I still can't go out on my own. I can't trust men at all. The police officer involved in the investigation still rings me up to see how I'm getting on. About a year ago he rang to let me know that the man was coming out of prison, but that he wouldn't be living in my area. That helped, and the officer said I should ring him any time I needed help. But I'm still scared, especially at night. That's why I spend as little time as possible at home alone.

My daughters went to live with foster parents. I contested the care orders. The social workers said there wasn't much point in my contesting because I'd lost them by neglecting them – which I probably did. It took months and months until the final hearing, with interim care orders time and again. While all this was going on, I was drinking like a trooper. I felt a failure. My solicitor was saying the same as the social workers – that it didn't matter what I did, I'd never get the children back with me again. Then I was found to have a heart condition, which didn't make things any easier.

In the end I had to trust what they were saying. I told my social worker that I didn't want to give up my children and I didn't want them to think I had. I loved them. I still love them. But if it was best for them, then I'd have to agree to their being adopted. I had to stop being selfish and think of what was best for them. But I'll never stop being their mother.

I have met the prospective adoptive parents three times, on access visits. They've had my daughters for about three and a half years. All the visits have been supervised by a social worker, and that's hurt me so much. Why couldn't they trust me? The court case is due to be heard in four months.

I last saw them last Easter, about nine months ago. It was so lovely and we got on very well. They both started crying. They'd never cried before, but this time they did. They didn't want to leave me. Afterwards I went to pieces. I started taking overdoses and cutting my arms ... to try to forget ... my carpets were soaked with blood where I'd cut myself. I did that about 20 or 30 times and have been in hospital a lot because of it.

Things are very different now. I've changed so much. I feel that I could look after them. My flat used to have hardly any furniture, bare boards, and stacks of bottles everywhere. I was so scruffy. My hair was long and untidy, I was a mess. I looked really old. I had no friends. But I stopped drinking 18 months ago with the help of Janice, who has become a close friend. I'd given her some keys and she came here one night and found me flat on the floor. I hadn't had a drink. I'd just blacked out. She did heart massage on me and rang for an ambulance. Apparently she saved my life. She's a great person and has helped me enormously. I also had a social worker, who saw the children as well. I wasn't always entirely honest with her, and used to cover up for Alan, but in the end I didn't. While they were still with us he was hitting them and knocking me around. I was knocked around as a child and sexually abused by my mother's boyfriend. I was in care from about the age of seven, as my mum had cancer. I didn't see anyone from my family for the two and a half years I was there. It was a horrible experience; they used to force-feed me. I didn't know what was happening, but I do remember thinking my mum didn't love me. After that I stayed with an auntie who was cruel to me. In many ways I've repeated my own history.

A cousin managed to trace me recently and told me I had two sisters who were trying to trace me. Then I remembered my mum having a baby in front of me in the front room. I was about seven. But it was so terrifying I must've repressed it. I thought she was dying. I was put in the home after that, separated from my brother. They found out my mum had cancer. My dad had joined the army and left home when I was about three. I saw him again when I was about 13. I'd run away from my auntie because I wanted to find my family. I was really confused. After that I had a kind of nervous breakdown. My mother died when I was twelve. I came to London when I was 16 and have been here ever since.

I didn't know how to be a mother. I love my children and tried my best to care for them. I miss them terribly. I haven't heard from them since last Easter. I've sent them a Christmas card and heard nothing. I always send them cards on their birthdays, at Easter and Christmas, and letters through the social worker. At first I had face-to-face contact with the adoptive parents. That was the agreement. I gave that up at Easter, almost a year ago, because it was too painful for me and I kept harming myself. I find it so hard to be apart from them and to think I'm never going to have care of them again. I wrote to the girls explaining why I couldn't see them any more at the moment. I said I'd love them to write and that I'd write to them and we'd send photos to each other regularly. That was the last I've heard. I've had no photos for the last year and a half and it's really hurting me. I feel I'm doing my best, I've given the adoptive parents the go-ahead to look after them. But I can't go on fighting.

I've lost all my children, although I still see my son. He came back when he was 15 and a half. He stayed with a foster family nearby. They were marvellous. Then he went into hostel accommodation. His dad died. We were going to get back together again. I visited him in hospital for the last four weeks. I still loved him. He didn't know what happened to his son – I couldn't tell him.

I've been helped a lot at my local hospital and have attended the industrial therapy unit as an outpatient for the last three years. I've also had a lot of help from Janice, who encouraged me to stop drinking. She helped me become aware of what it would mean for my daughters if I did manage to kill myself. She has also helped me become aware of nature for the first time. She took me out to the park when I was getting better and pointed out different birds. I started to see beauty for the first time.

I've told my solicitor that I think it's best if I don't see the girls. I can't handle it. I want to carry on living and do something positive for them. That's what keeps me going. I just hope that when they are 16 or 17 they will come and visit me. That's what I'm living for. In the meantime it's hard, I miss them like crazy, but I've made my decision not to see them face-to-face on access visits, and that has been forwarded to the court. Everyone I've been involved with knows how difficult it is for me to see them and supports my decision. I'd love nothing more than to see them, but I know I'll go to pieces afterwards. I've spent years fighting for them and getting rejected. I've written a letter to them telling them how much I love them but that I can't see them at the moment. I asked my solicitor if she felt my decision would help them and she said it would, by giving them a chance to settle down with their adoptive parents. I like the parents very much, and under the circumstances I'm happy that it's them who are looking after my daughters. I wasn't involved in selecting them, but then I probably wouldn't have been able to do so at the time. They're a lovely couple, very loving and down to earth. The only thing that upset me is that they are not being brought up in the Catholic religion. I wrote to my solicitor insisting they should; it took about a year to get a reply, which was that the girls did not want to be brought up in that faith. So I had to accept what I was told – that I wasn't well and I should let them decide.

I'm hoping that my solicitor will tell the court how I feel – that I have given the adoptive parents my two daughters and I want a little bit back, not much; just to exchange letters and photos from time to time to show me how they are growing and to show them that I am getting older, to prepare them for when we meet again. I need to know what they look like, how they're getting on at school. I haven't heard from them all last year and I'm worried that the letter I wrote has affected them.

In the absence of any letters or cards for the past eight months, I rang Margaret's solicitor on her behalf. She contacted Margaret's social worker and within a few hours he visited, then returned to his office and 'found' letters and cards for Margaret from her daughters.

11 Valerie

Valerie is the birth mother of Jodie, a mixed-parentage child placed with white adoptive parents, now aged 11. I made contact with her and Jodie's adoptive mother through Parent to Parent Information on Adoption Services (PPIAS) – a group set up in England in 1971 by parents who adopted children considered 'hard to place'. It offers practical help, advice and support to prospective and existing adopters and permanent substitute families.

Valerie, and particularly her mother Emily, wanted to maintain contact with the adoptive parents by way of letters. This was welcomed by the adoptive parents, who suggested it, along with the offer of more openness (face-to-face contact) should the birth family ever want to take it up.

Contact began as arranged, letters passed via the Social Services, but as their respective needs changed over the years, so did the nature of the contact. All parties are doubtful about whether the placement would have continued without this contact. Valerie and her mother first met Jodie when he was seven and have seen him twice since then in the last two years.

I was nearly 21 when I got pregnant in 1981 and Jodie was born in June 1982. I met Jodie's dad when I was 19. He was the only person I'd ever slept with. Within a few months of knowing him I was pregnant. That pregnancy was terminated, but I'm sure it's connected with getting pregnant again. No matter what people have said to me, I've decided for myself that I tried to replace that termination by having another baby – and realised, tragically, that it was the wrong thing to do. At the time I felt very, very confused – I let everyone decide for me. I let everyone organise things for me and just went along with it. The father was very immature, like I was. He was two years younger than me. He was quite excited about it at times, but neither of us was grown up enough to make any kind of decision. He was upset when he found out

I was going to have a termination, but eventually realised it was probably for the best. We still carried on seeing each other in spite of what everyone said. Our courtship was very stressful all the time, as we were battling against other people's opinions. My parents didn't want me to see him and wouldn't let him come to our house, so that caused problems between us. He is coloured and my dad is prejudiced, so it was always very difficult.

We kept on seeing each other and two years later I discovered I was having Jodie. This time I didn't tell anyone anything at all. I did a home-test which was positive. I was on my own at the time and I just sat crying for a couple of hours wondering what to do, thinking really this is what I wanted but what a stupid thing to do. I was in no better a position than last time. And how will I tell anyone? Something inside me told me it was going to be such an ordeal to tell anyone that I just shut it off. It wasn't happening. I didn't show much for the first few months and then I dressed to disguise it. Eventually my mother forced it out of me. I felt so young, I know I was still very, very immature for 21 in terms of going into the outside world and sorting out my own life. I don't know whether it's the way I accepted my mum and dad to be with me, or whether I really wanted them to be like that and cosset me. When I was little I always sheltered away from the outside world. I wanted to be inside with my mum all the time. It carried on when I grew up as well.

I was nearly six months pregnant when I finally admitted to my mum that I was pregnant. I think I thought it would just disappear one day. I was crying and told her I hadn't said anything because I was frightened of how everyone would be, of hurting them and causing utter chaos. Now looking back, having a baby isn't such chaos, is it? I couldn't tell my dad. I'm not really frightened of him, but I couldn't tell him. I remember mum asked me what I wanted to do and I said, 'I can't have him, can I? What will my dad do?' I actually said, 'I think I'll have to have the baby adopted.' I knew myself it wasn't what I wanted. I think I was hoping they would say to me, 'It's all right, you don't have to do that,' I think I was trying to tell my mum what I thought she wanted to hear – so that I wouldn't cause any more upset. From that day on, until I came out of hospital without Jodie, my dad didn't speak a word to me. Not one word. When I was little I went everywhere with him – even as a teenager in the school holidays. I didn't go out with crowds of girls, I went with my dad to the pigeons and up to the allotments to help him with the gardening. But he wouldn't speak to me at all.

It was a big relief not to have to cover it up any more and start to accept it myself. I was fine, apart from being tired. But the mental thing was something else altogether, looking back on it now. Ever since I was little all I wanted to do was grow up and have a family – and I'd done it all the wrong way. Not only was I having a baby when I should've been married, but I was having a mixed-race baby and I'd grown up with my dad being prejudiced. It didn't rub off on me because I didn't see Ron as coloured. His parents are Jamaican but he was born in England. When I went to his house his family welcomed me from the start. It was hard to accept that they could accept me but mum and dad couldn't accept him. So it was only in one part of my life that I was being accepted for what I was and what I wanted – I wanted to be with him and have a baby and get married – he never mentioned marriage, by the way! He thought it was a nice idea my having a baby – it gave him a sort of macho image, I think. My having a baby made him more of a man. I learnt that later. But according to the nurses, he did see Jodie when he was a couple of days old. He didn't see me, but I couldn't have seen him then.

I'd decided if I was going to have Jodie adopted then I'd got to stop seeing Ron – I had to start afresh. I needed strength to break away from Ron, which I hadn't been able to do for all that time as well as try and sort out what I was going to do with Jodie. But I still loved him and only stopped thinking about him all the time when Jodie was about three or four. I had such a strong feeling of wanting to do what my family wanted.

When it was decided that Jodie would be adopted, it was suggested I see a social worker to get things sorted out before he was born. She didn't talk about it in too much depth, but pointed out the positive and negative aspects and said she'd be in touch. We had a couple more meetings before he was born, and she told me what to expect. She didn't put any pressure on me. I think the strongest pressure was my dad not speaking to me. It's hard for him to talk about things, and perhaps I'm like him because I just shut it off as well.

If he'd been given to me straight after he was born, I know there's no way I'd have let him go. My mum was with me when he was born. I heard her say to the nurse when I was in labour, 'Is there any way when he's born that he can be taken away so that she doesn't see him?' I'd drilled it in to her that the baby should be adopted. I remember hearing the midwife saying something about a law that meant he couldn't be taken away within a certain time. I was quite drugged, but I remember seeing his arm as they put him in the crib. I think I must've fallen asleep after that. When I woke up he was gone.

For the first day I didn't know where he was. Then the nurses told me he'd been put in a a nursery and if I wanted to see him at any time they'd take me. I remember the next night I was soaked through with milk and it felt like the world had come to an end. It was about 2 o'clock in the morning and I could hear a baby crying. There was no one around, so I got up and went looking for him. There was a room with a glass panel in the door and two babies in it – one white and the other coloured. I saw him through the glass, then went running back to my room and cried for the rest of the night. I didn't go in and pick him up. I don't know why – except if I had, he wouldn't have been adopted. It sounds cruel to say I should have been thinking of him, but I knew that it was what I had to do. Otherwise, what would my dad think?

I saw Jodie again as I was leaving hospital. I had a look at him through the door of the nursery where he was. Then I collapsed. I went back home after the nurses checked out that it was what I wanted to do, but said I was free to come back and see him any time. Mum sat in the back of the car and dad drove us home. I don't know if my mum saw him or not. My sister went to see him and picked him up. I didn't go back to the hospital. He was there for ten days. The social worker rang and said she was taking him to a foster home in a nearby town.

I remember she asked me what sort of family I'd like. The most important thing I wanted was that he went to a mixed-race family. I wanted him to have the same sort of upbringing that he'd have had if he'd stayed with me and Ron. So he went to this short-term foster home while they looked. She also said if I wanted to go and see him, I could. But I couldn't – I couldn't make that step and go and see him and then walk away – I couldn't. Nor could I have touched him and then left. That would've been impossible. Nobody could've taken him out of my arms if I had.

I remember when I first came home being in a state of shock and numbness. I think it was too much pain and I couldn't handle it. I just had to shut it off altogether. That lasted for a few weeks. But my dad spoke to me as soon as I came home without the baby. So that made me happy, feeling I'd done the right thing, not hurting him any more – and that everything would be back to normal now. I remember a friend of his called round and was talking to him in the kitchen. Then he looked at me and said something like, 'How's the baby?' It was the first time he'd been mentioned. My dad said in a joking way – although his voice cracked as he said it – 'We sold him to somebody.' I think it was my dad's way, he didn't mean to hurt me, but it hurt ever so much. I can still feel it now.

After he was born nobody came to talk to me. Not even the social worker. It was like she'd done her bit now. It was like she just went through the motions when she first talked to me and it wasn't sincere. The only time I saw her after Jodie was born was when she came to collect me and take me to the court to sign the adoption forms. She got in touch a few times to say they were having trouble finding a family to suit my requirements as it were, and in the end they couldn't find a mixed-race family but they'd found a white couple. By then, he was six months old and I was so relieved there was someone out there who wanted him, it didn't matter any more. Nothing mattered. During that time I didn't visit, I was in a kind of daze – a trance. All I could think about was, 'I wonder if he's having his nappy changed,' or if he's crying, or getting any teeth; it was going round and round in my head all the time. I had a little dog that wasn't well and I spent all my time nursing her. I missed having something in my arms, even though I'd never picked him up. I was always thinking, 'I wish I was the one changing his nappy or buying baby clothes for him.'

I wished I'd had counselling after Jodie was born. I held a lot in. I talked to my mum and cried with my mum, but I think it helps to talk to a stranger, a professional person, as they can help bring out things that somebody too close to you can't because of all the emotions that get in the way. It's only been recently that I've realised that counselling would've helped. At the time I didn't ask for anything at all.

My mum mentioned him quite a lot during that time. I remember telling her that the social worker had rung and they still hadn't found any one for him, and she got up and was crying and said to my dad, 'Come on, we're going to fetch him back,' and she went to put her shoes on. She put on her coat and said, 'We're going to fetch him, it's not fair, he's in a strange place and he ought to be with us.' I think if my dad had reacted differently then, we probably would have fetched him. I sat there listening. My dad just sat there and must've said something quietly. I was

waiting for him to say something and then I could've let out my
real feelings.

The social worker told me about them, where they lived and
that they'd be coming up to collect him and would I like to meet
her. I said I'd love to. I also met their other child they'd adopted.
The meeting was very relaxed and comfortable. There was a kind
of bond straight away. It was strange. She said she'd already been
to see him and was going to collect him later. She spoke very gently
and my mum and I warmed to her straight away. She told how
much she wanted another child and about her miscarriages and
she made me feel very secure about how much she wanted him.
And she said she shared the same birthday. Her husband wasn't
there, I'm not sure why. Maybe he didn't want to be involved in
all the emotion – like my dad. It was a relief she was so nice. I
suppose if I'd taken an instant dislike to her it would've made things
a whole lot worse. But I didn't. She was lovely and we feel close
to her now. I didn't feel any jealousy, or that she was taking
something of mine. All I felt was a great sense of relief. It was
obvious in that short space of time he was going to go somewhere
where he'd be loved as much as I could have loved him. I don't
mean the material things. I just knew she was going to go back
to him and pick him up and love him. As we left I hugged her. I
felt I had to get hold of her and hug her. As I did I said, 'Thank
you,' to her. And she said, 'No, it's thank you to you.' And then
neither of us could speak any more and went our separate ways.

After that it felt a little bit easier for a while, having had six
months of not knowing what was going to happen to him. I started
to feel a little bit better knowing he was going to be somewhere
permanent and he now had a family. I still had the feeling of
wanting to hold him and change his nappy, but at least I knew
he was with someone who was doing that.

I'm really glad I met her. She talked about open adoption and
explained it to me. The social worker went out of the room for a
while and left us to talk. I'd never heard of open adoption. She
said she wanted us to always remain in contact, even if it was only
letters through the Social Services. I felt I needed it – to know what
was happening rather than just be constantly wondering, like I
was when he was at the foster home. While he was being fostered
it was always made clear to me that I could go and see him and
if I wanted to I could end it, right up to signing the papers. It
would've been very easy to go and pick him up, but I felt I had
to stop myself from doing such an easy thing in order to get

everyone else's lives back to normal – hopefully, for all the pain to go away.

Having the letters meant I had a proper picture in my head rather than not knowing. It was lovely being able to see what he looked like. It was hard trying to picture him before that. I wanted to put a picture in my head and until I got the photos I couldn't. I was all over the place before that. I don't know whether it was because I needed to feel this or not, but I felt he was in the place he was meant to be – with Brenda. And when I got those letters it all felt right. I didn't feel that I should've been in that place. It felt nice she was letting me know about him – I felt lucky that she was letting me know. You could tell in the letters that she loved him amd wanted to bring him up in the right way. That helped, knowing he was being looked after as I wanted him to be.

At first she wrote through the Social Services, so I didn't know exactly where she lived. Gradually she started to let us know about problems he was having. He'd got a zinc deficiency and was allergic to all milky foods and was becoming hyperactive. She was taking him to the hospital and letting us know what the specialist said. Then I started to feel guilt again, this was when it started to get bad for me. I felt I'd given her a baby that was causing problems and wasn't making her happy. At first what helped was that I was making her happy giving her a baby that she desperately wanted. Then all of a sudden she wasn't happy any more and was having a lot of trouble with him. So I piled all the guilt on to myself again. I also felt that his problems must've stemmed from my not having medical supervision all those months I was pregnant without telling anyone. I just felt unhappy a lot of the time. It wasn't the fairytale I wanted it to be. I knew he was safe where he was and was being looked after, but the main fear was that through my own actions, not only everyone at home had suffered, but now Brenda was as well. I thought he'd be a perfect child for her and she'd have 24 hours' happiness every day. I felt I'd messed it all up somehow.

I still wanted the letters because I was hoping in time everything would be right again. We'd hear every three or four months. She'd explain he'd calmed down because he was on vitamins and special foods. All through this my mum talked to me about it. It was only my mum that ever really talked to me about it. Looking back, she's helped me more than she could ever know. When the letters came I'd say things like, 'What have I done?', and she'd say that it was just a fact of life. The problems he was having were nothing to do with me. Apparently I had projectile vomiting as a baby. I felt better after my mum talked to me, but it seemed like I had a self-destructive thing inside me that would sneak up on me – I felt I'd done so much wrong. I'd brought a baby into the world and I'd made him like he was. Although I wasn't there, I was causing all these problems. Ron had moved to London with his mum. She didn't want me to have Jodie adopted. They had a much more relaxed attitude about keeping him. 'You've had a baby, just get on with it,' sort of thing. They rang a couple of times to see how things were, but that was it. I did see him a couple of years ago in a pub when he was visiting, but I didn't go all weak at the knees like I used to. We had a pleasant conversation and he left. He didn't mention Jodie.

Brenda's first phonecall was the second Christmas she had him and she also sent us a tape of him making a few words helping to sing Christmas carols. That was lovely. It made me cry, but I'm still glad I had it. I remember one phonecall when he was about four on Christmas Day and Brenda put him on the line and I just couldn't talk to him. My mum did. I wanted to, but it hurt too much even though I'd had letters and photos; I didn't want to hear his voice.

She's always said we could see him. I'd always imagined that when he was adopted that would be it, so getting the letters and photos was wonderful – I was so glad to have that. Then she started to gently get round to more openness. When he got to three or four she said, 'If ever you want to come and see him you're welcome.' It felt good to know she wanted that, and I felt very, very grateful because I knew in the back of my mind that somehow, some way we'd get to meet before he grew up and decided for himself who he wanted to see. It was too much to see him as a baby when he was a helpless, defenceless little creature that needed looking after – I was his mum and I'd got to see to him and then there'd be no chance of letting him go to somebody else.

But when he got to six or seven I had a kind of breakdown and started crying to my mum, 'I want to see my baby, I want to see my baby.' At first I could hear voices in the background saying, 'That won't do any good, it'll only make it worse, she won't be able to cope with it – she'll come back home and she'll be even worse than she is now' – I think it was my dad. I cried for two days. I've done a lot of crying in the past over it and there have been times when I've wanted to kill myself. And if I'd been brave enough I'd have done it. But it's a selfish thing wanting to escape the pain. I'm 33 and still immature. My mum knows I've wanted to die. But I decided it wouldn't do it, although it still goes through my mind – I still feel sometimes that I want to die. I don't think I'll ever feel completely happy – maybe I don't know how.

I'm not sure what triggered off the breakdown. For the first five or six years after Jodie was born I wouldn't let anyone come near me at all, apart from the family. I wouldn't get close to anyone, I wouldn't have a relationship with anybody. I shut off if anyone came near. And then I got involved with a married man. My feelings for him were quite strong. But again I was doing the wrong thing – I shouldn't love anyone that was married. We didn't have an affair, we just met a couple of times and walked in the forest, but we ended up feeling worse because all we did was talk about how negative our situation was and cry and come home feeling even worse. One day I realised I loved him and wished I was able to show it, to love someone else apart from my family, and it all just got too much for me. Also I wanted to have some kind of relationship with Jodie before he grew up, since I'd been given the chance to do it. It wasn't a planned thing where I suddenly woke up one morning and felt strong enough to go and see him. I'd just got to the stage where I felt a complete emotional wreck and sat there crying and it came out, 'I want to see my baby.' It came out from deep down inside, and all I could hear myself saying was I wanted to see Jodie. Nothing else in the world mattered. I couldn't calm down.

My mum rang Brenda, and she'd been wanting it so they arranged that we meet that Saturday. Until then I couldn't concentrate on anything else – I went to work but it was all mechanical.

We went down on the train. I didn't feel frightened, I didn't feel nervous all the way down. I didn't feel that happy either, it was more like I just had to do it. It was such a strong need. My mum came with me, which was wonderful because I knew I couldn't have done it on my own. She was a bag of nerves. We met in London, at King's Cross, and they came up from Surrey. I arranged the meeting and found out the train times and yet at the same time I was such a wreck!

I remember waiting for them and looking round. I knew what Brenda looked like and had seen photos of Jodie. Then someone tapped me on the shoulder and it was Brenda. I looked at her, then down at Jodie – and I didn't feel anything at all. I think I went into numbness – a state of shock. I didn't feel I wanted to grab hold of him and I didn't. I didn't go near him. I think my mum was watching me to see what I did. I didn't even touch

Brenda, like I do now. I just stood still and didn't speak. Then Brenda suggested we get in a taxi and go somewhere. I just followed them. I remember sitting across from him in the taxi and just staring at him and thinking, 'Stop staring at him, you'll make him feel uncomfortable.'

My first thought when I looked at him was that I saw Ron. And as he walked in front of us to get the taxi, my mum said he walked like my dad. All I could see was Ron. We went to Regent's Park, and I took Jodie and his sister on the swings. My mum sat down and talked to Brenda. He was just a normal little boy. I don't know what I was expecting. Then I just relaxed with him. I didn't feel I could be affectionate towards him. He felt like a stranger to me – a complete stranger. It was like meeting up with a child in the park you'd never met before. They wanted to be pushed on the swings, and I was quite happy to do that for them like I would any other children. I love children and have an affinity with them. I always talk to kids and it felt just like that. I wanted to push him on the swings and for him to have a happy day, but I didn't feel anything at all when I first met him. Perhaps I shut them off because it was too strong a force. I just did what I set out to do, which was to meet him.

I was very worn out going back on the train. My mum asked me how I felt and I said, 'I've been and done it now,' and cheered up on the train. I even had some British Rail sandwiches! It was like I was opening up after being shut off from everything for the whole day. But I'd gone and done what I wanted so much to do. I felt more contented, although I never feel completely contented, but I felt much more relaxed having gone through the barrier of that first meeting. I felt it would happen again sometime. The most important thing to me now is that I've got over the stage of constantly thinking of what my dad wants – even though I don't want to hurt him – I've got over that. My main feeling now is that as Jodie grows up, he knows if ever he wants me I'm there for him. He's already got a loving family, but if ever he needs anything extra he's only got to ring me. I want him to grow up knowing that. I'm sending him a letter soon to his school, together with a photo in a frame of us together when we met. I've had that had done specially for him.

We've met three times now. The first time was when he was seven, then again on his tenth and eleventh birthdays. The gap between the first and second time was probably because I felt that lucky being able to see him that I got on with things again and felt I ought to leave him alone to grow up in his family, and let them get on with bringing him up without me intruding any more. Then when he got to the age of ten, Brenda asked us again if we'd like to meet. He'd also gone to a new school, which she wanted us to go and see. It felt right to see him again. It was just a case of it feeling the right time to see him before I could do it. Now it feels like it'll be a yearly thing and that feels right. And Brenda said, 'Next year we'll have to meet at my house,' as if it was a matter-of-fact thing. We met last year and everybody felt comfortable with that.

I do feel it's very much up to her, and if she wanted to stop it then I would have to go along with what she wanted. I don't know what it would do to me, but I feel that she's the one that pulls all the strings. I don't feel bad about it, it's just how it is. I accept it for the way it is. But thank goodness we have a good relation-ship.

If I hadn't had any openness in the adoption, I don't think I'd be here now. I needed to know so much about his life that to know nothing at all would have meant I'd either be in a mental insti-tution and not be aware of anything any more, or possibly I could have killed myself. One or the other.

I feel it's very much an individual sort of thing, having contact. If a woman has given away her baby and she doesn't want any more contact again and she's finalised it, then that's her right. But I've been lucky and had the openness.

I feel my relationship with Jodie will get closer and closer as he gets more mature and more inquisitive. I think that's what Brenda wants as well. It would be nice if we could help Jodie to grow up understanding it all and help him not to make any mistakes.

I see him as her son. She has a right to tell him what to do and so on. The only time I've ever felt uncomfortable in the way she is with him was when we were in a café having lunch on the first day I met Jodie. I was 'in neutral' and Jodie was chattering away quite excitedly and Brenda kept telling him to shut up. I didn't feel mad with her, I couldn't ever feel like that with her, but I had a stange feeling inside that she's his mum, she's telling him what to do and she has every right to do that, but I wished she wouldn't speak to him like that. He was excited and I wished she'd just leave him alone. I like children to have manners, but he wasn't being cheeky or naughty, just rattling on a bit. But that's the only time.

Everything she does for him is right, his clothes, the way she cuts his hair. I look at them and think it's Brenda doing those things for her son. She's the one who's bringing him up, but I want to be a little bit selfish now and stand by him and put my arms round him and say how proud I am of him, but I don't feel I've got a right to say that because I haven't done anything for him. He played his recorder for us at his school and I felt ever so proud of him and I wanted to jump up and tell them all, 'That's my son doing that!' But I knew I couldn't.

The way it's worked out has been the best possible – apart from wanting to bring him up myself. I wouldn't have wanted it to be any different from the way it is now – it's quite special. I think it's worked not because of me, but because of Brenda being the sort of person she is and my mum being there guiding me along and deep down knowing what I wanted to do, like when I met Jodie for the first time, having her there. So I think it's due to Brenda and my mum between them, that has made things as they are – my mum's emotional support and Brenda's understanding about what it has meant for me. She's quite amazing – she wants to share him. In one of her first letters she said she felt she was bringing him up for us – that he was part of us. She felt he was my mum's grandson and that she should talk about him as her grandson and that I should talk of him as my little boy. When he was little she'd refer to me in front of him as 'mummy Valerie', Even now she says things like, 'Let's have a photo of Jodie's two mums.' That's how she talks – just very matter-of-fact. If she hadn't been like that and my mum hadn't been how she is, it would never have happened. I could never have done anything on my own.

But even now, eleven years later, all the feelings I have are still held in. They never go away. I didn't have counselling at the time because it wasn't offered, but talking to you today has made me see it is helpful to talk about it. Otherwise I'll still be like this at 65.

I don't feel I have entitlement to Jodie now, but I want to be able to feel comfortable with him and proud of him like I did when he played his recorder. I said to Brenda afterwards that I wanted to feel proud of him but I haven't got a right, and she got quite cross with me. She wants that, so I think it's only a matter of time before I let myself say, 'Yes, I am proud of him,' and, 'Perhaps I didn't make such a bad job after all!' Seeing your child's achievements is like seeing your own. If they're making a success of something, however small, you feel better about yourself.

Part Four
Open Adoption

A mother's spirit knows no abandonment,
no matter what circumstances
Produce separation or distances.
Our child will always know that you care.

Chris Probst, 'Our Child'

Open adoption here refers to a fully open relationship, with face-to-face contact between the birth family, the adoptive parents and the child while he or she is growing up. The families' stories in this section date from the 1980s in the UK and in New Zealand.

Like semi-open adoption, it is a verbal agreement between the two sets of parents reached before the placement is finalised and, again, there is no provision for the birth parent or child legally to enforce contact. Children of open adoptions have the same legal status as they would if brought up in a closed adoption.

Open adoption does not usually involve a third party, like social workers. The families communicate directly with each other. Initially, however, contact between them would have taken place via the adoption agency which, together with the birth parents, would have found a suitable family for the child.

This form of contact often means that a relationship can develop more easily between the families – one of mutual trust, goodwill and honesty – based on a commitment to do the best for the child. Also, direct contact means future communication can be more flexible and open to negotiation to suit changing needs over time; for example, birth mothers may want more contact in the first year or so after the adoption, and the child and adoptive parents may want more contact in the teenage years.

Open adoption as a practice has evolved in social work in much the same way as it evolved in the lives of the families it affected – beginning with one-off meetings and developing into more open arrangements. Many adoptive parents began to feel comfortable with the idea, to feel it was benefical for everyone involved, and adapted it to suit their own individual needs.

Conflicts can of course sometimes arise, as they do in other relationships, and some birth and adoptive parents experience pressure from family and friends not to have openness; as with semi-open adoption, they think it will make it harder for both sets of parents and, in particular, undermine the adopters' parenting. Adoptive parents in New Zealand have probably done most to promote openness; from their personal experience many know that birth parents are not forever turning up on the doorstep or disrupting the children's lives; they know the birth parent(s) as people and understand the personal cost to them of giving up their children and how much their welfare matters to them; they can see for themselves how much a part of the adoptive families the children are. According to one NZ study, even in the most open adoptions birth families do not customarily play any substantive role in parenting; this merely took the form of occasional alternative care offered at holiday times or by way of babysitting.[1]

It is not possible here to detail the numerous studies on openness from the UK, the USA and New Zealand, but rather to highlight various aspects concerning adoptive parents – for instance, they became increasingly more secure and less anxious about contact, especially after the adoption order was made; moreover, the greater the degree of openness, the more comfortable the adopters felt with it; this in turn increased their feelings of closeness towards the child. The placement of older children in particular was was much less likely to disrupt where there was contact with the birth family, including contact with siblings. Perhaps older children also need 'permission' from their past carers before they can begin to build a new relationship.

One small-scale New Zealand study shows that an observable pattern seems to have emerged showing that as adoptive parents feel more secure and willing to have contact, birth parents feel less need for information and contact, suggesting that openness helps complete the grieving process as well as that of separation.[2]

Nevertheless, open adoption is not a panacea for the grief and loss birth parents feel. Having knowledge of the child's welfare, and the reassurance that offers, may ease the pain of separation and loss – many say they would not have survived a closed adoption – but the grieving process is still profound. Although contact may help a birth mother to feel she has made the right decision, her feelings for the child do not diminish at the same rate that the adoptive parents' feelings for the child grow.

Nor should openness be promoted as an alternative to the social worker's primary task of working to keep families together. The current moral backlash against single mothers in the UK may mean that (young) pregnant women, without parental support, will be plunged back into similar conditions that existed in the 1960s. Single parents are no longer automatically entitled to permanent housing and there are proposals to curb benefits payable to them. In addition, there is an increasing number of infertile couples wanting to adopt children, and a corresponding decrease in resources to help keep children and their single parents together.

Openness in adoption has developed in the UK because it is seen to be in the best interests of the child. Birth families have benefited as a result. The nature of this communication between the two families rests on the attitude of the agency, which in turn may influence the adoptive parents. While recommendations in the White Paper of November 1993 support openness, it upholds the view that once an adoption order is made the most important objective is to support the new family relationship. Where adoptive parents oppose the prospect of openness, their views should have the greater weight.[3]

Legalising birth parents' access to their relinquished children is a concern of some professionals in New Zealand: some say that openness should be based on mutual trust and cooperation; others that openness should be reflected in the legislation. This would ultimately protect a child's access to both families. Also, relationships are more likely to work when parties can feel they are regarded as equals; it would exclude applicants who enter an agreement with the intention of stopping contact after an adoption order is made.[4]

Before the UK Children Act 1989 it was possible, though very uncommon, to have access written into the adoption order. Now the emphasis is on agreement between the parties before an adoption order is made and it is very unlikely a birth parent would get leave to apply to the court for access – a contact order – after an adoption order was made. In any case a court would be unwilling to prescribe contact and would prefer to leave it up to the individuals involved.

Attitudes to openness are very individual. They reflect personal beliefs about parenting, sexuality, the family and society. Nowadays family structure is changing – many children live in reconstituted families and relate separately to their divorced parents, their parents' partners or stepparents; our society is one where more and more emphasis is being placed on openness. This includes a child's need to know its origins and preferably to maintain those links, whether adopted or not. There has been little large-scale research done on fully open adoption, but what has been done largely supports openness as a a healthier and psychologically sounder means of building families by adoption. Any arrangement involving contact is a very individual one and works best when it is what everyone wants, where there is adequate preparation and counselling and genuine participation.

The families that have shared their stories have all been positive. This is not to say that there are no failures. They also differ in terms of the degree of contact. Those from New Zealand have a greater degree of openness, possibly reflecting the confidence in a system that has been underway there for much longer than in most western countries. Its lead can be linked to the Maori tradition of sharing the care of children among family members who regard those children as belonging not to the parents but to the whole community. This shared responsibility and decision-making is reflected in New Zealand's adoption legislation, which requires a meeting of the extended family to decide on a plan of care for a child in need of a new permanent family.

Most children involved in adoption today in the UK are older children, mainly those with special needs, whose parents often contest the adoption. Some professionals say that most parents can be helped to become involved in their children's adoption plan and should have at the very least updated information; that a child has a right to some kind of access to his or her birth family; that adoption is not the only secure alternative for those being permanently parented in new families. Others say that family links should be severed with adoption. In at least two states in Australia it is almost impossible to adopt older children because it is regarded as undesirable to break the genetic link.

In the UK the White Paper on adoption is recommending that openness should be the prerogative of the adopters; in New Zealand many adoptive parents feel that some form of openness should exist and those who decline are not yet ready to adopt. There, adoptive kinship is being promoted 'as a different and unique way to experience parenthood and family life based on "acknowledgement of difference", which will lead to honesty and openness in parent-child relationships'.[5] Much depends on the practice and philosophy of social workers to accommodate social changes in the family that are already well underway.

References

1. Rockel, G. and M. Ryburn (1988), *Adoption Today: Change and Choice in New Zealand*. Auckland: Heinemann Reed.
2. Iwanek, M. (1987), 'A Study of Open Adoption Placements'. Unpublished report, Wellington.
3. Department of Health (November 1993), *Adoption: the Future*. London: HMSO.
4. Iwanek, *A Study of Open Adoption Placements*.
5. Kirk, D. (1981), *Adoptive Kinship*. Toronto: Butterworth, quoted in Iwanek, *A Study of Open Adoption Placements*.

12 Heather

*I met Heather, Ben's birth mother, in Hamilton, New Zealand, through
my family, who were friends of the adoptive parents. They were
impressed with the way Heather and Lois, the adoptive mother, shared
the care of Ben after school and in the holidays.*

*Heather acknowledges she could have kept Ben, but chose to have
him adopted, not only for finanacial reasons but because she felt he
would be better off with a stable, married couple, whom she selected
from profiles offered by Welfare. She had the support of her family and
help from the professional workers. It was 1980 and fully open adoption
was not common practice. Heather had expected a traditional, closed
adoption after relinquishing her son, but the adoptive parents wanted
a fully open adoption. Maintaining a link with her son has been the
most important factor in helping to ease her loss and, ten years later,
she would not want to change things.*

*Heather's father also contributed to this interview as Ben's natural
grandfather.*

I was 18 when I got pregnant in 1980 and I felt my child would
be better off with two parents rather than one. I had nothing to
give him. I'd tried making the relationship with his father work,
but it lasted about six months or so and then we split up.

The father didn't show much interest when I was pregnant, but
a person like him shouldn't have children. He didn't want me to
have him adopted. He went to court to get custody and lost. I think
the reason he objected to my having Ben adopted was his hold
on me – keeping Ben was a way of keeping that hold on me. I
don't think it was the baby he wanted.

He was very possessive. He didn't want me visiting my mother.
She really hated him. He didn't like my closeness with my family.
I lived on a farm with him and I grew really skinny. He was
violent and he wanted full control over me. He might have done
the same to the child.

It was a relief he lost the court case. There has been one other case like this, but the father was a better person. I didn't want my son to know who his father was. I didn't put his name down on the birth certificate because I thought it would be better if he never knew. I would always try to put across to Ben the better aspects of his father if he ever asked me. The case was hard for the [prospective] adoptive parents as well. They had a lawyer, and Social Welfare was represented too – in fact there were five lawyers altogether in the Family Court. If the adoptive parents had lost custody, I think I'd have taken Ben as I think I'd have been the next best person – after them – to take care of him. Not that I wanted to get rid of him, or give him up. It was better for him.

I met the adoptive parents about a week or so after Ben was born. Welfare gave me three profiles and I picked them. She was a nurse and I thought he was a policeman, but he was actually a traffic controller. I was keen on the idea of her being a nurse and I didn't want to chop and change. I think they saw him and cared for him in the hospital from about the fourth day on.

I was put on a different floor from the other mothers, as they knew I was having my baby adopted – in case I heard the babies and changed my mind. My dad thinks it was because the father was causing problems and hassling everyone.

It was really hard before I had him to think about giving him up, but so much worse afterwards as your hormones are all over the place anyway. I did feel the hospital staff were there helping me, though. I remember the Sister came through and asked me when I was going to see the baby. When I said the fourth day she said this might seem like I was saying goodbye and that would make it worse for me. So I went down with her then and held him. He started crying, but it wasn't too bad.

I saw him when he was born, but only a glance, then on the second day with Sister and then again three weeks later. I was delirious after the birth. I had an epidural and didn't even know he'd been born. I remember saying, 'What's going on now?,' and they said that I'd had a baby boy. I didn't even know! I really didn't know what to expect, but I kept thinking, 'This is the one thing I can't get out of.' I had always said I didn't want anyone with me, but mum managed to get in, although at that stage I didn't care.

Looking back, I'm glad the Sister suggested I saw Ben that day instead of the last day. I was sad, very sad, when I left the hospital, but it was a decision I had made. It was a question of whether or not I could do it on the day. I signed him away, but I knew I could still change my mind up until then. But I couldn't. I wouldn't. I had to get myself a flat. I was still living at home then. I had no baby clothes. I had geared myself up for giving him away. It was better for him.

My family was fine about it. He was mentioned at home and they didn't make judgements or anything. It was agreed that I see him on the seventh day. It was the adoptive parents' idea. They wanted Ben to know his birth family right from the start. My own experience of children who were adopted was that they grew up with no idea of who they were and had a complex about it. Some of them turn out OK. I know of two children adopted by a family; one is OK, and the other denies the fact that he's adopted.

I knew it was going to be hard seeing him and saying goodbye, and the time after that as well. We were told, 'Whatever you do, try not to think too much about it' – birthdays and that. 'It's always going to be hard but the more you think about it, the more it'll tear you up inside.' I was told not to put it out of my mind, but to think positively about it – this was the lady who took the prenatal classes. Then afterwards a social worker visited to see how you were coping and feeling. I was fine because it was easier for me – I could see him again.

I met the adoptive parents on about the eighth day. I was happy seeing them and being able to see Ben. They made a time to see me again in the third week. Lois, the adoptive mother, was very anxious but she didn't tell me till afterwards, because the sixth week was fairly crucial. It was when I signed the consent papers. She was worried that I might change my mind. I remember telling her not to worry about my changing my mind as my hormones were all back to normal and she laughed. From then on I saw him every second week or monthly. It was their idea – especially Grant, the adoptive father. He had worked with and knew a lot of Maoris and knew their ways. Children belong to the community and are never adopted out of the family. Often it's the grandmother who takes care of them, so they always know who they are. But I think Lois was quite anxious about it all.

Ben has asked me a couple of times about being his mother, well, 'other mother', and I've said to him that we know who his real mum is – it's Lois. I'm more like an auntie really. But blood is thicker than water as well – he's still who he is, but he's their child, not mine.

I don't really think too much about it – like when she handed me the bottle that first time, I was just shocked that she offered me the chance to feed him because he was their baby, not mine, and I've always felt like that – that he's not really mine. He's my blood child but they've put their personality into him, so he's a mixture of theirs and ours.

It's great to be able to see him. That's all I want. That's what has helped me over the years – being able to see him and to know he's alive and well. We're like extended family. Lois is like a sister to me. I've never had a sister. I bought her a Mother's Day gift and I was really shocked when she gave me one. But maybe she was just as shocked. I gave her a vase with 'mother' written on it as my way of saying, 'You're the mother.'

I don't feel any resentment towards them bringing up my child. I'm able to see him all the time. I feel like his auntie. Sometimes I feel he's my blood son but I've never, ever felt jealous. Blood is thicker than water – I mean he's still my blood, he's still my child – or was my child. But if I had the choice tomorrow I'd never take him away from them. I just couldn't do it. He's theirs and that's that. The only reason I'd ever consider having him is if something happened to one of them. Even then, they might have their own ideas – they might want him to go to somebody else.

I wouldn't say I shared the parenting of him, but I do discipline him when he's with me and maybe in a different way. I tell him off more! When he's with Lois, she disciplines him in her own way. It would have been great if he'd had a brother or sister to learn to share things with. As it is he's an only child – there aren't children available in the same way for adoption any more.

It's much easier to keep your baby these days. But at the time it would've been hard on my family. I was sharing a room with my brother, so it would've been us plus the baby. Also I had no money and I was in a terrible state. Mum was five minutes late picking me up from the hospital and I was bawling my eyes out. My hormones were all over the place. Also I didn't feel old enough then, although I do now. I'm married now.

I don't know anyone who had their baby adopted, except those women in the hospital. I probably could have kept him, but it wouldn't have been the best thing for him. It wasn't just financial – you do get help from Welfare. I think it was the stability of having two parents for him. That was the main reason and that was more important than my own needs. I made that choice.

I don't think it's a big deal for Ben. I'm like his auntie and we've all pitched in to make it seem as normal as possible. He's always known who I am and we're like part of his family. They're hoping I might have more children so Ben will have a brother or sister. I think that's fantastic because legally he's theirs, yet they've made it feel like a family – they didn't say 'half' brother or sister. I'm sure the reason why mothers no longer give up their babies for adoption is because they never see them again.

As it is we see Ben about once a month. They used to live much closer but they've moved away, although not too far. When they lived here we used to share the care of Ben after school quite often.

It's so hard to imagine what it would have been like for us not to be able to see him or know his adoptive parents. I get a terrible feeling when I think about the fact that I was prepared to adopt him out to strangers. I'm sure I'd have had a lot of guilt and terrible sadness, never being with him – never seeing your own child. He wouldn't feel like mine or anything to do with me if he were with strangers. So I'm happy with the way things are – they're the best they could ever be. If there was a dramatic change in the law and everyone could have their adopted kids back, I wouldn't. It'd be a really cruel thing to do to Ben – and to Lois and Grant. I'm very happy with the way it is. Even though they are living further away, I know I can still have contact easily. I can ring or write to Ben. I've known them all this time and things are unlikely to change.

They have stayed with us several times. We're totally different people and yet it doesn't matter, certainly not to me. Politically we are different and in other things – I'm into horoscopes and they think it's a load of bull. They're communists – I was told that before I met them – and it doesn't matter. Ben can make up his own mind when he gets older. He can be religious, he can be a communist – it doesn't matter. It's funny but things have come out in Ben that they haven't instilled in him – like he's interested in horoscopes and witches and that sort of thing, just like me.

Ben used to cry when Lois went out to work but once she was out of sight he'd be OK. All kids are like that though, and it didn't bother me. He'd always stop crying once she'd gone.

I don't know anyone else in my situation. The older ones might never talk about it and the younger ones are taking the easy way out. But I don't think that's always fair on the children. I'm sure if everyone could have open adoption it'd be better on the children in lots of cases. They might then choose this way. My friends know about it and think it's great. He's my parents' only grandchild. But closed adoption must be like a death and you'd always be wondering, every day, every year, not even knowing if the child was alive.

I'd like my husband to be closer to Ben. He can be quite strict with him sometimes, but Ben doesn't seem to mind. He does join in and things, so it's OK. And he doesn't stop me from seeing him or anything. One of my brothers is very close to Ben. Lois thinks they look alike. They get on very well. My mother is very close to Ben as well and spoils him rotten. I guess we all do in our own way.

I know that open adoption isn't a legal agreement, and that they could cut me off at any time. I have thought about it from time to time. If that happened I would have to accept it and be happy with the time I've had with Ben. He knows who I am and could contact me later if he wanted to. I don't think shared parenting and having equal rights as a parent would be right either. That would be like fostering and it would be confusing for a child. They should be able to bring up the child as they like. The birth parents shouldn't interfere. It's important that everyone goes into open adoption with an open mind. I for one certainly wouldn't want to change things from the way they are.

Tom – Ben's Birth Grandfather

Ben was born on November 15th and we saw him just after Christmas. Lois first brought him over on Christmas Day. It was great. I never expected her to do that. She asked me if I'd like to feed him and she brought out the bottle. I just couldn't believe it. I didn't expect that would happen. She's always been giving like that. Then they extended the invitation to come round any time and we've had regular access to him ever since. It's great being able to maintain contact. It's worked out fantastically well – for all of us. He calls me 'grandad'.

Lois

Lois and her husband Grant wanted a fully open adoption after talking to adopted people and other adoptive parents. This was long before it was common practice among the white (Pakeha) population in New Zealand. Grant, in particular, wanted openness for the child's sake.

*Lois was very apprehensive to begin with, as openness challenges tra-
ditional ideas about the need for secrecy. She was fearful of becoming
marginalised by the birth mother and that the child might love her less.
But getting to know the birth family as people changed all that.*

Heather was expecting to have a traditional adoption where there
would be no contact. When we knew we were able to adopt a child
we spoke to quite a lot of people who had adopted children, or
who'd been adopted, and also to people who'd relinquished
children for adoption. With the exception of one person, all the
adoptees wished they knew why they'd been adopted, and who
they were and where they came from. The exception was a woman
who was hostile to her birth mother. So my husband suggested
we keep in touch with the birth mother. I was horrified to start
with because I was afraid she might usurp my rights – take over
my role. I had visions of her being more important to my child
than I was. It was irrational really, but that was how I felt. I then
tried to put myself in the other person's shoes and realised it'd
be great to know what was happening to the child.

Then we had news that we were getting this baby. We sent letters
to her saying we'd like to keep in touch and for her to see her son
from time to time. At first we imagined it would be a couple of
times a year, but it grew quickly into a very strong friendship. To
start with she said, 'I'll just be his auntie – I'll call myself auntie,'
but that's been dropped quickly and he's known who she is since
he was a toddler.

I described her to him as his birth mother – the woman who
gave him his life and who was strong enough to give him a
chance of having a family as she wasn't married. I've told Ben how
brave she was and how difficult it would have been for her to bring
him up as she would have been a single parent. It's not been hard
to be positive about her, because she's really lovely.

Our friends were flabbergasted at the idea of a fully open adoption,
as it was 1980 and not really underway as a practice. I think they
thought we were strange and that I was a bit mad. But one of my
brothers said he was really proud of me and thought I had great
lateral thinking! I didn't think it was that odd and although I was
a bit worried about it at first, that has long since gone.

If I hadn't known Heather I think I might have been very
anxious just walking down the street wondering if that woman
was Ben's mother. I would always have wondered whether that
boy was his brother, whether their child looked similar to our child.

That was in my mind while we were waiting to get Ben, actually – how I'd cope with not knowing who he was. So knowing who he is has been a great relief.

It's made it very easy bringing him up, because as it's open he's very aware of the whole thing – he's got no doubts about himself as far as his identity goes. In fact he's quite proud of the fact that he's got so many grandparents and uncles. None of my family is nearby – they all live in the South Island, so it's quite a blessing for Ben because it's like an extended family which he wouldn't otherwise have had.

I don't feel threatened by the idea that Heather might interfere in the parenting. When I met her again in her home on Christmas Day, she made it very clear to me that I was his mother and she wouldn't do anything to upset that. We talked about it and she was very clear. That relaxed me straight away. It's never been a problem. Although she's always been there quite a lot – and she's very proud of Ben – she's never pushed herself or hindered me in any way. I don't mind her having as much contact with him as she wants, because she's always been so careful about my feelings the whole way through. She's been marvellous about it. She doesn't have any children yet – but Ben can't wait. He's ten and he's our only child.

It's not confusing for him to understand who is related to who and it never has been. I'm his mother and all of his birth family have always been there for him. Kids just accept everybody. They don't sit down and try and work out who's who. He accepts them as part of his life. He does have a very strong bond with his birth mother, but if he fell over it would be me he ran to, not Heather.

I don't think he loves me any the less because his birth mother is around. He's very proud of what we did for him. He tells his friends about mum and how we let him see his birth mother and how she's important. I don't think he loves us any the less. I think kids just expand on their love.

Knowing his birth family has helped us in lots of different ways and has made quite a few things easier for us. Ben has had a few problems with dyslexia and has also had quite severe asthma, and we were able to trace that to the family background. If we hadn't known that, we'd have wondered what else was going to pop up. The letter we received from Welfare was very sketchy and included only a small paragraph on the birth parents. It was nothing to go on. That's probably more than adoptive parents used to get. It's good for Ben. It means he also knows his grandfather and is very proud of the fact that he's from Scotland. So he sees a strong link there.

As soon as we met Heather and got to know her she made it very easy for us to accept open adoption. She's a nice, honest, relaxed person. And the fact that we wanted her to know Ben means that she thinks we're great too. So we have a really good relationship. She selected us from a lot of couples. She visualised us both in uniform and thought we'd be great. She got my husband's job wrong but had made up her mind.

The social workers came round quite casually every few months after we'd been approved. We waited four years after being approved to get Ben. They told us that of those who apply, only one couple in 15 is successful, so we are very lucky to have a child. That was in 1980. It must be impossible now.

It was good that we had the birth family's approval. All I kept thinking about was the baby and Heather – and I was really quite sad for her. I was very aware of how she must be feeling. We were terribly excited, but I was also sad for her. There were two sets of feelings going on at the same time.

I know she hasn't any legal status as the birth mother, but I don't think there's any way round that because if we were tied together by law and something had gone wrong with our relationship it could have been very difficult. Shared parenting or guardianship might have been awkward if our relationship hadn't worked out.

I think our arrangement is the best thing we have ever done for Ben. He knows who he is. He's got no worries about himself at all. My husband had his mind made up from the beginning that we should keep in touch with his birth mother for his sake, and it didn't take me long to see that this was the best thing we could have done.

In my profession I have nursed quite a few adopted people with medical problems. They've got this big blankness behind them and it is quite a problem for them. One adoptive mother came into Waikato Hospital frequently with her adopted child who had terrible asthma attacks. She had no idea of the history and said she wished she knew more of the child's background – she was quite sad about it.

We never expected our son to be very like us and we didn't mind what he looked like. Strangely enough, he looks very like us – he doesn't look like his birth mother at all. He's got our colouring and our build, but I don't think that's very important. It doesn't change the way I feel.

At the moment he's having difficulty achieving and I just hope he'll achieve his best. He's also a bedwetter, which is something in his family – his uncles were too until quite late – so it's good to know that he'll grow out of it eventually. We just hope he'll reach his full potential, and we don't mind what he becomes. But knowing that there are problems there, we can just accept them.

I have talked with people who have closed adoptions and they seem quite indignant when I say that Ben has contact with his birth family. They feel the adopted child is theirs. We don't see it like that. We see ourselves as being responsible for him until he can take care of himself. We care about him tremendously. But people who deny the child is adopted are trying to pretend the child is something he isn't, and that's very artificial. Perhaps they're trying to deny their own infertility – I'm not sure. I think secrecy surrounding adoption is a hangover from the old days, and tied up with property laws as well.

Knowing Ben's birth family has given us so much. We were invited to Heather's wedding, Ben included. Everyone was completely open and appeared to be very comfortable with it, Heather as well. We've got lots of photos of her and Ben. Her husband likes Ben and makes him feel very welcome. We see ourselves as part of Heather's family and her family as part of ours. We're always invited there for Christmas and birthdays. On Mother's Day we always give Heather a gift to remind her that we're really pleased that she gave us Ben – and she always gives me a gift, which is lovely – and a Mother's Day gift from Ben. Heather's parents are his grandparents and that's what he calls them. They are very proud of him too. I think having to share Ben with the other set of grandparents was a little difficult for my husband's parents at first, as they'd waited a long time to have a grandchild. But that's long since been resolved.

Ben

Ben was quite happy to talk to me about knowing his birth family. I met him and his adoptive mother Lois in a rather noisy café in the centre of Auckland. Ben was on his way from there down to Hamilton, about 90 miles south, to stay with his birth mother. This was the second consecutive weekend he'd been and he said he was really looking forward to it.

I'm ten years old. Mum said you wanted to talk to me about seeing my birth family, 'cos children in England don't do that as much as in New Zealand.

I'm really glad I know my birth family because it means I've got two families to take care of me. So once one family has died I've still got the other one. It also means I can have lots of holidays with them all as well.

I'm with Lois and Grant because Heather got divorced and then she had me so she had to adopt me to another family. Then Lois said Heather could know me and she thought that was great.

I'd be sad if I didn't know Heather and her family. It helps me understand that people in the world are the same as me. I suppose it wouldn't worry me if I didn't know them, but it's really good that I do. I enjoy going to stay with Heather. Since we've moved away I stay with her in the holidays. There's some things I can do the same as Heather, like bending back my thumb, but I don't look much like her. We both like the same things though. I like strange clothes and hot food like chillies, and so does Heather.

I don't get muddled up knowing my birth mother. My mum is Lois but I'm glad I know Heather. I'm glad I know where my real mum is in the world. I can love them both. Heather's husband isn't my dad and I don't think he likes me saying he is. I've got enough love for both of them and it's not hard at all.

I wouldn't like to have to wait till I was 18 before I could know my birth family. That's not fair, because when you're really wanting to see someone or do something it's hard to just wait. Heather's always been there and that's good. And I can know my family – if I have brothers or sisters I can know them too.

And Heather's family are my relations – my grandparents and uncles. I'm the only grandchild. It's good they know me too. It wouldn't be fair for them to have to wait till I was 18 before they could know me.

I think I'm lucky to have two mums and dads. Other kids in my school who are adopted know their birth families as well. They think they're really lucky to know them too.

Last Christmas all my family came to our house – all my grand-parents, my uncles – all my birth family and mum and dad's families too. It was great. And I had stacks of presents!

At my new school my friends wanted to meet my birth mother when I told them about her. They wanted to buy her something special.

I see Heather as my special friend.

13 Ann

I had already interviewed the adoptive parents of Ann's daughter when I was in Auckland. Ann lives in Wellington with her partner and two young children whom she has had since relinquishing her first child for adoption.

Ann was very clear that she wanted her daughter to have a better life than she could offer her at the time, and that her gift of a child to the adoptive parents she chose for her daughter meant that they would be agreeable to her having contact while her daughter was growing up. Ann stipulated what she wanted for her child of mixed parentage (Maori/European) including the adopters to be present at the birth.

I was three months pregnant when I went to Welfare. It was 1982. I had been in a stable relationship living with the father, but things didn't work out. I had nowhere to live after I left him. My father was an alcoholic and my mother was continually nagging him – it wasn't a place to bring up a baby. I could see myself stuck on benefit and in a state house and the child being six or seven and me blaming her for the situation. I felt she deserved a good shot at life. So I went to Welfare and said what I wanted – stipulating things like wanting her to learn Maori; her father is Maori and there is Maori blood way back in my own family. Also I wanted the couple to be around my own age, as well as be prepared to be at the birth, because I believe that the first hold is your bond. In the meantime I made lots of clothes for the baby, as I felt there was no way I'd hand over a baby to someone and not contribute in any way.

Eventually Welfare showed me a file of a couple from Keri Keri – not in my area and miles up north – and asked if I minded where the child lived and if I wanted to have contact later on. I said that decision would be made after the child was born, as I wouldn't know how I felt till then. I was happy to have openness but wouldn't force it on them, but I wanted to know what was happening to her as she grew up. No way was I going to cry forever over a child that in the law's eyes never existed ... that you're just supposed to forget about. No way was that going to happen – I'd seen it happen before. The social worker was keen on openness and had had some successes.

I got myself all dressed up to meet them and make a good impression and they arrived in their jeans! I had my bag of clothes and mum had done some knitting. Two and a half hours later we were still sitting there talking. They were great. They couldn't have found better people. Cheryl was into spinning and weaving and they lived in the country ...

It was my mother's first grandchild and the whole thing upset her quite a bit. I wanted her to meet Cheryl and Bill, but she's very emotional so I didn't take her with me. I didn't want to embarrass them. I had to think about them too. Mum couldn't have looked after the baby. She isn't very patient with kids and she's 67. But it wasn't just that, or lack of finances. I wanted her to have a good shot at life, a stable home where she had a mother and father. I've seen too many people who'd kept their kids and regretted it. And kids asking questions about their fathers.

My boyfriend's sister wanted the baby. She couldn't have children. But I felt if she had her I'd never see her again, and that she would cut me off. Also I didn't really like them. And I thought what I was doing for them wouldn't have been appreciated. I would have been giving them the baby they couldn't have. They've split up now anyway, so maybe I had a sixth sense about them.

The arrangement was for me to ring the adoption worker when I went into labour and she'd ring them. But after two false alarms I phoned them myself. I had two friends with me and they were great. Cheryl and Bill were waiting as well. He chickened out and came in just after she was born. But Cheryl was really great and very supportive, saying, 'Come on now Ann, we want to see what this is,' and helping me. The staff were totally confused. I told them what was happening, that Cheryl was adopting the baby and that she was to be given the baby to hold when she was born. After she was born they went to give her to me and I said, 'No. Here you are, Cheryl.' She held her and said she was beautiful. I didn't actually hold her until that night after they'd gone. My friend kept saying, 'Oh, Ann, isn't she lovely? What are you going to do?' Then my uncle arrived and that was neat. I let Cheryl ring mum as I thought she had to ring someone and tell them she's got a baby girl! They had spoken on the phone before.

Then the nurses took me out of the delivery room and it was as if I didn't exist. They were trying to decide which ward to put me in and where to put the baby. I asked them what they were saying and they said they didn't know whether the baby should be in the same ward as me. I said, 'Hang on. This is my baby you're talking about and I'll be taking care of her while her other parents aren't here.' So I used to go down to the nursery and feed her and so on. But I got quite frightened that something might happen to her while I was looking after her and I'd have to tell Cheryl and Bill. She wasn't my baby – she was theirs.

The hospital had a room set aside for adoptive parents to learn to care for the baby and have some time alone with it. But it got to the stage where I'd take over when they went to lunch and so on. I was only in hospital for a couple of days. I asked Cheryl if I could show Huia, the baby, to some very special people. She wasn't just someone who was going to disappear off the face of the earth. I was proud of her – she was a lovely little baby. And she's a real neat little kid. An aunt came to visit her. She'd made something for her and put it in her cot, and got very tearful as her daughter had given up a child and didn't have any idea where it was. So it brought back a lot of memories for her. Then my grandmother wanted to meet the baby ... her twenty-seventh great-grandchild!

Cheryl and Bill were fine about it; none of their friends were there as they lived up north. Her family had been down and were not keen on me seeing them. I was a little bit hurt that I wasn't introduced to them, but I had to respect Cheryl and Bill. It turns out that we've got a good rapport with the whole family now. Also at that time I had ten days to change my mind.

I bought them a big bunch of flowers and a 'congratulations on your little daughter' card for them. Then I asked the hospital to remove my name from the cot and replace it with theirs. I was a bit worried that the baby's father's family might snatch her or something and I would've hated anything like that to happen to her. Also I kept saying to them, 'Don't worry, I'm not going to change my mind.' I was so happy with them and I could see how proud they were of the baby that I went to the lawyer's on the ninth day – but I had to wait till the next day before I could sign the papers.

I bought Huia a present that she would have all her life. I also wrote her a letter explaining to her why I didn't keep her. I said to Cheryl that just in case we don't carry on this friendship I want her to be given this so she knows why. I don't want her to grow up thinking I didn't want her.

It was as if they were friends I'd known for years and they'd had a baby. That's how I felt. They were a little bit reserved to start with. I think they were frightened that I was going to change my mind in those ten days. It did lay a little bit of pressure on me, but I kept telling them it was OK and when Cheryl admired the flowers and the card and the change of name I said, 'She's your baby and she should have your name on her cot.' I did all these things to reassure them. I'd had six months to get myself sorted out for this and I had a lot of support from the adoption worker. She was great and I could contact her at any time.

The open adoption situation just happened. It just flowed. I'd said to them I'd love some photos and I'd like a letter to know how she was getting on, but we didn't have any worked out arrangements. I'd taken lots of photos of us all at the hospital when Huia was eight days old.

I didn't know their surname to start with, but when they left it for me in case I needed to get in touch when I went into labour (for the second time) I felt they trusted me. And I felt very good about that. They had also explained that Bill was adopted at birth and was looking for his birth mother and that's why they wanted the openness. So I knew it was going to happen. I guess it was an invitation from them. I didn't want to put pressure on them. I said I'd love to see her as she was growing up – I could travel up there or they could come to me, which is what's happened. I think they understood how I would probably feel.

I got photos and letters from them and wrote back. It's not as if she's disappeared. It's as if our family's grown. And it's turned out uncannily that Cheryl and Tama, my partner, are cousins on his father's side. And also that his mother and Cheryl's were both founding members of a Maori culture group in Wellington and are friends!

When she was 13 months old they said they were coming down here. So we got my granny and mum, dad and sister and her baby together ... everyone was happy. It was neat seeing her. She was shy. And walking! I felt great meeting her. I was quite proud of her. And I didn't have any regrets because I could see she was happy – and I was happy for them all. Sometimes I feel so proud of her and what she's achieved. She's bilingual. I want to show her off. I couldn't have done what they have done – I could never have given her the opportunities that she's had, but

I'm very, very proud of her. I've seen her on average once a year and had lots of letters and photos. She'll be seven this year. Once we visited them and they looked after my three-month-old while we went out. Huia was delighted to see her brother – 'our other brother', as she calls him.

Tama, being a Maori, couldn't understand how I could just give a child away. I said I didn't just give her away. I handpicked them. But I said he'd find out when he met them. We stayed with them for two or three nights. It was good. I did feel sometimes while I was there that I was encroaching a bit on their lives – maybe we didn't want to overpower each other. And at that stage they had another child, Tom. We've now got Hutta, our second son, who's 16 months old. Huia hasn't seen him yet.

There are some people who don't agree with what I did. I've spoken to people about it, including prospective adoptive parents at meetings. The first meeting was when Huia was four months old. At one meeting when I went in they asked how many were in favour of open adoption and it was about half. When I left, the majority of them were in favour. I was able to explain that this is possible, and for me my daughter hasn't just disappeared, like so many who don't know where their children are, or how they are. If I hadn't had openness I probably would've been very different – a 'cot case', very emotional and very uptight. I would never have known where she was ... it would've been something that happened for nothing.

I don't think they would ever withdraw contact. I don't think they're that sort. I know them. I think Cheryl puts a lot of importance on my family having contact with Huia. She was really concerned when I told her mum was in hospital and they didn't know what the matter was. I asked if they could prepare to bring the children down ... mum looks on Tom as family too. His birth mother doesn't have contact, even though Cheryl and Bill want it. He was the result of an affair and she was apparently given an ultimatum by her husband – either get rid of this child, or you lose your other two sons and husband. So Cheryl and Bill have experienced both sides of adoption. They are very lucky people. They've got two children about 15 months apart. They're very lucky.

Having my other two children was a very different experience from having Huia as I was in a stable relationship. Tama told me he couldn't have kids, so that's how the first one arrived! They're special, but she's just as special. There's jewellery that will go to

Huia when I die which was passed down to me by my grandmother. And I would like her to have it.

When people ask how many kids I have, I say three. I've got a little girl living in Auckland. Huia calls me Ann, but I think she knows who I am. I must ask Cheryl next time. She calls my mother nana Rose. She arrives here in Wellington tonight and I'd really like to be able to say to them 'Can I take her home for a couple of days?' But then I have to think that Cheryl's family are down here and haven't seen her for a long time either. She has to be shared around. But Cheryl says she can't wait for the time when she can put her on a plane and send her to me for the holidays. Great!

Huia wants a pony. I rode horses when I was younger and my father was a jockey – and his father. It's in her blood. I'd said to them when she was born, 'Don't be surprised if she wants a pony.' She loves animals, like me, always rescuing them like I did. People say to me she's got my eyes. She's also interested in the same things as me, like animals. And she's very interested in the Maori culture. Obviously she's very young as yet.

I don't feel I need legal rights to see my daughter – we've got that rapport. I feel that anyone who relinquishes a child for adoption has done those adoptive parents a hell of a favour. The child is a gift, something they could never have. And I feel that too often adoptive parents are very selfish. They are also very frightened. They're terrified that maybe the child will say they don't love them any more. But that won't happen. You can't just cut off the love your adoptive parents have given you and vice versa. And how can you love someone you've never known?

I would never interfere. I think of them as my extended family and would never put them through that. How could I do that? I'm quite happy with my own family, with the contact I have with Huia, and I'm happy with Huia. I can't fault them. They're not like strangers – they're just like family. When it's birthdays or Christmas we buy presents for Tom as well as Huia. We don't just favour her.

And surely it's better while the child is growing up to have that person around so he or she can go and talk to them. It can solve a lot more problems than a person who may have a name but doesn't exist. For children in the closed system there must always be questions. But if they know their birth family, they know what they look like, they know their brothers and sisters (Bill has just found out he's got brothers!), it must make them more stable

– emotionally and physically. My daughter is growing up *knowing* who she is.

I am quite happy with the contact I have. I only ask that I have contact. I see myself as her mother – I'm just not her 'mother, mother' I'm her 'other mother', and she's my daughter. Cheryl is her first mother and I'm her second. If anything happened to Cheryl, like she dies or something, I would hope Huia would be able to come and talk to me and that I would be able to give her the same advice as Cheryl would.

There's a lot of people involved – all my family and Tama's and her adoptive parents' families too. And we've all been able to build up a relationship by getting to know each other. And building up trust as well. I think that was a fear initially. Cheryl's mother was worried I might change my mind and her daughter would be hurt. That's why it's important to get to know each other. Actually she [the grandmother] was down here with Tom recently and not Huia, but we all met up anyway at Cheryl's brother's place.

I think prospective adoptive parents should be told, 'This woman is doing you a favour ... giving you something you can't have. So instead of just taking the child, how about thinking of her as well?'

Huia is everybody's child – she belongs to all of us. She could never say that nobody loves her. There's loads of us!

I don't have any regrets. None whatsoever. If I'd kept her I might not have had these two lovely kids I've got now, and I probably would have still been on my own, a solo mother on benefit. And she would have missed out on heaps.

Cheryl and Bill

Through my family, I got to know of these adoptive parents who live in Auckland. They were friends of friends. I was a bit apprehensive about ringing them 'cold', as I knew virtually nothing about them and vice versa. However, they were very happy to see me.

Their experience of adoption covers every angle – Bill, the adoptive father, was adopted as a baby; Cheryl grew up in the Maori tradition of complete openness where relatives were concerned; and they have adopted two children, Huia and Tom. They have met both birth mothers of their children, but have continuing contact with only one of them.

Cheryl: It was probably my idea to have contact with the birth parents, as my mother was adopted by an auntie and it was open. Also I had a younger brother who was adopted and he always knew who his mother was. So I'd grown up in a situation where there was no fear or threat in openness. I'd seen it work and there was no threat to the person adopting the child. It was a Maori situation, so it wasn't uncommon. I thought it was very positive and healthy.

Bill: I probably had slightly more reservations about it, as I'd had no experience of it. I'm adopted myself and there was no openness then. But as I've got to know Ann I was sure it was the right thing. It was a gradual process.

Cheryl: The social worker approached us when Ann was about five months pregnant. Ann was given files of prospective parents to look at, including us, to choose whoever she wanted to meet. So we sent more information through the social worker to her. She did consider other couples, but I think they were older.

Bill: She chose us straight off, it seems, subject to meeting us. We were living in the country at the time and I think that helped. Apparently her mind was made up at six months.

Cheryl: As far as being chosen goes, I think it was always a situation of not quite believing. Even when we met Ann and right up to the birth, there was always the possibility that she would change her mind. And there's the ten-day period when the baby is in the hospital and legally they don't become yours until that time has elapsed. I think basically I protected myself from thinking the baby was mine until I felt that Ann was sure.

Bill: We did have a very good social worker, but that was before we went down to meet Ann. We didn't have any counselling at that time. Ann had excellent help from her social worker and we got to know her as well. We're still in touch with her to a limited extent.

Cheryl: Basically there was no counselling for us. The support was there for the birth mother. And her social worker was excellent. Ann was 26 when she had Huia and had really thought things out herself. Her family was very supportive too.

Bill: We met her mother and have become quite good friends and close to her. Her name's Rose. So Huia's got quite a few nanas. And she's her first grandchild.

Cheryl: We first met Ann just before she gave birth. We went down to Wellington to be at the birth.

Bill: She seemed to have things sorted out in her own mind. She was a very open person and made it clear she liked us there and then. And we liked her. So it was a good relationship from the start and quite easy.

Cheryl: Yes, there was that instant thing, liking – I think what was important for me was that she liked us straight off and that made me start to like her. I wasn't sure how I was going to feel about her.

Ann had specified that she wanted the adoptive mother to take Huia from birth and was to be there during the birth. I think she felt it was a very special time – that it was important for me to be there – and I think she was right. They're the moments you never have again with a child. I'd never been at a birth before, so it was neat!

We cared for Huia in the hospital for the ten days. They actually gave us a flat in the end and put the baby in with us, so everybody was really supportive. Ann saw Huia whenever she wanted to and she showed her to her family. It was a really hard time for her – she cried a lot. But she never lessened in her resolve. That first year must have been really difficult for her. She contacted us a lot during the first year and she needed the contact.

I understood it but I felt it was almost a burden ... that she was relying on me too much to support her, but then I understood it and it lessened. So it was OK. I think if it had intensified it would've been different. I suppose eventually I would've got in touch with her social worker to see if she could help.

I remember Huia's first birthday. I got really depressed and upset because it seemed that we had her at someone else's expense ... the cost to someone else had actually been quite high ... and on her birthday it really focused my mind back to what had happened, back to Ann. There was a lot of sadness there. I just couldn't feel happy on her first birthday, I could only think about the consequences of what had happened. But that has changed, because Ann is feeling so much better.

Bill: She's in a happy, stable relationship now and has two nice children. She contacts us reasonably regularly and we write to her and we see each other. They come and stay when they're up here. And Huia and Tom are going to spend a week with them soon. So that's great. We're really pleased. It's always been an open invitation anyway. It'll be the first time Huia's been to stay with them by herself and she's now at an age where she's quite happy to be more independent.

Cheryl: Huia does seem a bit confused in her thinking about Ann and me.

Bill: She doesn't see them as two mums, she sees Cheryl as mum and she knows she's come out of Ann's tummy. Now she's thoughtful about things when she sees Ann sometimes ... just like any kid really, she'll give it a moment's reflection and then burst outside back to the swing.

Cheryl: I'm not sure she's got the full picture yet. We've discussed it on occasions, explained it – but whether or not she understands, I'm not sure.

Bill: Since the adoption, we've had the three statutory visits from the social worker, just to see how things are going, and she was confident in us.

Cheryl: We never felt we were being assessed or there was any pressure on us, but our assessment was weird! After we made our application we had a visit from two Welfare workers. It was this heavy-duty number where they tried to put us off adopting. They gave us all the negative statistics. I didn't believe what they were doing at the time! I had a friend sitting in the next room and she could hear everything! They asked my why I wanted to adopt – and was it a good enough reason? They really gave me the third degree!

Bill's Personal Experience of Adoption

Bill: I grew up in the closed system of adoption. I didn't have any contact until recently.

My own experience was that mum and dad just told me my birth name. It was a good adoption, they were a good family, so it was more of a curiosity than a major concern. It wasn't really until I started adopting our kids that I began thinking about it more, and started searching two years ago.

I found my mother had died. That was really upsetting at the time as I was expecting to find her. But I found two brothers and a sister in the process who were also adopted out by the same mother. So we've got together in Wellington a few times. It's been quite amazing!

Cheryl: She died in 1966 at the age of 36. She was having a fifth baby and tried to abort herself. She died haemorrhaging.

Bill: That was eleven years after the last one of us was born. I was the second youngest.

It's been exciting getting to know each other, although one of us doesn't want to know, which is a shame, but the other three of us keep in constant touch. Three of us had been tracing. The oldest one, who's not that interested in us, it seems, started off. He didn't find any of us but found our birth mother had died and then found her sister. Then I started, with a lot of help from Cheryl, and couldn't find anything, but eventually did make some progress with Jigsaw in Auckland. At the same time, another brother in Dunedin was searching – and on a similar course to me. We came together bit by bit. Then Social Welfare said there's another child here somewhere. So we found him – that was the oldest and we met in Hamilton. Then Auntie Ruby, our birth mother's sister, said there was also a daughter somewhere. We didn't find her then, but we did find another brother. He was trying to find us.

One brother had written to our Auntie Ruby for information and we called in to see her the day after! She's found it quite hard to cope with all of us. She knows quite a bit but only lets out a little bit of information at a time. I think she thinks we'll write her sister off as a scarlet woman as well, no matter how we try to reassure her that that is not the way we think at all. But we can't convince her.

Cheryl: When the law changed here a flood of people started looking for their parents, but there was a lot of scaremongering and quoting obscure cases, and children always turning up on the doorstep! But I think the thing that convinced me was that I had a younger brother who was adopted and he was my cousin's baby. She had him when she was 16 and still at school. He grew up always in contact and knowing who his mother was. He grew up having the same amount of affection for her that you'd have for, say, an auntie. His love was for the woman who'd brought him up.

I think there is a lot of fear. When Bill started looking for his birth mother, his adoptive mother didn't handle it very well; she knew she was being silly, but she felt that he was hers and she didn't want to share him with anyone else.

Bill: She wasn't like that while I was growing up. She was happy to talk about what she knew, but she never actively encouraged us to go out and look. But once I did start, she couldn't handle it. But I carried on. A lot of people I know haven't told their adoptive parents in case it diminishes their relationship. They feel they can't discuss it with them. And it's a cultural difference too. I've really noticed that. There's much more equality in relationships in Maori culture between parents and children.

Tom – *aged five*

Cheryl: He doesn't have any contact with his birth mother, unfortunately. It doesn't seem to bother him much at this stage. He's aware of who Ann is, and Ann and her family have always treated him as if he's one of theirs too. They treat them both equally – what they do for one they'll do for the other. So that's good.

Bill: We've only met Tom's birth mother, Kathy, briefly, once. She had two older boys, about seven and eight – both really handsome. So is Tom. It's a shame he'll grow up not knowing them.

Cheryl: We met her when Tom was four weeks old. He'd gone to a foster home after the birth and it was really through the urging of the social worker that we met – in the botanical gardens. We had Tom at that stage and she wanted to meet us once and to see him once more. The meeting was very strange ... sort of clandestine, by the rose bushes.

Bill: It's a shame. She and her husband split up and she met this other guy and got pregnant with Tom. Then they decided to get back together again and he said the baby has got to go. Amazing conditions! I don't know how things have turned out for her.

Cheryl: She didn't specify a name for the baby, so we called him Tom. Huia's mum wanted Michelle in her name somewhere. His adoption had already been arranged, but they turned him down as he was too dark. That's why there was a four-week delay. In many ways it might have been a godsend, as it's better for kids to be in a family where there's lots of Maori contact. Cultural links are very important and particularly where there's a mixed marriage like ours ... and Tom feeling different having a Pakeha [white] father. Both the children are part-Maori.

Bill: It's a shame we're not in touch with her. It would be nice for Tom to see her and vice versa. I expect it's going to be more difficult for him not knowing his birth mother. But we'll try and make contact with her again later on. It was definitely good to meet her, even though it was only once; I'll never forget her, or her two boys.

14 Sue and Trevor

I was given Sue and Trevor's name by an organisation called Parent to Parent Information on Adoption Services who hold a register of families who have an open adoption in England and are willing to be contacted by other parents, etc.

They were quite happy to talk to me and welcomed me into their sitting room where there were lots of photos of their three children, Leanne aged five and a half, their baby Jake and two-year-old Nathan whom they relinquished for adoption six months after his birth. Sue mostly spoke for them.

We were 25 and 26 respectively when we had Nathan in 1988. Our daughter Leanne was four at the time. We were over the moon when we were told, after a long and hard labour, that we had a little boy. He was blue at birth, which didn't particularly worry me, and they said they'd give him a bit of oxygen in the Special Care Unit and left us to recover. About three hours later they returned and took us to a small, private room and I started thinking then that something must be wrong. Then they took us to the Special Care Unit and he was in an incubator with wires all over him and he looked lovely and pink and I thought, 'We can probably take him home now.' Then they said, 'The doctor would like to have a word with you, because he's got a few problems.' I immediately thought it must be heart problems. They took us into a little room with a nurse sitting on my side and the doctor on Trevor's and they said, 'Would you like to hold the baby?' and straight away I said, 'No.' I was putting up barriers and knew something must be wrong. But Trevor held the baby and kept trying to give him to me, but I wouldn't hold him at all. I couldn't hold him. If I loved him and there was something wrong it'd be better to keep away from him. I don't know why. And then the nurse grabbed hold of my hand and I thought, 'Oh, what are they going to tell us?' And he said, 'What do you think is wrong with your baby?' And I said, 'Heart.' Then he asked us whether we could see what was wrong and I immediately thought of Down's syndrome as that's the only handicap you can see. It hit me then. It felt like I floated up to the corner of the room and I was looking down on everybody and I couldn't hear what was being said. I remember saying to the nurse, 'Let him die.' I thought Down's syndrome was the end of the world. I know now it's not, but at the time I thought, 'He can't live like that, he's not going to have any sort of life.' I know now it's one of the mildest handicaps you can have. I wonder if I'd known all that I know now whether I'd have kept him. Two years on if they'd told me my next son was Down's I wouldn't have got rid of him.

My picture of a Down's then was someone really fat with their tongue hanging out – that's how I've seen them in institutions. It was the worst possible thing that could happen having this little baby grow up like that, and straight away I built up this barrier and I was frightened to death of him. I wouldn't see him. The nurses told me he wasn't going to die, so I said, 'Don't make me take him home then.' I don't know why I said that 'cos I love him to death now and I love all babies. I want to protect them and can't understand how people can let them go and yet I've done it.

We were so unprepared for it. There was a lot of help afterwards. The hospital social worker came the next day and saw us huddled up on the one chair and said, 'You'll make it. It's when you're on opposite sides of the room that I think you're going to have problems. But you'll get through this. Whether you keep the baby or not is a different matter.' She gave us lots of help and advice and books. When I came home I had two social workers visit me – one to tell me about adoption and the other what would happen if we decided to keep him. We went to the schools, we met lots of families and spent hours with them, all in that first week home. It was very helpful. But it was a bit onesided as we weren't put in touch with anyone who didn't keep their baby. So it felt like the emphasis was on that.

We were absolutely exhausted. We couldn't sleep and were given something to help us. I couldn't think straight. The baby was in hospital. He stayed there for a week. We did go and see him a few times and so did all the family. Then they said they had a foster family and I didn't want him to go there. I said I didn't know what I wanted to do yet. But either he had to come home or go into temporary care. I kept changing my mind. I wanted him and then I didn't. But we needed a breathing space.

I wanted to bring him home but something kept stopping me. All the way through the pregnancy I felt something was wrong. I wouldn't do the baby's room or get anything ready, not even a pushchair. Every time I'd say to Leanne, 'It won't be long and we'll have the baby,' and then I'd think I shouldn't have said that. At first we were going to tell her he died. We were told we couldn't say that. We spoke to the child psychologist, who said we had to be open with her and that way she'll accept it. She couldn't accept the fact that he wasn't coming home, nor could her cousins. Yet they're brilliant now. She tells everyone about her brother and they don't know what's she's on about. But she's had to cope with a lot and it's made her very grown up. She met some Down's children and understands they do need a lot of help.

It's affected us in different ways. I needed to talk about it all the time. Trevor's very quiet. He was working in a shop with ladies and they wouldn't talk about it with him at all. I think if he'd carried on working there, he'd have had a nervous breakdown. People don't know what to say. I used to cross the road rather than talk to people and they'd do the same. I was so unprepared. I felt like a child – I just didn't know how to cope with it. I wanted someone to help us. It felt like everyone would've agreed to anything we said – bring him home, leave him at the foster parents, anything. We didn't know what to do.

We decided at six months to go for adoption. We could've stopped it at any time. We were told that. Apparently Nathan went into a *Be My Family* magazine and there were over 100 families that applied for him. Everyone wants a new baby. I just wanted him to bond with a mother. It's such a special part, being a tiny baby, and it felt to me like he was in limbo. So I wanted the social worker to find him someone quick. If they couldn't and he had to go into an institution, I said I'd have him.

We said we wanted him to be in a family where there were other children, possibly another Down's child. The social worker did mention open adoption, but we didn't really know what that meant. I think at the time we felt that if we were the adoptive parents we wouldn't want the natural family visiting, although it might be slightly different with a handicapped child. Maybe it was also a way of protecting ourselves emotionally. Every time we saw him I'd be really high and the next day I'd get really down again.

When he was about six months old I began seeing a psychiatrist. I couldn't sleep. I couldn't eat. I thought about him constantly.

Everything I did was connected to him. I idolised him. He was in my mind all the time. We weren't seeing anyone then. The social worker came round occasionally but we were left to get on with it. We were advised to see the Community Psychiatric Nurse and he helped to put Nathan back in perspective – as a baby, not a god. So that was helpful and I saw him for quite a long time, until I was seven months pregnant with my next child. I was so terrified he'd be Down's as well – and was too scared to even look at him. Looking back, if I could've held Nathan and cuddled him and we'd been able to have a few hours with him as soon as he was born and then they'd have told me, my decision might have been different. By then, he'd have been my baby. But this way I'd seen him once when he was born and I was on pethidine so it was hazy. Then later I held him once but I couldn't believe he was my baby. I was sure they'd swapped him because somebody else didn't want him.

The adoption has been amazing right from the start. I was doing my ironing one day and happened to switch on the telly. There was the *Find a family* programme on and I immediately started crying. Then they played a video of this woman called Alex who had three Down's syndrome boys. So straight away I taped it because of the Down's. She was brilliant. She had a lovely room with Disney characters all over the wall. She sat on the floor throwing a ball at one of them and helping another do some colouring and I thought she was just great! She started talking and saying she'd adopted these three boys and she was a single parent and then she said she'd been approved for another one and that he'd been born and she was destined to have him. I thought how much I'd love someone like that! I never dreamt he would go to anyone like that, or to Alex. It made us decide he should go to someone who has other Down's children because they got on so well together. I showed the video to everybody as I thought she was just brilliant.

It was weeks later when the social worker came round again and he'd got it down to three families. He read out their details, using numbers for each family. It was good to feel we had some kind of choice. We expected to be told he was going to a particular family. They were fantastic to us. They went through the list and came to the last one who'd been selected because she had three other Down's children. I said to Brian the social worker, 'I know who it is,' and he said, 'You can't! She doesn't live round here.'

I said, 'She lives in Manchester, doesn't she?' He was gobsmacked! Then I put on the video of her and said, 'That's her, isn't it?'

Brian went to meet Alex and told her that I had her on tape and I'd been saying how much I'd love him to go to a family like hers. The first time he took Alex to meet Nathan she said she wanted to meet the birth parents. Brian rang me from the foster parents' and said she wanted to visit and I wasn't keen. They came round and she walked in and said, 'Get the kettle on,' and we hit it off straight away. We've never looked back. I love her to death.

I don't know why I didn't want to meet her at first. Perhaps it was just a normal reaction, or it wasn't my idea of what adoption meant. I know I felt guilty about her wanting my child and me not wanting him. I still feel quite mixed. When people ask me how many children I have, I say three and then I have to explain. I feel really guilty then because I'd never let a child of mine go now. I'd take in anyone's baby. I love babies. I feel people are thinking, 'How could you have let a baby go?' I can't understand it now. I do think it would be different now, but it felt right at the time. That's what we were told as well – that it would be right now but may not be in a year's time or whatever.

I know if we didn't have this open adoption I'd be a basket case now. Birthdays in particular – not being able to see him or know how he's doing, I would have been so upset. As it is, every year on his birthday Alex makes it a special occasion, she makes a special effort to involve me in what she's doing so I really look forward to it. Every now and again I wonder how I'd be feeling if I couldn't see him. I'd be feeling terrible. It'd feel like it was a death every year not knowing if he was alive or dead. I knew he had a heart problem and I'd always be wondering what is he doing and how is he getting on. Instead, I'm thinking that I'd better get the cake ready!

One of the things we specified before open adoption was a possibility, was that should he die we wanted to be informed. They agreed to that. But we're not sure how openness really happened. No one actually said anything outright. When the adoption was going through we had a visit from the guardian *ad litem* [social worker appointed by the court] who said if he didn't agree with this open adoption he'd stop it. That upset us as that was what we were moving towards. I suppose it was new to him too and he was a bit wary of it. For us, in our situation, open adoption is by far the best. Having a handicapped child, he's not going to really understand our relationship but we'll be special to each other. We'll be just like any other relations.

I don't think we'd hassle Alex if she lived close by. In fact she was ill recently and so were the boys. I said if we lived nearer I'd look after him for you and she wished I could. I'd have looked after all of them. We ring each other quite often. I remember the first Christmas she had Nathan she rang and said, 'Thank you for giving me the best Christmas I've ever had. He's absolutely fantastic.' She was thanking us for letting her have him! We were so chuffed that he had bonded with her. We could have kept him for a couple of years, but our greatest worry was not being able to cope. And it would've been much harder to give him up when he was older. This way seemed best.

Our daughter regards them all as her stepbrothers. They do feel like family, especially Alex. I can talk to her about anything. And it's OK talking about Nathan to other people. They get all sad, but I don't feel like that. I know where he is and I can ring Alex any time if I want to. We see him once or twice a year when Alex hires a cottage near here so we can all see him. It must cost her a fortune! We feel it's OK her deciding when and where we see him – that's all part of the adoption. Legally we've got no claim on him. He's Alex's child, so it's just an agreement. I feel I take a back seat. She's his mum. I see myself as his mum and so does his foster mum. She's still in touch with him. I don't feel any more special to him than them. I just carried him. He doesn't still feel like my baby. Ann, his foster mother, still gets upset when she leaves him, but I don't. I just feel high. I love it. I think I've managed to come to terms with it and it all feels right. I've never had any doubts about him being with Alex.

I think open adoption is great. I've seen birth mothers on TV programmes still grieving 20 or 30 years later – they're still feeling that same pain as they did the day they let that baby go, and to them it's still a baby. They haven't seen it at all the different stages growing up.

I don't think Alex would stop us seeing him. We're too close. But if she did, then we'd have to accept it. But I'm sure we'd never put her in a position where she'd feel it was necessary. We phone about once every three or four months – she rings us more often than that. She does most of the running and we feel that's OK. She rang us recently to ask our advice about a birth mother and adoptive parents wanting open adoption and the social workers objecting as they lived too close.

I would like to help other people. I wish the social workers would contact us when they come across anyone in the same position as we were. Couples who don't know what to do. We were taken to meet families with Down's children and that was really helpful, but we never got taken to families who'd given them for adoption.

Open adoption has been the best possible thing for us all and it has worked particularly well since we all fit so well together. We all get on so well. That has helped enormously to make it work. We never disagree on anything. She asked me if there was any special way I'd like her to bring him up. She'll do things like ring me up and say he's biting. I could then tell her all the children bite in our family. And on another occasion she took Nathan to the doctor's and he asked if there was asthma in the family. Alex said she didn't know but would ring the birth mother and find out. She couldn't have done that if it wasn't open. The doctor was amazed and gave her a list of questions to ask me! It was good to be able to help.

I see our future as carrying on like this. As Alex said, she'll never have to explain who his mum is, as he'll have always known you. She's got lots of photos of us. He may understand; it's hard to know. We've found someone who suits Nathan as well as us. I guess it all depends on how much the adoptive parents are genuinely willing to give. When adoptive parents are being assessed, openness should be an important part of that and there should be a lot more emphasis on the benefits of it. In spite of that, it hurts like hell to give up a baby for adoption, openness or not. To be able to see him or know how he is, is a tremendous help to us. We also want to know how Alex's other children are getting on – and her mum – because they're just like family to us, and we're part of their family too.

15 Joanne

I met Joanne in 1991. She had her daughter Jennifer seven years previously when she was 18. When Jennifer was two, her father contacted Social Services as he was concerned about her care. She was admitted to hospital with serious injuries and subsequently went to live with foster parents. Her father remarried and for a while Jennifer went to live with him, but it didn't work out so she went to live with another set of foster parents called Margaret and John. They have since adopted her. Joanne has a legal right to see her daughter regularly as a condition of the adoption order – unusual for 1989 (just before the Children Act came into effect). I interviewed the two mothers together at their suggestion at the adoptive parents' home.

I still say to this day that I did not touch her. I was having to go out to work all day and my boyfriend – who was not Jennifer's father – was living with us and looking after her, as well as a babysitter. Nothing was ever proved. My mother always said that if I hadn't been living with him then things might've been different: he was up on charges of actual bodily harm and it was while she was with him that she hurt her face with a bottle. There were other injuries as well. She was taken into care.

Most of my support came from my family, especially my parents. There wasn't anyone else around. Social Services did try to rehabilitate us for a short time. My boyfriend and I used to go to a family centre while Jennifer was with her first set of foster parents. Her father went on different days. I found it very hard to be natural there because there were always people watching you all the time. I felt I was being judged and that this was about whether I'd get Jennifer back. I found they weren't very understanding and there were so many social workers coming and going. You'd get to know one, start to relax with them, and then they'd be gone. But at least I had some contact with Jennifer, although it was frustrating always being questioned by a social worker while I played with her. I think it was only about an hour that we had at the centre once or twice a week. I felt grateful to be able to see her but a lot of the time I didn't really know what was going on. I suppose I felt very unimportant and that nobody cared about me. The focus always seemed to be on Jennifer.

I did find it very hard to cope with. I was working in a restaurant from early evening till late and I was also working at the hospital as a domestic, including the weekends. I had a mortgage and bills to pay and was barely managing.

I wasn't involved in any assessments of how we were doing or anything; at least, I don't remember them. Jennifer went to her father's but I don't think she was wanted there, and eventually came here to Margaret. I didn't feel very involved in what was going on. I wasn't sure how long she was going to be here for.

I came here and saw her about once a week with my mum and a social worker. Once I got to know the social worker I found it easier to relax a bit more. Then my father wanted to see her too, so we were able to take her out on Sundays. My father was held to be responsible for her.

At first I was very bitter and angry – a lot of anger was directed at myself. I always wanted her back and I'd have to walk through their front door every week with a brave face, having smoked about ten cigarettes on the way over – and again after I left. I felt my parents were on my side but that's all. I could talk to mum but not a lot.

I wouldn't say that I couldn't stand Margaret – it was just that she had what I wanted. And other children of her own.

After she'd been there about three or four months I went to Social Services about having her back. They held a case conference and it was decided she should stay with Margaret and John until she was 18. I remember getting a letter telling me that and talking about adoption. I went absolutely demented.

Some time after that I decided to apply for a revocation of the care order. It went to court and a social worker was appointed. She recommended that my daughter should stay here with the foster parents as she'd spent half her life with them already and couldn't remember being anywhere else. I was really disappointed because I wanted her back. It meant I had to try and pick up all the pieces and start again. It all felt very final.

I had been seeing her once a month on a Sunday because I'd moved away, although I'd have liked to see her more often. But that was thought to be best.

Being able to see my daughter means a lot to me. But it was very hard to start with. I was always so upset. I could only see her every six weeks at Margaret's and that was supervised again by a social worker. It was also very hard to accept the idea that they wanted to adopt her. It meant I couldn't relax and had very mixed feelings, even though we were always made to feel welcome. I always felt I was walking away with nothing. It's still hard when I visit, although it is a bit easier now. I tend to dwell on it less than I used to and make myself get on with other things. I realise now I have to carry on with my own things – my own life.

But I did contest the adoption. Jennifer was adopted 18 months ago when she was six and a half. I remember it was very hard all sitting there in court together, facing each other. I suppose that underneath it all I knew she was happy with Margaret and John. But it was still very hard. I felt I'd lost everything. All those weeks and weeks of worrying and wondering and most of all hoping. I suppose one thing about the adoption was that it finally put a lid on further hope and anxiety. Although it wasn't what I wanted and I found it very, very hard to accept, at least I finally knew where I was in all this. The important thing is that I still have contact with her.

The adoption order gave me the right to have access, which is uncommon. That helped enormously. In spite of that, though, I did feel a lot of pain at the loss of my daughter. It was only when I started to see it in a more positive light, and accept it as being the way things were, that I think I began to get something out of it. I didn't want to lose contact and although I didn't have what I wanted, my daughter, it was better than having nothing at all. At least I can see her, know how she's getting on and what she's doing at school. Otherwise I'd never know what had happened to her and I'd always be wondering.

Since the adoption there haven't been people around like social workers, which has helped as we can now make arrangements direct. Margaret might ring up and invite me over to tea. Or sometimes I've just popped in. That would never have happened before the order.

I don't know what I could've done differently except when I think back to the beginning. It was then that I should have taken notice of the marks and bruises and taken her to the doctor straight away. I'm not sure what stopped me at the time.

I don't know if I see myself as being like any other relative to Jennifer. It's hard to say at this stage. I always feel very welcome but I used to feel evil, just sitting there quietly – maybe it was my anger I was keeping down.

I don't want to have any more children – whether that's because the right person isn't around or my experience with Jennifer, I don't know. And would they take my next child away too? It's always in the back of my mind – and I couldn't go through all that again.

I enjoy being with her, although I'm only a small part of her life. It also means she knows who she is while she's growing up and she knows her family. I think she understands why she was adopted, I'm not sure. She asks a few questions, like the colour of her eyes when she was a baby. She may want to know more when she's older. I always try and answer as honestly as possible to help her accept things as they are.

I still see her every six weeks or so. That was a time suggested in the court as a rough guide. But I can also see her sooner. And my parents see her too. Their attitude has changed over time. Dad didn't used to like visiting, but that's changed. All the tension and pressure has gone since the adoption. They definitely see her as their granddaughter. And they see her as often as her adoptive grandparents.

It's hard to say whether I still see her as my daughter. I know it hurt when I was no longer called 'mummy' but Joanne. That really did hurt at the time. She stopped calling me mummy when she was being fostered, and after she was adopted she wanted my permission to let her call the adoptive parents what she wanted. So she calls me by my first name, although sometimes she calls me mummy if I'm with her for a while. Actually it was getting a bit difficult, when Jennifer called out 'mummy' Margaret and I would both turn round! Then we'd look at each other to see who she was referring to! Her photo is by bedside. I still think of her as my little girl, but she's not really because she's adopted.

She visits me at my place on her own as well as with Margaret and John. One of our nicest days out was a day trip with my nephew and niece as well as Jennifer and her adoptive parents.

Unlike most other birth mothers, I have a legal right to see my child. If I wasn't happy about the amount of contact, I could take it back to court. As things are, they fit the access around me and my working week. We work it out together. I feel I could just pop in and see her if I wanted to and I know it'd be OK. I would never have done that before the adoption – just popped round. No way!

My parents do too, and it's always fine. I suppose I see Jennifer's family as part of my family.

When Margaret rang to tell me about you visiting I said I'd prefer we spoke to you together. We both know how we felt at the time and all that's gone on since then. At the adoption I remember Margaret and I hugged each other in the waiting room. Also once when I was visiting Jennifer and she said I could see her on her own ... I just burst into tears.

I am quite happy with the way things have worked out. If I hadn't had open adoption I think I'd have cracked up by now. It's helped me come to terms with what's happened. I'm not left always wondering where she is and whether she's all right. At least I know.

Margaret and John

I made contact with Margaret after reading an article she wrote in the Guardian *on her experience of open adoption. Fully open adoptions like this one are rare in Britain, particularly where the birth family is given legal access in the adoption order, much like a divorcing, non-custodial parent. Although the adoptive parents became reluctantly embroiled in a contested adoption, they wanted the birth family to continue having access to Jennifer in the same way after the adoption as they had done when she was being fostered by them.*

Jennifer was two and a half when she came to us and about four and a half when Joanne applied for a revocation of the care order. We were very worried that there could be a cycle of revocations and we felt the only way to stop it would be adoption. We'd already been considering it in the long term, but we didn't want a contested adoption. What we'd been hoping was that when she'd been here a long time and our relationship had grown with Joanne we'd go for adoption with her consent. We hadn't got to the stage of talking to her about it – we were just about to when she applied for the revocation.

We were asked if we could take her on permanently as they didn't want her to have to go to another set of foster parents. She'd had quite a few changes since living with her father and the previous foster home was not working out. We were approached to offer her a permanent home. It was mentioned at a much later stage that we might like to apply for custodianship, which had just come in then, but we felt we'd rather adopt than have custodianship because it is revocable and it didn't offer the security she needed – like having our name. So in a way the revocation precipitated the decision to go ahead with the adoption when we did.

Jennifer was thrown by the revocation because obviously she had to speak to the social worker appointed by the court – the guardian *ad litem*. She didn't know what to say because she likes to please everyone. When she first came she was very insecure. She desperately wanted to be given security and we knew we shouldn't be saying, 'It's all right, you'll always be here' and so on because there's a small chance that that may not be the case. So although it was wrong, we needed to say those things. Within about six months she became much more secure. There were always mixed emotions with access visits and two and a half years later we were having to say to her, 'Mummy would like you to go back and live with her.' We had to prepare her for the fact that things might be changing and going through that made us realise that we couldn't carry on in that way. Our whole world was turned upside down. When we first took her we knew there was a possibility of a revocation, but by that time we thought it had all calmed down. It was a complete bolt from the blue when we got the solicitor's letter. Poor Jennifer, who is always wanting to please everyone, just couldn't. In the end she said, 'It'd be very hard to leave,' and she didn't want to go. We had a very good guardian *ad litem* who was able to talk to everyone without upset. She was very perceptive and went to a lot of trouble.

She was the same guardian who was involved in the adoption. We didn't actually apply to adopt, as we didn't want to contest it. Instead, the local authority went for a freeing order to dispense with Joanne's consent and free her for adoption. We understood (wrongly) that the local council would apply for the freeing order and they would have to have the fight and having got it they would say we want to place this child for adoption. The battle's already done. Then it turned out at the last minute it wasn't the appropriate case to apply for a freeing order, so suddenly it became a hearing for the adoption rather than a freeing order. So Joanne was contesting the adoption instead of the freeing order.

We had tried to get over to Joanne at a meeting after the revocation that we wanted to go for adoption with access. It took a long time to get that across. I think she felt she wouldn't have access because that's what normally happens. Access was the right thing to happen. Jennifer wouldn't have wanted to lose contact with them. All she needed was security and our name.

She was five years old and enjoyed seeing them. Every now and then the social workers would say things like, 'Even so, we ought to stop the access,' because they were worried about getting it through the court. But we wouldn't agree as there was no way we wanted to tell her she couldn't see her family.

We desperately didn't want a contested adoption – to be arguing over a child, stealing someone's child. That's how it would have felt. But we could also see the right thing for Jennifer – she desperately needed the security of knowing she could never be moved again.

Openness was made easier for us as we'd always fostered so we were used to seeing parents of the children we were caring for. You get this training as foster parents that says how important access is and how vital it is for the child to know its family and its roots, otherwise it's going to fantasise some fairygodmother character. All the arguments pro-access for fostering seemed to exist for adoption as well. There didn't seem to be any difference. Nothing is going to make Jennifer think I gave birth to her because I didn't. I see myself in a caring role, the mothering role, and am therefore automatically her mother, whether or not there is a piece of paper.

If the child is tiny then the option exists of pretending there isn't anyone else. But someone of Jennifer's age is not going to forget her family and she is going to know she's adopted and want to know more. Her natural family hasn't vanished. They are there and important to her. How could you explain to her why they weren't there any more?

In fact her family are a real asset, now that our relationship has improved. They have all the information. Jennifer was having trouble learning to read and her grandmother was able to give us some useful family history which we'd never otherwise have had. Jennifer was curious about whether she'd been born with brown eyes or whether they'd turned brown later and we were able to say, 'Next time you see Joanne, ask her.' So there's no room for grudges or fantasies.

I don't worry that she might love us any the less because she's in touch with her natural family, although we tell her off from time to time and they don't because they don't see her that often! I think perhaps there has been an element of competition, but as we've got to know each other better that has gone.

I think our feelings were fairly mixed after the adoption. There was relief for ourselves, but our contact with Joanne and her parents wasn't that different. In fact the very first time they came after the adoption we had a barbecue and Joanne looked ten years younger. It was as if someone had taken a great weight off her. She was a different person. The case took a year to come to court and when it did the judge at one stage was too busy to hear it. Try explaining that to a five-year-old! The strain on all of us was tremendous. With the case pending for so long, we felt we had to be careful about what we said in case it was used as evidence. That was why at one stage we went back to supervised access, so there was an independent witness to what was going on.

Some of our friends think we're a bit odd! They went through the traumas in the beginning with us because we had to have someone to talk to, especially when the revocation was pending and we were worried. It is an unusual situation and not the norm so perhaps I'm not surprised that people find it curious and might think there are easier ways of doing this. You get a stronger reaction if they realise it was a contested adoption. The whole concept of a contested adoption raises a lot of feelings in people – how can you possibly adopt a child without its parent's consent? Of course we don't explain how she came into care in the first place. Most people don't know that. Even so, it was something we always said we wouldn't do. But we got ourselves backed into a corner over it. We were aware all the time and with absolute confidence that we were doing the right thing for Jennifer, but we were aware that we were inflicting a lot of hurt on the way. In a way it was also the right thing for us, but then you worry because of that and think maybe she doesn't have to be adopted, maybe it could work as it is, and did people make right decisions eight years ago? But of course you can't step backwards.

A friend was enquiring after Jennifer the other day and she was amazed when I said she was going to tea with her mum. Perhaps they're worried it'll all go wrong for us or she'll love us less or they'll steal her away or something. Since the adoption I don't feel she's ever usurped my role or criticised me or anything like that. There haven't been any problems at all. We did go round to her house one evening at her request without Jennifer to talk about the names. That was to clear the air about who she called mummy.

I don't think Jennifer gets confused about her relationship with Joanne and me, I think it's more about split loyalties. She did start saying 'my real mummy' – I think she heard it from somebody else. So we talked about the fact that if she was her real mummy what did that make me? After that we didn't use that word, it was too confusing – we used 'first mummy'. We've also got her life storybook with pictures of Jennifer with her birth mother and so on, her original birth certificate with their names on and her adoption certificate with our names on. That's how we explain the adoption. She was very upset when she saw the birth certificate because it didn't have our names on. But it was a very useful way of explaining the adoption. I think she was confused when she was younger and would go round telling people she had two mummies. She's more settled now and only one of us is called mummy. I think the name was quite important. Maybe as she gets older she'll get more awkward, but at the moment she tells various people. Apparently she told her class she was adopted and had been to see her first mummy and that does rather floor people. Being adopted they can cope with, but having the first mummy around they don't quite know how to react.

The only time it was awkward for us was when she started telling this old man about how she'd been hit in the eye and we could see him looking at us and wondering! I think she forgot to tell him we'd adopted her.

We would've wanted Jennifer's family to have access regardless of what sort of relationship we had with them if it seemed to be in her best interests. We're getting on like a house on fire now, but we weren't early on. Jennifer's grandfather wouldn't come into our house to start with because it upset him too much. We didn't feel relaxed with each other. We knew we could be in for a lot of problems by continuing the access, which was why the social workers were a bit uneasy. They weren't sure if we could handle things. As far as the adoption went, we were saying we thought access should continue. Luckily everything has worked out well. As a parent you have an absolute right to say what you think is best for your child. We don't really have that right as far as access goes, but she clearly benefits from it.

If she hadn't had access to her family after the adoption order it would have been impossible for us to explain where her family had gone. The guardian *ad litem* took her out to lunch and asked her what would she like her to tell the man in the court? Jennifer said she wanted her name to be the same as ours, to stay with us forever, to carry on seeing her family and while she was there to tell him she didn't like her teacher! Apparently it was all relayed!

Having openness doesn't influence our lives enormously – or Jennifer's, although I think it might if there was no contact. I'm sure she'd react differently and that in turn would affect us. It is odd being a mum and having another mum about – it's a funny relationship, and where it wasn't easy early on it's much easier now. Because it's going well it means we don't feel the need to stick to the letter of the agreement about access. Joanne asked if Jennifer could visit for tea tomorrow and that's fine.

I know I'll never have to say to Jennifer that I don't know something about her family. They are there, although she doesn't see her dad. I've spoken to him twice on the phone and I can get in touch with him if I need to. He's adopted himself which means she can't trace her family back on his side. She does see her father's adoptive parents, who couldn't imagine having had his parents dropping in! They are very supportive and she sees them quite regularly. They have the information about him even though she doesn't see him. I think he's pulled back because it's uncomfortable for him – he's failed.

Jennifer was so pleased on the day of the adoption. She was so delighted to have our name. She went wild. She told everyone. Half of them thought she was ours anyway. After about ten minutes she asked when she'd be seeing her birth family, like she was just checking up that she'd be still seeing them.

I do feel openness has to be in the best interests of the child. It isn't always, like where the child doesn't want to and is actually saying so, maybe in cases where he or she has been sexually abused. I don't think the child should have to see that man again, whatever the man says. It might be a good idea though to keep the name and the contact if the child should want it in the future. One always needs to listen to the child.

At the moment the norm in adoption is secrecy and that should be out of the question. I do think that grandparents are in a great position to be the contact with an adopted child. All children have grandparents in varying numbers and they have all the information. They can provide a contact into the natural family for the child without the emotion of the real mother or father. They have a lot to offer. Obviously they must get hurt as well, and have no control over what happens to the child. Jennifer's have been a valuable link for her. We've picked up a lot through the life storybook, like where she was christened and so on. We got a lot of information about her dad via her grandparents, as our relationship with Joanne wasn't good enough at that stage and it wouldn't have been appropriate to ask questions. We also got a lot of photographs.

The judge was a shrewd old man. He said he 'wouldn't write access into an adoption order at all, but since you're all telling me to – I will.' It is written on the order as 'reasonable access', which was debated as Joanne's side was saying they wanted to go back to a day every four weeks and we said to keep it as it was – every six weeks for two hours. We also stood up in court and said we weren't going to do that anyway – it'd be according to what we all wanted. He responded saying every six weeks for two hours and also anything else that it is considered reasonable by the adoptive parents, like grandma's birthday etc.

Our feelings over having a contested adoption lasted. Even though in the end we were glad we'd done it, it wasn't what we wanted to do. But as our relationship with Joanne has improved, those feelings have dispersed. It all feels natural and works extremely well, just like we hoped it would. In retrospect, any other arrangement wouldn't have worked as well. Of course Jennifer loves all the extra attention she gets as a result, and her family seems to us like 'in laws'. As Joanne's dad said in court, 'I'd never have met them otherwise. But bearing in mind we're stuck with them, we're getting on OK!'

16 Kathy

*Kathy is a birth mother and an adoptive parent. I met her through Social
Welfare in Auckland and later at an adoption conference in Wellington.
She is involved with a support group for all parties to adoption.*

*She is hoping she will eventually be reunited with her daughter, who
is 15. She has been unable to have any more children of her own and
has adopted two children, Alisha and Alex. She now knows both the
birth mothers well and some of their extended families, although the
first adoption was initially 'semi-open'.*

I used to get really emotional talking about my experience of having
a child adopted. I could hardly get a word out. I'd get a lump in
my throat and start to cry. But the more I've talked about it, the
easier it's become, so that now people probably think I'm hard
because I don't cry so much. But it's like being healed of something
awful. I really felt I was going nuts for years after my daughter
was born. I felt I was hiding a mental deficiency in myself, because
when I was on my own I was constantly depressed and miserable
and when I was out with other people I was my 'good old Kathy'
self, constantly laughing and giggling, a real joker. Yet the other
side of me was so maudlin and I had huge, big, black moods. All
I wanted to do was to go into my bedroom and curl up like a baby
on the bed and bawl, and nobody could make me feel better. That
was until I started talking about it, and since then every time makes
it easier. Now I'm involved in Adoption Support Link and I talk
there.

It's just like a huge wound that's healed up. In some ways
meeting my daughter now would be a lot different from meeting
her a few years ago. It would have been that big emotional thing
– whereas now I'm scared that when I meet her I won't cry or
anything. And I want to!

It was like when I adopted Alisha and the telephone call came
and they said they had a little girl. At first I didn't believe them.

193

Then I was sick. I vomited. I was so excited about the whole thing. I always thought I'd rush up there and bawl all over her. But it wasn't like that at all. I was cool and calm, but I loved her from the minute I saw her. But it was so different from what I imagined. I think I cried after I came home with her and it was real. I cried then. But I could imagine how adoptive mothers could pretend the child was actually theirs, because when I went to get her the hospital suggested I stay in overnight with her – and even I pretended! I had her in bed with me and I cuddled down and the nurse came in and said 'What's that baby doing in bed with you?' And I said, 'She's my baby now and I'll do what I like with her!' It was like, 'I'm going to do this now 'cos I wasn't allowed to do it before!'

But once I got her home I really started thinking about the birth mother, because it was a closed adoption. It just sort of worked its way up to open adoption. This was 1983.

When we first met her birth mother it was to talk to her for about an hour so that she could see whether or not she liked us. She'd chosen us out of a number of files, five I think, and we just had the one meeting. I was pretty nervous to start with and although Jacki isn't the sort of person I'd choose as a friend, without sounding awful, we got on very well and talked for about an hour and a half. They had to call it to a halt!

She had an appointment at the solicitor's which was a bit rushed. She was very angry with Social Welfare – she hated them and never told them anything. In fact they said she was a very quiet girl, which made me wonder if she was the same person – she talked so much! And lots of words beginning with f... She said the solicitor treated her like dirt. I thought things would've changed by now. She said if she hadn't met us before she went there she would've said, 'Up the lot of you,' and changed her mind.

She came up to the hospital to say farewell to her daughter. That wasn't made any easier by the social worker sticking her head round the door just as Jacki was saying her goodbyes and holding back her tears, and asking, 'Hasn't that baby been out of her bassinet long enough?'

We agreed that would be it and we'd send photos and letters to her. But I found that I was writing hundreds of letters, which went through Social Welfare as we weren't meant to know where she lived, and I thought, 'What is the point of all this writing?' Alisha was about seven months old. I thought, 'I'd be happy for her to come and see how she's getting on and share her with us.'

Who suffers from having more than one parent loving you? They have grandparents. So I suggested it to Ron, my social worker, as all these letters were killing me!

Jacki was very reluctant as she's adopted herself, so she felt it wasn't right. We met at a pub and discussed it. She wasn't very keen. But when she came home and got to the door she almost pushed me aside and said, 'Where is she? where is she?' And it grew from there.

I didn't feel a bit threatened, but I must admit that now, because Alisha is so much like Jacki, even when they haven't seen each other for six months there's an instant bond. She's normally a reserved child and doesn't go up to people very easily, but with Jacki it's just an instant thing. She never seems shy. And sometimes when she's on Jacki's knee with her arms around her neck having a kiss and cuddle, I feel a sort of twinge. She knows she grew in Jacki's tummy and she calls her 'my special lady'. She's definitely got a tie there. My adopted son Alex doesn't bother that much with his birth mother – he never makes the first move, but then he's a lot younger. But Alisha would be very resentful if we said there's no more Jacki coming around. She's a very special person in her life and has a special place.

It helps me too. I can see so much of Jacki in her! I know it's not something I'm doing wrong. I know it's her personality. I always thought you brought up a child a certain way and that's how that child will be. Well, Alisha has a really strong personality and it doesn't matter how you deal with her behaviour, she'll go on and on for hours rather than give in. And Jacki's exactly the same! But it's neat that way. I love knowing about her. It helps me to understand her.

I feel we would always have the final say about something. I don't see Jacki as interfering. She can be a bit bossy. It's her personality. Once she said, 'Don't get Alisha's hair cut, it looks really nice like that,' and I thought, 'If I want to, I will.' I say that to her now and we have a joke about it. At first I found it hard, like over Alisha's name. I was always going to call her Alisha and then we met Jacki and found out she'd called her Rebecca in hospital. So we decided to keep that as her middle name. Then we thought Alisha was quite popular, so maybe we'd call her Amy. When we met her at the hospital and she asked us what we were going to call her, we said 'Amy'. She went, 'Ugh!' Then when we said Alisha she said, 'That's really nice.' So actually I was quite relieved because that was the name I'd always wanted for her. It was my great auntie's name.

If she falls over and hurts herself, it's me she runs to, not Jacki – it's always 'mummy'. The other day she said, 'I don't have to 'cos you're not my real mummy.' So I said, 'OK then. Come on. We'll pack your things and I'll ring up Jacki and maybe you'd like to go and stay with Jacki.' Then she wailed, 'No, I don't want to go to Jacki's!' I know she's just teasing me, trying to hurt me as kids do. I guess I do feel hurt sometimes, but when she's not well or whatever, I'm the one she cuddles up to. And she wouldn't do that if she didn't think I was her mummy.

For some reason she thought David, my husband, was her birth father because we'd never really talked about it. She happened to be looking through her brother's photo album and saw his birth father and said, 'Daddy's my birth father, isn't he?' When I said he wasn't she wanted to know who was. I told her all I knew, which was only his name, and she wanted his photo. She's asked me quite a lot about him and I don't know. Neither does Jacki actually. Apparently they worked together briefly. We'll have to try and find out more about him.

Adopted Son Alex

Vicki, my adopted son's birth mother, already had two other children aged seven and 14 months. She's 27 and quite young for her age. She was living with her partner, who was violent, and they broke up. I think she just needed someone to love her. She was on the pill and ended up pregnant with Alex. I feel really sorry for her, because she handed her other son over to the birth father while she was pregnant, as she was very ill, and she's trying to get custody of him now. He's about five. Things are getting better for her and she's got her life much more together now. She's met someone really nice and they're getting married soon. But at the time she couldn't cope with two, let alone three, but she didn't ever want to lose contact with him. I think someone had talked with her about open adoption and she decided right from the beginning that was what she wanted to do. She didn't want an abortion or anything.

She's got a very good relationship with Alex. I don't think she gets very emotional about him. She did in the beginning, but now she can come and see him and give him a love and go off. And I say to her, 'Would you like to have him for the weekend?' and she says, 'No thank you.' It's not that she doesn't want him, it's that she doesn't feel she needs that sort of contact with him. Jacki doesn't either.

I think Jacki's found the whole thing harder to come to terms with. She's become very religious now, from an angry person to a reborn Christian, so we get the 'halleluiahs'. It's taken over her whole life. It used to be embarrassing before, when she'd be saying 'f...' all the time; now it's 'Halleluliah, praise the Lord' all over the place! And Vicki has become a Seventh Day Adventist.

But I believe birth mothers need a lot of support afterwards. Not just support groups. They need care and attention. I guess they're vulnerable and are attracted to a safe and caring environment with people who are good to them and not judging them.

With Vicki the adoption was open from the very beginning. She chose us from our file and photos. It felt like she'd already decided on us before we met. We went to Social Welfare to meet her. We met her in the lift going up. We kept looking at each other and finally she said, 'You wouldn't be Kathy and David would you? I'm Vicki.' She was very friendly, so we already had a good rapport before we arrived!

We did have a bit of bother with Alex though. He was put up for adoption and then they decided there might be something wrong with him. They said he had dismorphic features, strange to look at. He was an ugly baby actually, not very pretty and would roll his eyes up and drop them down. They felt he may not grow up completely normal as he got older. At first we were doubtful about being able to cope with that sort of thing and whether we were the right sort of parents for him. And then we talked to the paediatrician, who said he felt something was not quite right although nothing was showing up on tests and he felt he may grow up to be a bit slow. When we looked at him that was it! We decided, 'Who cares!' We just wanted him!

He has had lots of difficulties. He's a very attractive little boy now but he's very slow at speech and wasn't toilet-trained until three and a half. They did think he was intellectually handicapped until recently and I felt really sad for him. When I told Vicki I think she thought I was saying she'd given me defective goods or something. It was awful. I tried to reassure her that we love him no matter what, so I was really relieved for her when he was assessed as normal. She was really worried and kept reassuring me that everything would be all right! But I didn't want her to have to reassure me. I wanted to reassure her!

We have a really neat relationship. We ring up and chat about everything else and then we remember Alex at the end! And I feel protective towards her and want to help her, make sure she gets along. She brings out the mother in me. It's sort of like having a big sister to Alex. She's a super person. Her daughter comes and stays with us, usually for a couple of nights. And she always comes to Alisha's birthdays. It's just like having a friend whose kids come to see you. It's no big deal. She's nine, but I don't think she really understands about Alex. Vicki said she tried telling her when she was pregnant that she wouldn't be bringing the baby home, but it's as if she switched off, and even though Vicki has talked to her since it's like she doesn't want it to sink in. But she does come and play with Alex and says, 'I love Alex because he looks so much like my other brother.' And they are the spitting image of each other. Also, there's heaps of similarities. So I think Vicki's going to have to talk more to her because Alex is already saying he came out of Vicki's tummy. So he knows!

Birth Grandparents

Jacki's mother – Alisha's grandmother – wasn't involved to start with and she didn't think it was a good idea that Jacki see Alisha. We met them at Jacki's baptism. She'd asked us not to bring Alisha as her parents would be there. They came up and spoke to us and we got on really well. Jacki moves around a lot and I'd lost her address, so I wrote to her mother some time later. She wrote me a beautiful letter back and since then we've kept in touch. We write, not ring, even though she's not far away. I always send her photos of Alisha and she loves getting them, but she doesn't want to see her in person. I think it might hurt too much. She said in her letter she's always thought about the birth mothers of her two children, but never the birth grandparents. She recalled in her last letter how distraught they were to see Alisha at the hospital as they felt this would be the last time they would see her – their grandchild.

Jacki said she always felt like a kitten in a litter, as her adoptive parents, who already had another child, just decided they wanted a daughter. They rang up and said they wanted a blue-eyed, blonde-haired daughter and within two weeks of ringing Welfare they went and picked up Jacki. She's always had a big chip on her shoulder about being adopted and felt she fitted what *they* wanted – and off she went to them. But she felt she was never matched up to anyone in terms of her mother's background, personality, wishes, etc. and that there should have been more care about those things. She's always felt the odd one out. She's definitely different from her parents. She doesn't have much in common with her father. She loves her mother. I think she may have been given a lot materially. Her father never cuddled her or loved her. She's always had fantasies about her birth mother being beautiful and rich. She's been trying to trace her mother and found out where she was living when she was born. The family had moved but she found neighbours who remembered them and told her that the father was always shouting and screaming at the kids. So that was Jacki's mother's family. Apparently they were English and emigrated from New Zealand to South Africa.

The report from Social Welfare about her mother was awful. They said some terrible things. They described her as uncooperative, cheap, wore too much makeup. I thought she'd be devastated but she wasn't. She's entitled to the report. Another friend got a report saying her mother was a very plain, unimaginative little girl. I wonder what they said about me? I remember seeing my social worker for about five minutes. She didn't explain anything to me, any alternatives like fostering or anything. How she could have assessed me in that time, I don't know. And you weren't your normal self anyway. On top of all that you were terrified of Social Welfare.

Alex's Paternal Birth Family

My son's birth story is really complicated! Vicky was actually friends with the birth father's mother. She was a big, Maori grandmotherly sort who lives along the road. She befriended Vicki to start with and used to take her shopping and things. The father was a bit of a fly-by-night. After Alex was born, Vicki asked if the grandmother could see him. I said I didn't mind, thinking we'd go to Vicki's house and the grandmother would be there. We ended up going to the grandmother's house as she'd made morning tea. She was a great big Maori lady, obviously the matriarch. She asked us all these questions and wasn't very happy because my husband was a different tribe from her family. That never came up at the adoption, which surprised me. Then she looked at Alex and said he was strange-looking and then went on about how she would've adopted the child herself if it'd been a girl. Then she happened to mention that the birth father would be popping round to pick something up and he'd be here soon. I kept thinking, 'We'd better get going' – I didn't know what to expect. He arrived just before we left. He was very odd. He rushed in, had a look and rushed out saying, 'He's got funny eyes,' or something. Then we left and he came after us with a huge bear and said, 'You left this behind.' We said it wasn't ours so he took it back. It was almost as if he wanted to give it to us but couldn't. So he took it and went. And that was the only time we ever met him.

I didn't mind meeting them, but I'd rather have met them on my home ground. I wasn't sure what was going to happen and they kept looking at Alex and wanting to hold him and I had this horrible feeling they were going to run off with him or something. They asked if I minded if they bought him presents and clothes, but they've since moved away and we haven't heard. I can't connect Alex with them. He's such a loving, gentle, demonstrative child. I think they were annoyed because they didn't have any say in his adoption and it's generally very much against their culture. Children are always kept within the family. It was interesting meeting them though, and I've got a photo, although Alex doesn't look like them. He looks like Vicki. But the father lives near us, so we see him quite a bit. When you have open adoption you tend not to think about all the people involved. You think of the mother but not birth fathers or grandparents.

Adoption Support Link Meetings

Some of these women have never, ever talked about their experience with anyone before and they may have had a child 30 or 40 years ago. It really affects me, as some of them are still so emotional about it. It takes them all their courage to start talking – and they're crying. And almost all of them have gone through broken marriages, psychiatric treatment – and it all seems to come back to losing their child. It's hard to believe the agonies they've gone through. And if they never get to talk about it in England, then what's happening to them? That's when I started to look at my own life and to realise that before I was able to talk about it I must've been hell to live with all those years, always bawling and crying about babies, affected by anything to do with them.

Some of these women have never told their husbands. It's so important to talk about it and it can be very healing. You can see the change in them after a few months of attending the groups. One lady found that her birth son had died. He was only 22. He'd died in a car accident about six months before. But she said that even finding him dead was better than not finding him at all. She is a very churchy lady and had never told anyone. She started telling people and lost people that she thought were friends ... but the difference in her! She was very nervous before. She said, 'I can tell people now when they ask who that photo is of – I tell them.' Apparently the adoptive parents were awful to her and wrote terrible letters, but her son's two sisters made contact and said she was not to believe what their mother had told her about her son: that he did want to make contact, he did want to meet her, and they gave her lots of information about him including photos of him growing up. She has come to terms with it and her own self-esteem has really improved.

Kathy's Birth Daughter

I think having talked about it a lot has been a very healing thing. If I'd met her a few years ago I guess that in itself would have been healing. I think I'd have imagined that's how I'd have solved all my problems – by meeting her. But now, because I've talked about it so much, it's almost a non-event. I mean I really want to meet her but I want her to want to meet me too. I honestly don't know how I'll feel when it comes. I'm hoping it'll be a letter to start with so we can build up a friendship before we meet. Talking about it in the support groups has helped me to become more emotionally mature and has helped to heal me emotionally. But I'm not sure how I'll be when we meet. Some people say that all the anger and hurt about what happened comes to the surface when they meet their child. So although it's lovely, it's also a reminder of all the pain and misery they suffered. I really, really want to meet her but I don't want to think about it too much till it happens.

Talking about it, especially in a group where nobody's judging you and everybody's in a similar situation, is really important. Also a lot of adoptees that come to our group are really angry about their birth mothers deserting them, and when they see or hear how emotional it was, that their mothers loved them and cared about them, they see it differently. Especially men. So they're being helped too. Like one guy who came and said, 'My birth mother was 27 when she gave me up! How could she not cope at that age! She just didn't want me.' But we've got birth mothers who were 30 plus and still didn't have any support or choice, and when they hear that it helps them to understand.

We don't get a lot of adoptive parents, unfortunately, but most of those who come have got adolescents. They think that their child doesn't love them any more because they're going through that rebellious stage – or sometimes they just want to look for their birth parents. So listening to the birth mothers they can see they don't want to take their children away from them, they just want to know what's happened to them and see how they've grown up. And the children really want to fill a hole and satisfy their curiosity too. But the adoptive parents that have come have been great and have helped their children search. But there is the other variety who don't feel that way. We had one woman who never, ever changed her point of view and having that baby had been like having her own. Breastmilk had come into her breasts, she'd loved him so much. And how could that child now turn and go and look for his birth mother? I think Social Welfare had persuaded her to come. She only came about three times and then set up a group of her own for adoptive parents to stop adopted children looking! I don't know if it ever succeeded.

The reunions I've come across seem to vary from extreme love to quite casual relationships where they see each other on the odd occasion. I don't know what that's about. Perhaps just different personalities. I like to think mine will be really emotional! When I wrote the first letter to my daughter I wanted to say 'My darling daughter' and pour out all this gush and I thought, 'God, I'll probably terrify her!' It was really hard to stand back and say, 'Dear Melissa' and tell her I loved her without too much emotion. You're at the stage where you just want to hold her and say that these last 15 years have been hell and I loved you from the minute you were born, but you're not quite sure if the other person's going to accept all that. Mind you, a friend of mine loves all the gush her birth mother tells her ... where her parents walked before she was born, all the things they did together ... she loves it. But I guess she's like that too.

I know I'd have made contact by now if she was living away from home. At the moment it might make it awkward for her. Another thing is, you love that child you gave birth to, but when you see the adult it's a stranger, it's not the baby that you loved. You have to learn to love that person all over again. Or not. And that'd be very hard, if you don't love each other. Perhaps that's part of the reason I'm reluctant to do it. But you do have that really exciting moment when you've found each other and then you have to get to know each other. Even my parents said they'd love to meet her. I think it's been hard for them because they've got no granddaughters. My sister and I both had daughters adopted out, then she had another one after she was married and that died of spina bifida. And I've never had any. Our family is very into history and genealogy and that's what I want to give her. I think my family's quite interesting and I'd love her to know about it. My grandfather is meant to be the illegitimate son of Sir Arthur Conan Doyle. My great-grandmother was his housekeeper and she was the most austere-looking woman! You couldn't imagine her … it might be a whole lot of guff, but it's interesting! My grandfather actually worked for him as a pageboy and we've got beautifully handwritten references saying he was a good boy. Although my adopted kids will find them interesting, there won't be a connection there like my own daughter. And I'd like her to have the old family jewellery that's been handed down. My adopted kids are having other stuff, but the family stuff I'd like her to have as I think that's important.

Alisha is six now. She was shocked at an American TV programme we were watching recently on adoption about how their records are sealed and the birth mother could never find out about anything. She said, 'Is that what really happens, Mummy? Don't they ever get to know who their birth mummies are – or even see them?' When I said they didn't, she said, 'I'm glad it's not like that here. I'm glad I know who Jacki is!' Even Alex seems to understand. I'm sure they're happier knowing. And so are we.

Appendix

Useful Names and Addresses

Natural Parents Support Group
Doreen Ward
10 Alandale Crescent
Garforth
Leeds

Post-adoption Centre
5 Torriano Mews
Torriano Avenue
Kentish Town
London NW5 2RZ
Tel: 071-284 05555

NORCAP (National Organisation for Counselling Adoptees and Parents)
3 New High Street
Headington
Oxford OX3 5AJ
Tel: (0865) 750 554

BAAF (British Agencies for Adoption and Fostering)
11 Southwark Street
London SE1 1RQ
Tel: 071-407 8800

Grandparents Federation
Moot House
The Stow
Harlow
Essex CM20 3AG
Tel: 0279 444 964

PPIAS (Parent-to-Parent Information on Adoption Services)
Lower Boddington
Daventry
Northamptonshire
NN11 6YB

Birth families and adopted adults can register a wish for contact by writing to:

Contact Register
General Register Office (Adoption Section)
Smedley Hydro
Trafalgar Road
Southport
Merseyside PR8 2HH

NORCAP also holds a register which has been in existence for a number of years.

When writing to any of these organisations it is helpful to enclose a stamped addressed envelope.

Adoption counselling is now required to be made available by local authority Social Services departments. There are also several post- or after-adoption counselling centres in the UK. Their addresses can be obtained through your local Social Services office.